EXPERT SYSTEMS PROGRAMMING

*Practical
Techniques for
Rule-Based
Systems*

EXPERT SYSTEMS PROGRAMMING

*Practical
Techniques for
Rule-Based
Systems*

*Ken
Pedersen*

WILEY

John Wiley & Sons

New York • Chichester • Brisbane • Toronto • Singapore

Library of Congress Cataloging in Publication Data:

Pedersen, Ken, 1957–
    Expert systems programming : practical techniques for rule-based systems / Ken Pedersen.
      p.   cm.
    Bibliography: p.
    ISBN 0-471-60069-5.—ISBN 0-471-60068-7 (pbk.)
    1. Expert systems (Computer science)   2. Rule-based programming.
I. Title.
QA76.76.E95P43   1989
006.3—dc19   89-30391
    75113   CIP
10 9 8 7 6 5 4 3 2 1

Figure 8.4 is from "Uncertainty and Evidential Support," Bruce G. Buchanan and Edward H. Shortliffe, in Buchanan and Shortliffe, eds., *Rule-Based Expert Systems* © 1984 Addison-Wesley Publishing Company, Reading, Massachusetts, Figure 10–1. Reprinted with permission.

Chapter 9 is adapted from material published April 1989 in *AI Expert* magazine with permission.

TRADEMARKS

dBASE IV is a registered trademark of Ashton-Tate.

M.1 is a trademark of Teknowledge, Inc.

1-2-3 is a registered trademark of Lotus Development Corp.

Personal Consultant is a trademark of Texas Instruments, Inc.

Guru is a trademark of Micro Data Base Systems, Inc.

LEVEL5 is a trademark of Information Builders, Inc.

VP-Expert is a registered trademark of Paperback Software International.

KES is a trademark of Software Architecture and Engineering, Inc.

Exsys is a trademark of EXSYS, Inc.

OS/2, Presentation Manager is a trademark of IBM Corporation.

Microsoft is a registered trademark of Microsoft Corporation.

RuleMaster is a trademark of Radian Corporation.

ADS is a registered trademark of AION Corporation.

The . . . new class of knowledge engineers organizes and encodes knowledge in forms dictated by expert system shells. They generally do not have an academic background in artificial intelligence; they often have no programming experience. . . .The "old type" knowledge engineers tend to migrate to research labs or to cutting-edge development projects. The new breed of knowledge engineer . . . can be trained quickly, and they are capable of building many useful expert systems. This is a very fortunate turn of events, since the universities are unable to produce [the other kind of] knowledge engineers fast enough to meet the rising demand.

Edward Feigenbaum, Pamela McCorduck, H. Penny Nii
The Rise of the Expert Company

Preface

If you aspire to be one of Edward Feigenbaum's pioneering "new breed" of knowledge engineer, this "how-to" book is for you. *Expert Systems Programming* takes a first step toward filling the gap between expert systems theory and the needs of developers using rule-based expert systems shells. It is targeted at *first-time and early developers producing small- to medium-scale systems.* It is designed to fill the void that exists among software documentation, tutorial books that explain "what are expert systems," and academic literature. We do this by showing an approach that can help you win the advantages of expert systems while avoiding and minimizing their drawbacks. The book is a how-to survival guide designed to get you through those first projects in a practical, no-nonsense way.

This book does not try to make you qualified to develop large expert systems or those dependent on other representation schemes. Nor do we discuss the dynamics of managing projects in which many developers are involved. Instead, the book delivers a high level of specificity on the topic of building rule-based expert systems with the commonly available shells that make up the largest selling segment of the expert systems market today.

It is only recently that the nonacademic expert systems developer has begun to win respect. While many people talked about the eventual possibilities of AI research, the vast infrastructure of conventional developers have been ignored and snubbed. This is exactly the group who have problems to solve today, and therefore one of the groups that can gain the most from expert systems.

Both as a consultant working with inexperienced professional developers and a Purdue professor teaching student developers, we bring substantial insight into the common obstacles people encounter in learning expert systems development for the first time. We do not provide exhaustive analyses of the theoretical foundations of various expert systems techniques and concepts. We do show a path to usefully deploying these tools, thereby leveraging the conventional development experience you may already have.

Expert systems tools provide a powerful approach to solving classes of problems that conventional software (like COBOL and C) address poorly. What is often missing is an answer to the question, "How do I get started?" This outcry has two parts. First, "What are the key issues in choosing a domain?" Second, "Are there technical guidelines for the programming work itself?" This book is a response to that outcry, and those two topics are its central focus.

In order to accomplish this goal, we focus exclusively on rule-based systems whose primary search strategy is backward chaining.* Some products that fit this definition include (but are not limited to) LEVEL5™, EXSYS™, Guru™, VP-Expert®, KES™, M.1™, and Personal Consultant Easy™. This does not mean that our focus is better than that of others. It does mean, however, that to give the specific advice we offer, a set of starting assumptions is needed. "Expert systems" is an umbrella term that covers wide, diverse, and—in some cases—untested territory. A book on an umbrella topic can't say anything too specific, and must say too much. Therefore, we've chosen the most common and most often used representation approach: rules. Moreover, we do not cover all the representation possibilities available in advanced rule systems. Notably lacking among these is the use of "frames" representation.

The topics we do cover are those of mainstream commercial interest. Of particular relevance are expert systems projects that address diagnostic, selection, and classification problems. We help the reader evaluate whether his or her project can be implemented using the facilities covered in this book. Our goal, then, is to define a world in which the reader has a good chance for success, using a "walk before you run" approach geared toward producing positive results. The path produces tangible results, and helps make for a strong introduction of the new technology into environments that have little previous experience using it.

Expert Systems Programming uses a generic syntax that can be easily translated into most rule-based shells. Thus, it doesn't take advantage of features unique to one product. The syntax of most rule-based shells is relatively simple. While programming languages and "productivity" software like 1-2-3® or dBASE IV® have large and unwieldy syntax and grammars, many rule-based expert systems require knowledge of about ten verbs to get started. A well-written production rule, the major construct of a rule-based expert system, is almost intuitively readable to the casual, untrained reader.

---

*We define this term later, but for more knowledgeable readers, we also cover forward and mixed chaining features that many shells offer. However, the search strategy we build upon is the backward chaining approach.

The challenge instead lies in the fact that expert systems use a methodology of software development different from that of conventional methods. While these approaches are not necessarily difficult, they are often counterintuitive for the conventional programmer. The challenge has two main parts. First, define the project properly. Set proper goals, frame the problem, and manage expectations. These organizational issues affect the success of expert systems inside the company and are as important in the "real world" as creating the software. Second, acquire, organize, test, and maintain the knowledge destined for the expert system. These are the technical questions such as, "What does a well-written rule look like?", "What do I ask the expert?", "Exactly what happens inside an expert system?", and "What's the best approach for developing and testing the knowledge base?" Syntax and grammar play minor roles for these major issues.

The method we use is tailored to a realistic, practical approach to the kinds of projects that rule-based expert systems shells excel in addressing. The generic syntax enables us to demonstrate the essential architectural, design, and development issues, while giving examples relevant to most tools. Most of the important technical issues raised by today's popular commercial tools can be described and demonstrated in terms of a limited, product-indifferent grammar. Such an approach offers the benefit of giving a broader view of expert systems development that prepares developers for using any tool. Once these issues are well understood, the reader has built a foundation for using "extra" features while preserving the integrity of the knowledge base. These "extras" often lead developers, especially new ones, to produce poorly structured knowledge bases that depend on clever programming technique instead of solid design. These features can distract and lure you into writing "spaghetti" knowledge bases that are virtually impossible to test and maintain.

For those who maintain the need for syntax in the form of the actual tool, we provide a Glossary that cross-references our terms to those of the major rule-based tools named above. Where useful, we also provide examples using syntax of some of the tools popular at the time of this writing. Finally, the Appendix discusses the specifics of how these products handle some of the important topics covered in this book: uncertainty, handling unknowns, rule selection, knowledge sourcing, and rule processing.

This book will help you:

Understand the Basic Essentials. What are the general facilities available for expert systems development? How are these used? How do I choose the right project?

Create Well-Structured Knowledge Bases. You will learn how to make the expert system as easy to read and maintain as possible. Push procedural content out of the knowledge base. Make it as Englishlike as possible. Write well-structured rules.

Make Knowledge Bases Portable. We describe the essentials of expert systems development, using the general facilities available in almost any shell. If you use our guidelines to grasp and equate this syntax to your shell, you will produce highly portable knowledge bases, which can more easily be moved among shells and hardware platforms. Once you understand our system, you will have captured the essence of how virtually all rule-based systems work.

How Do I Work with Experts? What are the fears the expert may have about the project? How do I acquire knowledge? How do I evaluate where I stand?

Make the Knowledge Base Easy to Test. The more Englishlike and non-procedural your knowledge base, the easier to test and maintain it is. We discuss the software facilities and principles of building bases that are as easy to test as possible.

CHAPTER SUMMARIES

Part 1: Getting Started

Part 1 familiarizes you with the topic of expert systems, defines basic terminology, provides guidelines for choosing a project, defines the basic components of expert systems, discusses how inference engines work.

Chapter 1: Introduction. This chapter defines some basic terminology. We also summarize some of the reasons why expert systems development is a timely and important topic.

Chapter 2: Selecting a Domain. One of the most critical events in the expert systems development cycle is selecting and formulating the right project or knowledge base *domain.* This chapter explores the key questions you should ask about your proposed project in order to ensure that it is both technically feasible and that it will benefit your organization.

Chapter 3: Understanding the Basics. In this chapter, we explain the basic building blocks of rule-based systems. We look at the differences between conventional programming variables and their expert systems counterparts: attributes. We discuss attribute properties and show those that are most commonly used. We look at the component parts of rules and show some common forms and variations.

Chapter 4: The Inference Process: Backward Chaining. Here we examine how inference engines use rules to draw conclusions. We look at the basic steps that almost all rule-based inference engines take, and show how these steps relate to the way an actual expert might approach solving a problem.

Chapter 5: Forward and Mixed Chaining. We look at some common types of expert systems problems and define their salient traits. We examine these traits and show how backward chaining is not ideally suited for processing all types. We define forward chaining and look at an example of how it works. We also examine how forward chaining may be simulated in shells that do not offer a solely forward processing mode. We also discuss how mixed chaining can allow the use of both approaches in a single consultation.

Part 2: Technical Topics

Part 2 investigates specific technical issues that may arise during your development efforts.

Chapter 6: Handling Unknown Information. One way in which expert systems display humanlike behavior is by reasoning in the face of the unknown. The expert system can inform the user when a problem cannot be solved. It can reason about whether a particular piece of information is known or unknown. It can accept unknown responses from users and pursue alternate lines of reasoning. In this chapter, we examine this capacity more fully, and show how you can use it to let your expert system capture and reason about unknown conditions.

Chapter 7: Handling Multivalued Information. One of the traits of real-world problems is that their causes and solutions can have more than one plausible value. A key benefit of expert systems shells is their ability to represent multivalued information and to process those multiple values without programming logic supplied from the developer. In this chapter, we examine this aspect of expert systems development.

Chapter 8: Handling Uncertainty. In this chapter, we show common certainty factor algorithms and discuss their limitations. We explore how to evaluate whether you should use certainty factors and some common implementation approaches.

Chapter 9: Integration. Expert systems cannot survive as islands. They need to connect to the outside world. In this chapter, we look at some of the possibilities.

Part 3: Designing the Knowledge Base

Part 3 describes the development process. You start by interviewing the expert and acquiring knowledge. This is translated into a prototype. The process of this translation is examined in depth. We discuss techniques for refining performance and testing the knowledge base.

Chapter 10: Knowledge Acquisition. This chapter gives a method for structuring your first knowledge acquisition efforts. We look at guidelines for managing the common biases against expert systems that experts may have. We show a simple three-stage model for understanding how experts articulate their knowledge. Then we offer communication techniques you can use in all knowledge engineering sessions. Finally, we look at the *what* of the first interviews: the goals you set and topics you cover during those early sessions.

Chapter 11: Prototyping. Having completed the initial interviews, you now move to the rapid prototyping stage. Here we discuss the structure of the rapid prototyping development method. We look at how to organize and encode the results of your initial acquisition efforts. Then we present a method for working with the expert to correct and expand the prototype until the system meets the goals you set for it.

Chapter 12: Guidelines for Development. This chapter discusses knowledge base organization. We cover here those principles you should keep in mind when developing rule-based expert systems, regardless of the domain. By applying these principles, you can avoid many of the testing and debugging problems that many developers needlessly encounter.

Chapter 13: Fine-Tuning Consideration Order: Once the knowledge base correctly represents the knowledge of the domain, you may want to fine-tune the order in which it asks questions or reduce the number of fruitless paths it pursues. During the prototyping and development phase, you focus more on getting correct results than on tailoring when certain questions are to be asked. When it comes time to deploy the system, however, these fine-tuning points become important.

Chapter 14: Testing the Knowledge Base. Here we look at techniques that make knowledge bases easier to debug. We present a method of writing "structured rules," which loosely borrow from the well-accepted principles of structured programming. We also look at the importance of testing early and often.

Contents

P A R T   O N E

Getting Started

1 | *Introduction*

This chapter defines the basic terminology used throughout the book. We also summarize some of the reasons why expert systems development is a timely and important topic.

Expert systems are one of a group of disciplines often labeled *artificial intelligence* (AI). AI aims to make computers capable of displaying behavior that is considered intelligent when observed in humans. As the definition implies, it doesn't so much define what goes on in the computer as the *effect* the computer or computer software conveys to humans—that of "humanlike" behavior. The common belief that AI is inherently some set of magical techniques should be banished once and for all. Where specialized techniques are used, they are used because they have taken a step along the road to producing a more humanlike impression. If the impression of humanlike behavior could be produced with a COBOL program, then to whatever degree it succeeds, such a program could be considered artificially intelligent.

AI encompasses four major areas: vision systems, robotics, natural language processing, and expert systems. Vision systems are computer systems skilled at recognizing patterns, objects, or scenes and processing those data in some manner. Robotics research tries to create "general purpose machine systems that, like humans, can perform a variety of different tasks under conditions that may not be known a priori."[1] Natural language processing aims to make computers capable of handling language couched in the vernacular of everyday speech. These are all valuable disciplines. However, in the last few years, expert systems have won the most attention from the mainstream data processing community.

---

[1] *Encyclopedia of Artificial Intelligence*, ed. Stuart C. Shapiro (New York: John Wiley & Sons, 1987), 2:923.

Many definitions of expert systems have been put forth; we group them into two broad groups. There is the *how they're implemented* school that describes expert systems in terms of the techniques and tools used to build them. One such example is, "Expert systems are computer programs that use inference techniques." If the defining component of AI is the impression of humanlike interaction, this definition of expert systems is inadequate because it focuses on techniques rather than the end result expert systems produce. The definition excludes software that doesn't happen to use those few anointed techniques even if it produces results identical to software that does. For example, what about expert systems tools that convert finished knowledge bases into self-standing C programs? After being converted to C, are they still expert systems?

Other definitions focus on the *human knowledge* aspect: "Expert systems are computer programs employing human knowledge to solve problems that ordinarily require human intelligence." This seems more promising. Phrases like "human intelligence" match our intuitive idea of what artificial intelligence is. However, terms like "knowledge" and "intelligence" are difficult to define in a manner that is useful in a business setting. If you've come up with the definitive definition of "human intelligence," step up and accept your Nobel prize. While the discussion is interesting, we prefer to leave it to the disciplines of philosophy, cognitive psychology, AI research, and neurophysiology.

Instead, we opt to downscale the definition of expert systems to one that can be applied as a criterion for business use. Here it is:

> Expert systems are computer programs that give the appearance of human-like reasoning for problems ordinarily requiring expertise.

We inherit the "humanlike reasoning" phrase from our definition of AI. Again, it refers to the ability to provide the impression of human interaction. The key part of the definition—*for problems ordinarily requiring expertise*—means that the problem requires a human for its solution and that a small group of people performs much better than their peers. "Expertise" can refer to the very rare and specialized expertise of a disease diagnostician, or the more common but equally human knowledge of a shipping clerk who has learned the best way to ship freight. The common denominator here is that the problem requires humans, and the expertise is based on insight and experience.

The fact that expertise can come in many forms is an important point. Many seemingly mundane tasks make excellent expert systems targets. If the shipping clerk retires, that departure may leave a gap in know-how that could cost the company money. Likewise, if the production line is often held up because of poor diagnostic skills, the result is lost productivity. Expertise is indifferent to environment. We'll talk more about "expertise" later.

HUMANLIKE BEHAVIOR

We've defined expert systems in terms of their ability to exhibit "humanlike behavior." At least six traits help define what we mean by this.

Symbols

Perhaps the most important quality of humanlike behavior is the knack for manipulating symbols. Computers excel at processing scripts of exact instructions. Humans don't seem to operate primarily in this way. Instead, people use symbols to encode the world and their experience. These symbols are then used in rich and varied ways.

One way symbols are used is to solve problems using rules of thumb. The AI word for "rules of thumb" is *heuristics*. A heuristic is useful because it often, but not always, helps solve a problem. Contrast this to *algorithms*. Algorithms solve a problem using a consistent, precise set of steps. Because of their adeptness at processing lockstep instructions over and over again, computers have traditionally been used to solve problems that can be described algorithmically.

Programming languages have been designed to ease this job of controlling the computer algorithmically and telling it exactly *what to do*. To distinguish between this approach and that used by most rule-based expert systems development tools, we refer to the former as "conventional programming" and the latter as "declarative" or "nonprocedural" programming. Declarative programming focuses on telling the computer *what to know*, that is, encoding the knowledge the system is to represent.

Languages like BASIC, C, COBOL, FORTRAN, and assembly language fall into the conventional category, although dialects of these languages are appearing that offer some of the features that characterize the declarative approach. Similarly, most expert systems tools offer some type of procedural control, however primitive those features may sometimes be (we discuss this later). The line between the "conventional" and "declarative" will continue to grow more fuzzy in the future. For purposes of clarity here, though, we assume that the distinctions are clear-cut.

Conventional programming works fine for telling a computer what to do *every time*, but it is not so good at letting you represent knowledge that applies "most of the time." While rules of thumb may not always solve a particular problem, humans use them extensively because these rules work in an imperfect, pragmatic world. The ability of rule-based expert systems to express rules of thumb as rules plays a big part in helping them display humanlike behavior.

Uncertainty

Another humanlike behavior is the ability to deal with uncertainty. Conventional languages easily represent "yes" and "no," usually mimicking an "on" and "off" switch. However, most computers have no idiomatic way to represent "maybe." Many real-world problems don't have simple yes or no answers. Yet humans somehow still manage to reason in the face of that uncertainty. The fact that most expert systems support the representation of uncertainty is one way in which expert systems differ from conventional programming. We look at uncertainty in Chapter 8.

The Unknown

The way in which most computers represent everything as "yes" or "no" leaves out another capacity humans have: the ability to reason about the *unknown*. Humans often find alternate paths when important information is missing. Most conventional languages have no way to handle unknown cases. Most expert systems tools do. They let you reason about what is unknown, pursue alternate reasoning lines when data are missing, and can return a conclusion of "unknown" when the expert systems' knowledge doesn't cover a case. This character of being able to "know what it doesn't know" enables humanlike handling in the face of missing information. This topic is examined in Chapter 6.

Explanations

Another trait distinguished as humanlike is explanation behavior. Experts must defend and explain their reasoning ("*How did you reach that conclusion?*"), or justify why information is needed ("*Why are you asking that?*"). This kind of interaction also satisfies a more general characteristic of social interaction, namely the ability to engage in dialog. Expert systems usually offer explanation facilities that can answer "how" and "why."

Explanation facilities are important features not only for producing humanlike appearance, but also because they offset suspicion and increase acceptance of software meant to supplement or replicate human advice. Not all solutions are obvious or unambiguous. Without explanation facilities, such advice may seem arbitrary or random. If expert systems can justify their requests for information and explain how they arrive at a conclusion, chances are greater that users will accept the results. Thus explanation facilities address human acceptance factors beyond the production of humanlike interaction.

Multiple Conclusions

The ability to make multiple conclusions is a humanlike trait. Many problems humans solve can legitimately have two, three, or more answers. This aspect of human problem-solving differs from conventional computer programs which usually calculate *"the* answer." Problems can have more than one solution because they are ill-defined. They may have areas that deal with human preference, unknown data, and uncertainty. At other times, there simply is more than one answer. Most expert systems shells allow more than one value for a given factor, often reasoning and manipulating those multiple values without direct "programming." We discuss multivalued information in Chapter 7.

Tailored Advice

The final humanlike trait we mention here is the ability to tailor advice or conclusions. By *tailoring,* we mean acknowledging factors determined during the consultation in the final conclusion. For example, consider these two groups of recommendations from an expert system that evaluates expert systems problems:

Group One:

- The expert systems topic is recommended.
- The expert systems topic is not recommended.

Group Two:

- The expert systems topic is not recommended because it depends on common sense and such problems are difficult to define.
- The topic clearly contains economic payoff. However, you haven't yet narrowed the subject matter enough. Define exactly what it will and will not include. Be more concrete in defining what a finished system is. Get a set of examples and cases that, when the expert system solves those problems, the system will be considered complete.

Clearly, the second group of recommendations seems more humanlike because it gives more information, recognizes what the consultation wrought, and gives a glimpse of the underlying reasoning. Such recommendations are more useful and more acceptable to users, since the expert system is not just recommending from "on high."

Human experts mold their advice to the needs of the situation. Their recommendations take into account seemingly minor considerations that can have a powerful impact on the acceptance, effectiveness, and implementation of otherwise mundane advice. Remember this observation: the more detailed and concise an expert system's advice, the more it imparts a humanlike impression. This helps win user acceptance.

IMPORTANCE OF EXPERT SYSTEMS

The real question of course is, "Why develop expert systems at all?" Many data processing shops have survived thirty years without expert systems. Why start now? Why are expert systems *needed*? This question takes on added urgency when held up against the existing application backlogs of many MIS and data processing shops. Developer resources are expensive and in short supply. Maintenance and support are costly. Why throw something new into the pot?

The need for expert systems is different from the need for conventional software. Conventional software's main focus has always been the automation of repetitive tasks. Usually these tasks are well understood and already performed in some noncomputerized manner. Their benefits can be concretely estimated because they do the job faster and do it with fewer errors. The bottom line is improved productivity. In this framework, the computer is a traditional twentieth-century machine in the broadest sense of the industrial revolution: it produces faster and more efficiently than the manual methods that preceded it.

The advantages of expert systems are quite different. Expert systems technology aims at improving *qualitative* factors. This qualitative nature is one reason why corporate America has had difficulty in justifying expert systems on a large scale. The expert system doesn't replace twelve payroll clerks and do the job 29 percent faster. Instead, it helps make better decisions, enforce consistent methods, and preserve the imprecise, but undeniable, expertise its employees develop. For those companies with old world viewpoints, it can be difficult to put a number on this kind of value.

Nevertheless, technology continues to change the way many investments are measured. Many companies now accept the reality of smaller, diffused markets. Many believe that customer service, though expensive, is vital to winning and keeping loyal customers. Many companies see that knowledge and information increasingly define a service-based economy in which production is not the determining edge. All these points of view somehow reflect attitudes that put high value on *qualitative* factors that numbers alone cannot represent. Technology is increasingly becoming an integral, inseparable part of many businesses, so much so that many industries must completely rethink themselves. The new view sees its business as not just using technology, but *becoming technological.* As a snake and its mode of locomotion are inseparable, forward-looking businesses are fusing themselves with new technologies so that the two become one. In this world, expert systems can play a vital role.

The key benefit of expert systems, then, is their "get ahead" value. The expert system is a tool for adding new capabilities that did not before exist. You can use expert systems to improve customer service by automating a help desk. Expert systems can diagnose and maintain your incinerators better and thus keep them running at capacity longer. They may help make better acquisition decisions. But before any of these uses can be realized, those who justify, approve, and support expert systems must see them in the light of winning new advantages that become strategic assets. Arguably, one reason for the slower than expected acceptance of expert systems is the slow development of this realization. Thus we continue to see gradual evolution, not revolution.

Are Expert Systems Development Tools Better?

The hype of recent years has led to the colloquial claim that expert systems are *better* than conventional software. We've defined expert systems in terms of their ability to express humanlike behavior as identified in the six traits discussed above. They use symbols and uncertainty. They allow reasoning about the "unknown," with multiple values. They can explain their reasoning. They can tailor conclusions. Thus a more precise way to think of the relative advantages of expert systems is that they excel at handling problems requiring this behavior. If a problem can be better solved using such capabilities, software that makes it easy to do so has a built-in advantage over software that doesn't. Since conventional languages like COBOL, BASIC, and C as of this writing do not commonly provide these facilities, expert systems tools are preferable for this class of problems.

Another way in which expert systems shells top conventional tools is in the development method they enable. As we will examine in Chapter 10, the problem of *knowledge acquisition* is one of the more challenging issues of developing an expert system. Because it is difficult to acquire all the knowledge before coding begins, a method called "rapid prototyping" has found acceptance in expert systems development. Most shell development environments are designed to let testing start very early in the development process. This trend is slowly gaining steam in the conventional languages. It is an established fact in expert systems work. Prototyping is explored in Chapter 11.

Expert knowledge can be both declarative and procedural. The solely step-by-step control that conventional languages offer lacks an easy way for encoding declarative know-how. Expert systems excel at coding knowledge declaratively. We show you in this book how to structure declarative knowledge so that you can control the inferencing process. In this way, you get excellent declarative ability, usually with enough procedural control to do what you want.

Rules—the basic building block of rule-based expert systems—seem a natural way to summarize much of what we know. They can be added, changed, and deleted with less impact on the workings of the program than with most conventional programs in which any change to the program's logic runs a high risk for entering "bugs" into the program. Rules are usually independent, and are often easier to understand (more *transparent*) than equivalent knowledge expressed in a procedural manner. This effect is enhanced by the simple, Englishlike syntax many shells utilize to encode rules. The modular, easy-to-read nature of declarative rules written with Englishlike syntax can make an expert system easier to read for nonprogrammers, and easier to maintain for the maintenance programmer.

These facts weigh heavily in the favor of expert systems tools *for problems requiring the impression of humanlike behavior.* They don't replace conventional software, nor are they as a category better. But for a given class of problems, they provide a path for getting to where other tools do not travel.

Other Benefits of Expert Systems

The need for producing the impression of humanlike behavior is what drives the choice of expert systems tools. From this core observation come a number of benefits that one should be aware of when considering an expert systems solution.

They Make Intangible Assets Tangible. Expert systems projects can be expressed as "rent-or-buy" decisions. When companies hire an expert, they essentially rent that expert's knowledge for the time he or she is employed with the firm—an inefficient, but inevitable, investment compared with capital equipment and other more tangible investments. When the expert retires, dies, or otherwise leaves the company, the lease term is over. The investment offers no lasting return except to the extent that other replacement experts have been trained, thus beginning a new "rental" period.

Producing an expert system that captures the expert's knowledge allows a company to "buy" that expertise and turn it into a corporate asset. The expertise can continue to be applied after the expert leaves. A previously intangible human phenomenon is now a tangible software entity. Like a capital investment, it will require ongoing maintenance. But the essential quality is that the company owns and controls this resource, and can dictate its use.

They Don't Have Lapses. Expert systems out-perform human experts in at least one respect. Expert systems don't suffer from bad days, problems at home, burnout, or job frustration that may make them perform poorly. They don't get distracted or skip steps. Expert systems approach each task in a consistent manner.

They Are Readily Replicated for Distribution. Once expert systems are completed, you can theoretically deploy them at any number of sites, to any number of appropriate purposes. This may dramatically improve employee productivity and provide substantial payback.

They Can Give Advice When the Human Expert Is Unavailable. Expert systems are available around the clock. Not only don't they quit or ask for pay raises, they don't get sick, take days off, or have too many people competing for their time. This "always available" aspect make expert systems especially useful for supplementing human experts.

The fact that expert systems can be constantly on the job suggests one of the most common roles for expert systems: the screening system. Some problems of expertise are characterized by the 80/20 rule: 80 percent of the problems are easy. They waste time that the expert could otherwise devote to solving the 20 percent of the problems that challenge him or her. These are the problems whose solutions benefit the organization most. By off-loading the 80 percent to an expert system, you make the more accessible parts of the expert's knowledge available to nonexperts. The expert has more time to address the "hard" problems.

Training. Expert systems can serve as excellent training tools because of their ability to explain their own reasoning. Nonexpert performers can engage in consultations to improve and test their own performance. Users can learn by asking *how* and *why*.

Standardized Problem-Solving. Organizations may have several experts who solve similar problems differently. This may cause political, support, reliability, and other problems resulting from the conflicts and inefficiencies of using different methods. An expert system using several experts may be able to reconcile different methods, or create a standard defining the organization's supported method. This is especially useful for areas like data processing, accounting, and other professions in which the technical nature of the work makes standardization desirable.

Staying Current. One final point we make here is not so much a benefit of expert systems as a benefit in learning about rule-based expert systems technology. Expert systems techniques are rapidly infiltrating conventional software. They represent a problem-solving paradigm that can be used to address a wide variety of problems. Organizations and developers who gain a working knowledge of rule-based expert systems have significantly widened their perspective on software problem-solving. They have also taken a valuable first step for understanding object-oriented programming, object-oriented data bases, and the kind of programming that new operating systems and environments like OS/2 imply.

Expert systems are one tool in the continuum of software development. They excel at providing the capacity for humanlike behavior. Rule-based tools are one approach for developing expert systems. They excel at capturing the experience and rules of thumb of excellent performers. In the next chapter, we look at specific guidelines for choosing and evaluating expert systems topics. From there, we go on to examine the inner workings of rule-based expert systems themselves.

2 | *Selecting a Domain*

One of the most critical events in the expert systems development cycle is selecting and formulating the right project or knowledge base *domain*. A "domain" is the subject area explicitly included within the scope of an expert system. Aspects included within the expert system are said to be "within the domain." Portions outside its scope are "outside the domain."

There are many reasons why choosing the right domain and setting the right expectations are so important. Here are a few:

- Expert systems shells enable you to address problems requiring human-like behavior. Beginners sometimes choose problems that might better be implemented using conventional programming tools.

- The term "expert systems" is a broad one. There are many different kinds of expert systems. Your chances of success are increased by choosing a more manageable type. Topics lending themselves to the rule-based approach tend to be easier to develop than many other types of expert systems.

- Expert systems projects often have a relatively high profile within the organization. Success is important to the individuals involved.

- You may be engaging in one of the first expert systems for your organization. Its success or failure may influence the future of other such projects.

- Some domains are like icebergs: they look small above the surface, but the deeper you explore, the larger they become. You may discover that the problem has become amorphous and hazy. In this case, your chances for success are greatly reduced.

- There may be many domains that provide significant payback but are technically difficult. The best return on investment comes from finding the best mix of economic payback and technical feasibility—especially for novice developers.

CHOOSING THE RIGHT PROBLEM

When evaluating candidates, we look at three important criteria: economic return, expert need, and suitability. The first two points deal with the realities of business data processing: resources are scarce and time is precious. You want to get the best return on these assets by choosing projects that most benefit the organization.

If your domain passes the first two tests, you must then examine whether it can be successfully implemented. Rule-based development software is only one in a continuum of software tools. It is well-suited for problems requiring humanlike behavior. It is your responsibility to make sure that you choose problems that match the tool.

We now look more in depth at the issues of selecting expert systems domains. We then look at dealing with technical and organizational issues often encountered once a domain is selected.

Economic Return

The horizon of potential projects is enormous. The question, then, is where to start. The best starting point is to analyze whether the problem will produce an adequate economic return. By starting with economic return, you make it easier to gain and maintain management support. Technology is important only insofar as it increases productivity. By choosing those projects that hold the potential for increased productivity, you make your expert systems project important by virtue of its contribution to the basic role of all companies: to provide return on investment to their shareholders. From this perspective, economic return is *the* most important criterion to apply to any technology. The project may be completely suitable from a technical standpoint. But if it does not provide economic return, so what?

Here are some of the more important questions to ask in evaluating whether an expert systems project holds the potential to provide an economic return. Some of these points overlap. This is understandable, since the eventual goal of all productivity increases is higher profitability. View these various points as different surfaces on the cube of profitability and those relationships will appear logical and proper.

Does the Knowledge Provide a Competitive Advantage? Over time, many companies develop areas of specialization which help distinguish them from their competition. The specialty is often based on the experience of key personnel in solving some class of problem the company has addressed and successfully solved.

In a law firm, it may be understanding some class of legal problems. In a consulting business, one or more employees may have broad experience helping clients solve particular kinds of problems. In a mail room, the mail clerk may have researched all viable options for shipping company freight and overnight mail. The key trait in all of these examples is that the experience and expertise of the individuals performing the task provide some unique ability to generate business or reduce expenses for the company.

Any knowledge that represents some unique competitive advantage can be considered as a target for expert systems implementation. The knowledge has proven value. The firm has already paid for the development of that expertise. By encoding it and making it more broadly available, it may hold the potential for leveraging that advantage by enhancing the performance of other employees.

Are Workers Bogged Down in Trivial or Repetitive Tasks? A person we know was in charge of selling his company's technology product to several important governmental agencies. The individual is an excellent salesman. He works hard at cultivating demand for what he sells. Unfortunately, part of the selling job also included filling out the legions of lengthy forms that the various agencies require. Being relatively new to government sales, he was fortunate to inherit an assistant who understood exactly what were the various significances of these forms, what were the effective methods of completing them, and how to classify the firm's products in the most advantageous way.

Things went well for several months. The two made a terrific team. Then the assistant was hired away by a competitor. The salesman was forced to take over the form-filling. His selling time was cut in half as he had to learn by trial and error how to handle the paperwork responsibilities of the company. His progress was impeded by his lack of knowledge for completing them effectively. What happened? The salesman's production plummeted and he eventually quit.

This is a good example of how a competent individual can get bogged down in the details of a task. Although the paperwork completion was a subsidiary component of the job, it was an essential activity that required some expertise in itself. The salesman became bogged down in that subtask on the way to his larger goal, making him only fractionally as effective as he might otherwise have been.

Many jobs include diverse activities. Often some of those are themselves subspecialties with various levels of competence. An expertise shortage in one of them may keep personnel from meeting the larger goals of their job.

Are Costly Mistakes Made? Actions that cost money or waste time are mistakes. If many mistakes are made, you have either an incompetent em-

ployee or a difficult task. If good performance requires skilled decision making, then the task may be a candidate for expert systems implementation.

Mistakes can be onetime, large money losers (for example, a bid that is
calculated incorrectly), or common judgment errors that pervade the entire
organization (choosing the wrong overnight carrier for an important piece of
correspondence). Either is a legitimate candidate for expert systems.

Is a Consistent Decision-making Process Needed? Some important tasks
may have more experts (actual or self-proclaimed) than are good for the
company. Consistency is lost when personnel perform important tasks in
materially different ways. An expert system may be able to provide consistency.

There are many reasons why consistency may be desirable. One camp may
be unwilling to support the method used by another. Junior personnel don't
know which approach to adopt. Customers and other outside parties become
confused by different messages coming from the two sides. Good results may
be difficult to duplicate.

Because they approach problems consistently, expert systems can provide
the foundation for establishing a standardized method for approaching problems. Expert systems can play the role of an impartial, unequivocal standard
for measuring *method* as well as results. Thus they may arbitrate disputes
about the best way to approach a problem.

Is There a Need for Training? In some cases, a company's long-term future
depends on being able to replenish its supply of expertise. This is done by
recruiting and training a pool of junior replacements for the time when more
mature experts are promoted or move to other tasks. Expert systems may aid
in this training because of their ability to explain why information is needed
and how a result is reached.

Does the Company Need to Understand the Problem Better? Some kinds of
expertise are scarce. In extreme cases, a company may even be held hostage
to the talent or knowledgability of one of its employees. Not only may the
expert be the only one who can competently solve the problem, he or she may
be the only one who really understands the decision factors involved. By
committing this knowledge to an expert system, the company not only ends
up with a new expertise source, but in the development process learns valuable new information about analyzing and quantifying the problem during the
knowledge engineering process.

Is There a Centralized Repository for Knowledge? Some knowledge evolves
quickly and impacts many areas of the company. Sometimes this leads to

Table 2.1. Economic Considerations in Choosing an Expert Systems Topic.

Does the knowledge provide a competitive advantage?

Are workers bogged down doing trivial or repetitive tasks?

Are costly mistakes made?

Is a more consistent decision-making process needed?

Is there a need for training an expert system might meet?

Would the company benefit from a better understanding of the problem?

Can the system become a centralized repository for knowledge?

inefficient and error-prone duplication of the research and application of that knowledge throughout the firm. Expert systems can be an excellent way to maintain and communicate important, rapidly evolving knowledge. By maintaining this knowledge centrally, the company can dedicate a resource for keeping and supporting it. Unanswered questions are put to an expert who does the research and formulates a response. The expert then works with the knowledge engineer to update the expert system. The expert system provides a centralized, coherent way to communicate this new information—a way that saves the company money in time, support, accuracy, and user satisfaction.

Expert Need

Once economic return is established, we next look at expert need. Expert need can be seen as an extension of the economic return question. The economic need analysis establishes that the domain deals with a topic that can contribute to the company's financial results. The expert need analysis contains three steps:

- Establish that the task requires *expertise* for its solution
- Establish that nonexpert performance is inadequate
- Establish that there is a shortage of expertise, but that it does indeed exist

If the task does not require expertise, it may be technically unsuitable or the organization may not have a critical lack of talent for doing that task. If the nonexpert performance is acceptable, why bother? If no experts are available or committed to the project, it may be difficult to get, test, and maintain the expertise. The following questions address these issues.

Does the Task Require Expertise for Its Solution?

Is There a Large Difference Between Best and Worst Performers? One of the characteristics of expert behavior is that a few perform better than the vast majority of the population. This can be shown graphically, as in Figure 2.1. The bottom 80 percent of individuals perform at essentially the same low level. The next 10 percent do only marginally better. Finally the top 10 percent show an increase in competence, with the final 1 or 2 percent showing dramatically higher performance several orders of magnitude better than even the lower part of this top 10 percent.

When a population's task competence approximates the curve in Figure 2.1, you've found a topic which can be said to have experts. By choosing such a topic, you have the chance to exponentially increase the performance of that 90 to 99 percent of the population who are nonexperts.

When evaluating this point, distinguish between performance differences that result from lack of training and those that result from lack of expertise. The first refers to topics in which almost all untrained workers perform poorly, and that—conversely—the average trained performer executes competently. Expert behavior, on the other hand, denotes the above-average performance of an elite group whose performance stands out from a larger pool of otherwise trained, competent workers. The expert behavior emerges from the greater aptitude, experience, and other intangible skills that make these individuals consistently perform better than average.

Is the Problem Poorly Structured? Poorly structured problems are complex, poorly understood, and made up of many isolated facts. They are difficult to model or quantify. When a problem is well understood, it can often be solved using a set of lockstep instructions. Such problems can usually be implemented with conventional software.

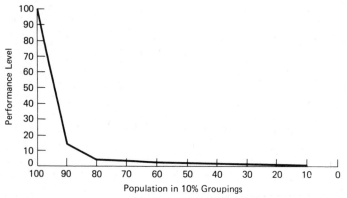

Figure 2.1. Typical Performance on Tasks Requiring Expertise.

Human experts excel at solving problems whose traits are unordered and inconsistent. Much of an expert's performance in solving poorly structured problems stems from his or her ability to ask the right question, attend to the relevant factor, and recognize the key symptom among many. The expert applies "best guesses" based on experience and insight. These "best guesses" can often be expressed as rules.

Is Nonexpert Performance Inadequate?

Do Nonexperts Perform Poorly? While experts may perform much better, their performance may not have much meaning if the performance of nonexperts is nonetheless acceptable. For example, there may be experts who understand the implications of an obscure portion of the tax code much better than the general population of accountants. Yet this may not mean much if the majority's superficial understanding is adequate for most of their clients.

On the other hand, if those nonexpert accountants are inadvertently violating tax law or losing their clientele money, this lack clearly becomes more critical. Then the lack would be a positive indicator for establishing expert need.

Is There a Shortage of Expertise, and Does It Indeed Exist?

Are a Few Key Individuals in Short Supply? When an organization becomes dependent on a tiny pool of experts, these people become a bottleneck for growth, and their shortage threatens critical areas of company performance. Therefore, if you find an area in which critical know-how is in short supply, you have found powerful evidence for expert need. Conversely, even if nonexperts perform poorly, there may be little need for an expert system if there is an adequate supply of experts.

One sure way to determine expertise shortage is to observe which people in your organization are constantly in demand for their knowledge. Is progress on various tasks held up because these individuals are overworked? Do certain employees constantly travel because only they can provide some advice or service? One sure tipoff: you have to fight to get appointments with the expert, or the expert shuffles and reschedules your appointments. When this happens consistently, it is likely you have identified an area in which there is a shortage of experts.

Is There an Expert Available? Having a shortage of expertise and having no expertise are very different situations. Without *any* reliable access, it is difficult to create an expert system.

Most expertise is local and specific to a particular environment. The development process requires an expert who is integrally involved in the project from the beginning, and who remains with it until completion and perhaps on from there. Thus it is difficult to bring in expertise from the outside unless you are working in a domain that is rather generic and you get a long-term

Table 2.2.   Expert Need Considerations in Choosing an Expert Systems Topic.

Is there a large difference between best and worst performers?

Is the problem poorly structured?

Is nonexpert performance inadequate?

Are a few key individuals in short supply?

Is an expert available?

commitment for that expert. Unless the domain is especially stable, you should probably avoid domains in which an expert is not locally available. Strive to identify topics in which the experts will be around for the long haul.

Suitability

After you have established a genuine shortage of expertise in some area that impacts the economic prospects of the firm, you must evaluate whether the domain is suitable. You have established the value of the project. Is it practical to produce it?

Evaluating the technical suitability of a proposed project is one of the most difficult tasks a new expert systems developer must undertake. You have no experience evaluating the special issues of expert systems development. What do you look for? What is and is not important? Moreover, the consequences of mistakes at this stage are missed opportunities and failed projects down the road. Therefore, it is important that you take the time to understand the issues the following questions raise. As you interview the expert to establish project feasibility, make sure that you answer these questions for yourself. We look now at the key questions you should examine about the domain that help you decide whether it can be successfully implemented.

Is the Domain Well-defined? Perhaps the most important question to examine is how well-defined the topic is. It is important because many problems that require humanlike interaction are like icebergs. We see the obvious high-level issues rise above the water. However, underneath may lurk questions and issues not readily sensed. Without a clear understanding of how these issues interact to form what we see above the water, we are not likely to succeed in building a successful system.

Unfortunately, this question is also one of the most difficult to answer. It is part of the power of the human mind that we are often not consciously aware of exactly how much we know, how we know it, and what factors go into reasoning and formulating judgments. This means that the issue requires serious and thorough analysis to define exactly what the expert system will and will not include.

If you are the expert, this analysis may be more difficult. Because you already know what you aim to encode, you probably take for granted significant portions of that knowledge. Superficially, you may believe that the domain can be lifted out of the context of your background in dealing with the topic. This is exactly what to strive for: a topic which can stand by itself without reliance on background knowledge and other factors that we will discuss momentarily. Commonly, though, as you begin work, you start to realize that new unanticipated factors are used in solving the problem, forcing a broader thrust than originally anticipated. When this occurs, it is a danger signal. The project becomes too large and may lose its focus, exceed its deadline and budget, require representation of certain unsuitable types of knowledge, and be difficult to test.

To define the domain, define the cases the expert system will solve *as specifically as possible.* Lay out detailed descriptions of common and essential problems and their symptoms that you want the expert system to address. Create a document that defines these cases and describes the types of recommendations and examples of those recommendations that the system should provide. Also spend time thinking about what the expert system *will not* handle. Write out these in detail, too. Definitions of what the system will not do are also essential. This exercise is valuable because it helps you and the expert conceive of the kinds of problems that may not be practical to solve with software.

Make sure you can describe what you are trying to accomplish in one sentence. If you cannot, you may be trying to accomplish two projects instead of one. The statement should be a catalyst for answering some hard questions. For example, the statement, "This expert system diagnoses 50 percent of the calls received by the Information Systems help desk" generates the obvious follow-up, "which 50 percent?" This, then, needs to be laid out in case study fashion. Goals that go after 50 to 75 percent of the occurrences of a topic's problems are good in that expert systems rarely solve all the cases of a problem. If you can establish the value of this kind of a goal, you probably have a good chance for success, while leaving the possibility of expanding its scope in the future.

By defining the domain in detail, you win two advantages that dramatically increase your chances for success. First, you set reasonable expectations from the start. If the expert system goes after 50 percent of the domain's possible cases, you establish a partial solution as a win. By establishing the value of this partial scope, you define in people's minds what success means, and manage the overly high hopes that expert systems projects sometimes unleash.

Second, you create a finish line for yourself. Unlike conventional analysis where the final result is somewhat easier to define,[1] knowledge-based systems development runs the risk of going on forever as the expert identifies and unpeels new and more complex layers of knowledge. To avoid this, you must create a tangible goal. The notion of an acceptable goal has a way of evolving over time. Your written definition serves as a defense against this. Use the definition as an agenda for negotiation: relate changes in the goal to the required adjustments in manpower, budget, and time that you require to meet those changing standards.

In Chapter 10, we show you interviewing techniques for defining the domain. Try to define it as concisely as possible in a manner that will still be useful. Such an initial definition may sometimes seem too narrow at first. Chances are it will expand as work proceeds and you learn more. You can usually expand a definition more easily than you can narrow one. Moreover, if you define a project too broadly, you will probably find it difficult to complete or find yourself forced to a level of superficiality which makes it useless.

Is the Problem's Solution Dependent on Common Sense? When you think about what's below the waterline, you should think specifically about several points. One of them is the role of common sense in solving the topic problem. We take common sense so for granted that we don't always realize how large a role it plays in our everyday behavior. Why do we jerk away when someone holds a heavy object over our foot and lets go? Tied up in this image is a complex array of experience and knowledge about gravity, pain, the relationship between heavy falling objects and injury, and knowing how to contract our muscles in highly precise ways to effect movement. This kind of knowledge is common sense.

In his book *The Society of Mind*, Minsky says this about common sense:

> If common sense is so diverse and intricate, what makes it seem so obvious and natural? This illusion of simplicity comes from losing touch with what happened during infancy, when we formed our first abilities. As each new group of skills matures, we build more layers on top of them. As time goes on, the layers below become increasingly remote until, when we try to speak of them in later life, we find ourselves with little more to say than "*I don't know.*"[2]

Topics that largely rely on common sense for their solution are usually poor candidates for expert systems development. As Minsky points out, our ability to acknowledge and articulate how we use common sense is usually poorly developed. The amount of knowledge necessary to approximate a common-

---

[1]There are two reasons why traditional systems are easier in this respect: they tend to automate well understood processes; they produce outputs that can be "objectively" judged.

[2]Marvin Minsky, *The Society of Mind* (New York: Simon & Schuster, 1986), 22.

sense understanding of the world is large enough to push at the frontiers of what today's development tools can do.

Evaluate whether or not your domain candidate depends on common sense. Does it rely on implied relationships among physical objects in the world? Is there a large body of assumed knowledge about the way psychological, sociological, mathematical, or other complex but somehow intuitive systems work, on which the expertise is based? If the answer is yes, the domain may depend too much on common sense.

Does Solving the Problem Depend on Sense Data? Another "below the waterline" factor you should examine is the role of sense data. Like common sense, we often take for granted just how much our reasoning relies on our senses. If the expert depends extensively on visual or auditory or other sensory cues to solve the problem, this expertise may not fare well as an expert systems topic. There are two reasons why this is the case.

First, people *interpret* what they see and hear, and people simply interpret the world too differently. This may make aligning the expert's impressions with the user's difficult. Second, we process much more information than we can verbally describe. Many nuances simply don't show up in our verbal descriptions of the world.

Consider an expert system in which the expert's interpretation of subtle shades of color are critical to a diagnostic procedure. This would probably not be a suitable topic. What if a user is color-blind? How can we be sure that users in general will properly match the shade in the same way the expert does? Further research would be necessary here, but this need should be a warning signal.

Limit the role of sense data in your expert systems topic. If shapes, sounds, colors, or other sensory inputs are required for solving the problem, make sure that the description of this data is as factual and objective as possible. For example, show pictures of symbols that users can choose instead of asking for descriptions of those symbols. This will help ensure consistent input among users.

Is the Domain Stable? If a domain's knowledge changes too rapidly, it probably should be avoided. All knowledge evolves, albeit at varying rates. Often experts will underestimate how fast it does evolve. This is because they subconsciously update their knowledge incrementally as they factor new experience into their decision making. Unless there is a dramatic change from time to time, experts are likely to say the domain doesn't change much.

Your maintenance plan must factor in the upkeep of the expert system over time. If the projected topic changes too fast, avoid it. You will end up spending your time encoding a moving target. Users will perceive it as constantly out of date, and you will find it difficult to define what the acceptance criteria are.

Are Performance Standards Realistic? Domains in which wrong results or recommendations can lead to the loss of life or of large sums of money are usually poor candidates for expert systems. People resist the use of software as a source of expertise when the results are too weighty.

The resistance has several fronts. One is legal. Some industries, especially those that can somehow affect people's health, are regulated. Must the expert system be licensed? Are there special regulations regarding expert systems? Do these regulations regard an expert system as an instrument or a tool? Must a medical expert system pass a medical exam? Must an expert systems shell get FDA approval? Who is legally liable for bugs in the expert system? These are all issues that must be considered if the expert system impacts human life or financial health.

Another issue is accountability. When a decision's impact is large, someone must be accountable. Relying on expert systems may make accountability difficult to establish. Users and management alike may feel uncomfortable allowing software programs to make decisions that affect them so deeply.

Another question is that of social interaction. While the system may provide excellent advice, it does not console, empathize, or encourage. If the domain is one in which the stakes are high, the beneficiaries of the expert advice may find these factors as important as the advice itself.

When expert systems errors can cause major financial loss or loss of human life and limb, carefully consider the role the expert system will play and the strategy for winning acceptance of that role.

Does the Problem Rely More on Heuristics Than Algorithms? How does the expert perform the task? Does the task rely on a precise, lockstep series of steps taken the same way each time? Can the expert's good performance be reduced to an algorithm? Can a concise flow chart be created which captures how the problem is solved? Is the number of possible solutions small enough that you can easily examine and test every potential solution? If so, you may be better off using conventional software to implement the project.

If the domain can be reduced to a predictable series of steps, conventional programming languages like BASIC, C, and COBOL give you better control over the processing of the problem. They often perform better than the same solution implemented with expert systems tools.

Expert systems excel at solving poorly structured problems. This means that the solution probably cannot be represented as a formula because there will be many factors and too many exception conditions. The problem space may be so large that every possible solution cannot be practically considered. Instead, the expert uses rules of thumb to narrow the number of candidates from a palette of possibilities. In some cases, the essence of the expert's behavior is using such rules of thumb to eliminate irrelevant or impractical paths from consideration. By skillfully representing this tree-pruning knowledge as rules of thumb, you capture the expert's problem-solving acumen. If this approach describes the expert's strategy, then you've found evidence in favor of the expert systems approach.

Does the Expert Deal More in Symbols Than in Numbers? This point is somewhat related to the one above. There are many kinds of expertise. The kind that expert systems shells handle well are those in which the expert represents the problems in terms of concepts or *symbols,* rather than of numbers.

While numbers are a particular set of symbols, they are symbols that operate under precise and well understood laws which can be expressed algorithmically. Specialized tools have been developed to solve problems in which mathematical symbols can represent the problem. Conventional programming languages have adequate facilities for representing numbers and generally pay attention to providing good performance in the process. An expert system can be thought of as a system for representing specialized symbols required to solve a nonnumeric problem. The problem may have inconsistencies. The shell is specially designed for representing problems that have this inconsistent nature.

Expert systems traditionally have handled numeric information poorly. In the past, many could not perform even basic arithmetic functions. Today the situation is better, but it still varies greatly among development tools. Many that provide numeric handling perform at a relatively slow pace when compared to conventional tools. If there is a substantial demand for arithmetic processing, you should evaluate whether a shell will perform adequately in this area.

If the thrust of the expert's method is quantitative, it is likely that the project can be better implemented using conventional languages or off-the-shelf software. However, if the essence of what she does is to manipulate nonnumeric symbols in a manner that cannot be readily expressed algorithmically, then the task may well be suited for the expert systems approach.

Can Results Be Evaluated? When you add two and two you get four, no matter whom you ask. Numbers and algorithms are wonderful in this respect: they return the same result every time. Their results are easy to evaluate.

The problem is not always as clear-cut when dealing with human knowledge problems. Some expertise areas are easy. For example, some diagnostic problems are easy to evaluate; you test the diagnosis with a remedy. If it fixes the problem, the diagnosis is correct. However, other kinds of expertise involve recommendations that are not always so easily confirmed. In some domains, different experts may give differing advice. In others, remedies may not work consistently for all subjects. In still others, like configuration or planning problems, it may be difficult to differentiate between an arbitrary solution, a good solution, and "the best" solution.

Is there some definite way to evaluate the results the expert system will produce? There are three ways to answer the question. If the expert system produces results that can be readily confirmed (as in many diagnostic problems), the answer is an easy "yes." You simply implement the recommendation and see if the system resolves or improves the situation.

If you cannot feed results back to determine objectively whether the system improves the status quo, another option is to adopt a "case method" of evaluation. This method entails creating or identifying a set of cases *before* development starts. When the expert system can successfully solve those cases, it is finished or "debugged" for that stage of the development cycle.

Finally, you can have the expert judge whether the results are right or wrong. This could be one expert or a committee of experts. When considering this method, assess how confident you are that the expert is consistent in the results she or he produces. If more than one expert will serve as the judging source, verify that they indeed agree on what a correct result is.

There are many reasons why it is important to answer the question of evaluating results. First, if different experts disagree about what a right solution is, you—as the systems developer—are in the "no-win" situation of trying to satisfy various conflicting parties. Second, if expert systems give results that can be interpreted in differing ways, there is a high likelihood that the recommendation your knowledge base provides will be disputed or rejected. Such a situation would be a strong argument in favor of tightening the scope of the domain or even rejecting it.

You must be able to evaluate results. As an expert systems developer, you may sometimes find it difficult to differentiate opinion from expertise. If the validity of the system's results cannot be evaluated, those results may be an opinion. Unlike humans, expert systems are not good at defending themselves from the attacks of parties with vested interests in promoting particular methods or conclusions. Your role should not be to defend an expert's reason-

Table 2.3.   Considerations for Evaluating the Suitability of the Topic.

Is the domain well-defined?

Is the problem's solution dependent on common sense?

Does solving the problem depend on sense data?

Is the domain stable?

Are performance standards realistic?

Does solving the problem rely more on heuristics than algorithms?

Does the expert deal more in symbols than in numbers?

Can results be evaluated?

ing, but instead to capture and encode it. Therefore, don't choose topics that have this "opinion" character. Inadequate work in refining this area early can lead you to create a system whose results are merely the subjective opinion of the expert—which may be the target of disputes, depending on the whims of those involved.

Technical Issues

This book looks solely at rule-based representation. Rules are a popular form of representing knowledge in expert systems. Rules are relatively easy to construct. They enable rapid prototyping; testing can begin with just a few rules. Rules often seem a natural way to summarize much of what we know. But like anything, rules mean certain tradeoffs. They have limitations. We now discuss some of the limitations of rule-based approaches, with the goal of heightening your acuity to their weaknesses. The goal of this discussion is to help you choose domains which leverage the many benefits of rules while avoiding those for which rules are poorly suited.

Rules Require Sufficient Knowledge. If you conceive of all the knowledge in a domain as a line, each rule represents one point on that line. The job of the developer is to acquire knowledge and create enough "points" so that a line of reasoning can be tied together (see Figure 2.2). If the expert cannot articulate his or her knowledge, too few rules will produce a system that answers "UNKNOWN" more often than is acceptable. If the domain is defined too broadly, the line becomes so long that encoding and testing all the rules representing it becomes too large a project.

Using rules, developers run the risk of creating arbitrary, incomplete systems that appear pointillistic at close range. Such systems risk reflecting an incomplete or inaccurate picture of the domain. This fact points out the importance of concise domain definition, and of making sure that there is indeed enough knowledge available to solve the problem.

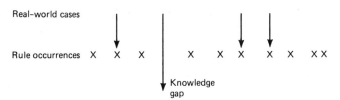

Figure 2.2. Depiction of Knowledge Gaps in a Set of Rules.

Rules Model the Domain Implicitly. One of the underlying assumptions of the rule-based approach is that the expert's use of rules of thumb can solve the problem at hand. This assumes that the expert does not have a mathematical or other model which algorithmically generates solutions or solution candidates. Instead, the expert relies on experience and intuition to deal with situations he or she has encountered over and over again. The technical jargon for this process is the so-called "recognize-act" cycle. The expert *recognizes* certain situations, and *acts* accordingly. These acts include activities like asking questions, inferring intermediate steps, and choosing what next step to take or knowledge to apply. This *recognize-act* approach is central to rule-based systems.

Problems that rely on *explicit* modeling may not be suitable for rule-based systems. By explicit modeling, we mean that the target of the expert's reasoning is represented in such a way that its elements or behavior is simulated in some manner. For example, one might create a model of a factory to test its performance under certain capacity loads. Each production line might be represented by showing how each machine or other component of that line interacts with others. The expert's knowledge is then encoded in such a way that it can be applied to this model.

Rule-based systems usually represent the expert's useful insights in recognizing and remedying certain conditions in the domain. It does not usually model how the domain works. As the rule-based system comes into existence, it starts to implicitly portray the domain by virtue of the accumulated facts and rules that describe the expert's reasoning. If this implicit *recognize-act* approach is not sufficient, then a strictly rule-based approach may not be the right one.

Rules Do Not Easily Model Objects in the Domain. Rules alone are not well suited for solving problems in which many objects interact. One easy way to determine unsuitability is to detect whether there are three instead of two significant levels of description.

For example, an expert system diagnosing flu in a patient revolves around reasoning about various kinds of symptoms in that patient. The physician may reason using two levels of description about the patient, considering:

1. The patient's various symptoms; and
2. each symptom's value or values.

An oversimplified rule he or she might formulate might look like this:

RULE 89
IF   glands = swollen
THEN diag_evidence = flu

The reasoning about these various symptom-value pairs is what makes up the essence of the expertise. The premise *glands = swollen* could be expanded to spell out an important assumption. The assumption is that there is only one patient. The world this expert system is concerned with deals only with one patient at a time.

If we expand the problem to include knowledge that predicts or explains the spread of flu throughout a population, the representation job becomes more complex by an order of magnitude. This complexity results because we now need to add a third level of description. Reasoning about this problem now includes three major factors:

1. Each patient's
2. various symptoms and behaviors; and
3. their value or values.

This kind of rule may now be necessary:

RULE 89
IF   patient-X-glands = swollen
AND   patient-Y-glands = swollen
THEN diag_evidence = flu_has_spread

In the jargon of expert systems, the representation scheme has grown from an *attribute-value pair* to an *object-attribute-value triplet*. The expert system may now need to reason about interactions among members. It may need to be able to reason without a priori knowledge of exactly how many members exist. The knowledge may include reasoning about complex interactions among individuals, each individual's symptoms, or even about subgroups of individuals. This may require a mode of reasoning that rule-based systems have difficulty representing.

The addition of a third dimension may dramatically expand the amount of knowledge needed. It may balloon the number of potential solutions that must be considered. If a two-level problem can be represented as a line, the addition of multiple objects adds another dimension. Thus now we must create enough rules to tie together a line of reasoning in a plane (see Figure 2.3).

Because of their added complexity, such problems fall outside the scope of this book. While there are rule-based expert systems tools that can represent three levels of description, these tools often require greater expertise and experience and their use is difficult to generalize. Other paradigms, such as "object-oriented" or "frames-based," may work better. For new developers, we recommend that such projects be approached only with the greatest care. If your organization lacks experience, you may decide to use experienced consultants or choose another problem. The decision to use a strictly rule-based

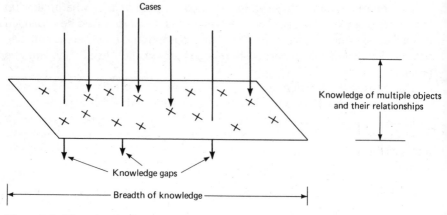

Figure 2.3. Three levels of description increase the technical challenge.

approach to problems in which the major targets of reasoning contain three or more levels of description should be made with the greatest caution.

Rules Do Not Model Time. For domains in which representing time is vital to solving the problem, rule-based approaches may not be adequate. The finer the resolution required, the more this rule of thumb is true.

For example, an expert system which simulates an airstrip for purposes of scheduling the gate assignment of planes requires time to be a major and deciding factor in evaluating whether the system works. The clock plays a major part in deciding *what* action should be performed *when* and is consulted on a minute-by-minute basis. Unless the shell has specific facilities for representing time, a solely rule-based approach is almost certainly not the right approach for this.

On the other hand, if only coarse time divisions are necessary, representing time may not be a problem. If the domain compares before and after results, or uses large chunks of time like "morning," "afternoon," and "night," such divisions should easily be represented.

The problem of dealing with time is analogous to the problem of modeling objects with rules because it adds a third level of description. If the expert reasons about the patient's symptoms while the diagnostic process is in progress, the expert can assume that "time = now." If the diagnosis includes considerations from last week's therapy, the expert system might yet handle the problem with rules comparing *last_weeks_swelling* and *todays_swelling*. However, if the expertise includes reasoning that involves progress over many days or hours, there may be too many "time units" to explicitly represent. At this point, the knowledge engineer must likely resort to strategies that specifi-

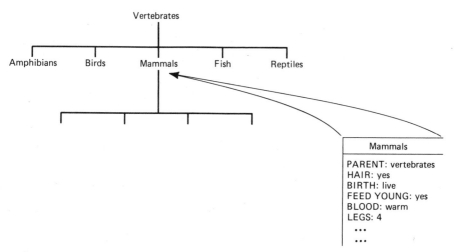

Figure 2.4. A Class Hierarchy.

cally use time as an integral part of the representation approach. An approach that uses only rules may fall short or complicate the development project to the point that advanced tools and skills are required.

Problems of Hierarchy. When the objects of reasoning tend to fall into hierarchical relationships, strictly rule-based systems may prove awkward and cumbersome unless they have an "inheritance" mechanism. For example, an expert system that identifies animal classes based on observations about specific biological traits might use a hierarchical representation of those classes that is best represented using frames. Figure 2.4 shows a fragment of how such a hierarchy might graphically appear.

Each level in the graph has traits that occurrences below it on the graph inherit. By organizing these objects to represent this hierarchy, an object occurring below an object may inherit the traits of those parental objects. The developer need not write rules that specifically assign those traits for every instance that falls below it on the graph. If this were the case, it would force the creation of redundant rules like the following:

```
RULE giraffe_is_mammal
IF   giraffe = mammal
THEN giraffe_blood = warm
     giraffe_birth = live
     giraffe_hair = yes
     etc. . .
```

RULE mouse_is_mammal
IF   mouse = mammal
THEN mouse_blood = warm
        mouse_birth = live
        mouse_hair = yes
        etc. . .

Although some development tools (PROLOG, for example) let you write expressions that can represent the above knowledge in a general way, few rule-only shells support this capability. If your topic exhibits hierarchical relationships, you'll need a shell with facilities for representing hierarchical relationships. This is usually found in shells that offer "frames" representation capability.

Problem Space Must Be Pruned. The number of possible positions and moves in a chess game is so large as to be virtually inexpressible. Thus chess players don't consider every possible combination. Based on their experience and recognition of good and bad positions, the best chess players weed out unpromising lines early and concentrate on the fewer possibilities with promise.

This ability to recognize promising lines among vast numbers of unpromising options or solutions is a characteristic of expert behavior. If the expert system had to consider each conceivable combination that occurred along the road to solving a problem, it would probably never solve it. This is called "combinatorial explosion." The number of possibilities increases exponentially, since each new branch itself contains many branches.

Combinatorial explosion not only threatens the efficiency of human thinking, but can also bring a computer to its knees. Therefore, it is important that you evaluate how you can avoid combinatorial explosions. How does the expert avoid extensive examination of unpromising lines of exploration? Can you develop rules that eliminate groups of possibilities from consideration? If the problem has large numbers of potential search paths, you must gain a firm understanding of how the expert avoids looking at all the possibilities or giving too much attention to unpromising candidates.

Solutions to the Problem Are Preenumerated. The possible solutions to some problems are known beforehand. For example, an auto repairman knows that cars won't start for one of several possible reasons. The answer is chosen from a relatively small group of common causes with which the expert is familiar. The job, then, is to track *which one* of those problems is causing this or that particular car failure. The expert reasons "backwards," asking questions whose answers will help him or her match those causes to the symptoms for this particular car.

Table 2.4. Considerations for Evaluating the Technical Suitability of Rules for the Topic.

Can you get enough knowledge for rules to be effective?

Does the expert use an explicit model of the domain to solve the problem?

Are three levels of description required to represent the objects in the domain?

Does solving the problem require a finely granulized representation of time?

Are objects in the domain hierarchically organized?

Can the problem space be pruned?

Are the solutions to the problem preenumerated?

Domains whose possible solutions can be named are said to be "preenumerated." Such domains can have solutions as easy as yes/no or confirm/deny. Or, they may have as many as five, ten, or more possible recommendations. Expert systems addressing such problems use a strategy of narrowing down the candidates until ultimately one fits the situation better than its competitors do. Typical kinds of expert systems that rely on this approach are diagnostic, classification, debugging, repair, and selection. If the domain you examine has a preenumerated solution set, this is evidence in favor of the domain's suitability.

Dealing with Organizational Issues

The organizational issues of successfully producing and deploying an expert system may be much fuzzier than the technical issues. Yet these issues may impact the success—and perception of success—as much as any technical consideration. You should consider how these questions may impact you and your project.

Get Organizational Commitment to Learn and Explore. Before you conquer a new land, you must explore it—even if you believe it to be the promised land. Not until you explore its peaks and valleys can you know which parts of the land are worth settling on, which areas will reap the best harvest.

If you are new to expert systems development, you should be working towards getting management to provide a period of relatively low expectations so that you may familiarize yourself with expert systems tools and techniques, with the privilege to make false starts, mistakes, and errors. As you make mistakes, you learn. As you learn, you bring an equity of knowledge to the environment that qualifies you to take on challenges that can pay back the learning time you invest many times over.

Get an environment in which you can learn. If you are expected to produce weighty results from the beginning, you are falling into a trap prescribed for failure. Sell the organization on a period in which you produce several prototypes. The prototypes serve as a proof of concept and as a learning experience. They provide the chance for the organization to absorb results, and discover what is and is not reasonable to target in a production system.

Lower Expectations. Expert systems have been the target—and victim—of hype and overwrought promises. If you allow yourself to be caught up in unrealistic expectations, you will become their victim.

An expert system is just computer software. As the saying goes, "it's all ones and zeros." There is nothing magical about expert systems. Expert systems do not write themselves. They produce no more than is put into them. They produce errors if the knowledge contains errors. Expert systems are not panaceas.

Both management and the user of the expert system may tend to view expert systems as something different and unique—something of a cross between a person and a computer program. All the human factors that arise in the integration of computers into a new environment can become doubly critical with an expert system.

It is important that you create an environment in which expectations for the expert systems project you choose are coherent and rational. The benefits of expert systems technology are real. The idea that they magically solve problems is not. Help users see the expert system as just another computer program.

Think Small, Think Incremental! Before you learn to run, learn to walk. When choosing the first expert systems project, it is usually wise to choose one which is relatively small. Additionally, it may be useful to build on some expertise or system in which the organization already has experience. This is one of the reasons that data processing "help desk" applications are popular: the developers often are already somewhat familiar with the domain. This puts them on familiar ground from the start.

One way to "think small" is to reduce the number of unknowns or new tasks in the first development effort. For example, find a source of clearly documented written knowledge as the first expertise source. This reduces the challenge of knowledge acquisition and allows you to focus on representing knowledge and using the expert systems shell facilities. Another possibility is to try to automate one small independent segment of a human expert's reasoning.

By "think incremental," we mean that you may find it easier to build on something that already exists. For example, if the organization already has an EIS (executive information system) or DSS (decision support system), you might try to build an expert system that performs a small portion of the executive analysis that human experts perform on that data. By adding to or building on some existing system, you may find it easier to gain acceptance for the expert system.

Establish the Role of the Expert System. What role will the expert system play? Broadly, you should try to establish one of three roles for the expert. The first role, *advisor*, is the least demanding. An advisor system may serve as a "reality check" system, helping experts and other decision makers check their preliminary solutions to domain problems against the expert system. If the two opinions coincide, the expert's opinion is reinforced. If the advisor system disagrees with the expert, the expert does further research, thinking, interrogation of the advisor system's line of reasoning, etc. The role of the advisor system is to ensure consistency, to act as a "sounding board," to be a training system. It is not expected to perform up to the expert's standards. This is also an appropriate role for expert systems which deal in domains affecting large sums of money or decisions which could possibly cause human injury or loss of life.

Peer systems work as the equal of the humans who consult them. The human may have some knowledge in the domain, but not enough to reliably work through the problem alone. His or her performance may not always be optimal. The expert system's role may be to suggest viable solution candidates from which the human makes the final decision. In this role, the expert system is a decision support aid which can explain its reasoning, or ensure that the right questions are asked. However, it differs from the expert role in that the human user plays an essential role in the final decision. Human and expert system work together toward a solution.

Finally, expert systems may play the *expert role*. Users consult the expert system to address problems they deal with inadequately without the expert. They have no substantial knowledge about the problem domain. The expert system has the final word. When expert systems play the expert role, there is little tolerance for error. The expert system must be complete within its defined domain.

For early projects, the technically easiest and usually most readily accepted role is that of advisor, followed by peer, and finally expert. Because they keep the human user in the decision loop, advisor and peer systems are less threatening. Because the expert role makes greater demands for accuracy and completeness, the domain must be precisely defined, and the system extensively field tested before deployment into that role. Therefore, consider starting with advisor systems first.

The moves from advisor to peer to expert represent a logical evolution for an expert system. As users become familiar with the expert system, they come to accept it. Thus after successfully fielding an advisor system, you may decide to upgrade its role. Thus the three roles are not mutually exclusive. There can be overlap and movement up the ladder over time.

If the eventual goal for the expert system is for it to play the expert role, treat it like a new employee. First train it. Give it a small amount of responsibility and expect it to make mistakes. When it does, correct it. As it gets better and its (human) peers accept it, promote it. Finally, when its performance is proven, the move to the expert role will seem natural. Trying to force it on the user community is like trying to impose a new boss on a group of established employees. Either the boss will go, or you'll need new employees.

Get the Right Expert. Where does the expertise for the expert system come from? Usually from a human being. Therefore, the human expert plays a decisive role in determining how good the finished expert system is. Finding the right expert is a critically important step in creating a good expert system.

What should you look for in an expert? The expert should be articulate. Many human experts are poor at explaining how they reason or arrive at conclusions. The experience and background they bring to bear is such a part of their fabric that they have difficulty separating the knowledge they assume anyone should have from the high-level concepts they use to eventually reach a conclusion. For this reason, many experts believe their domain is easily described, because it depends on a few simple decision factors. Upon further examination, the knowledge engineer finds that these "few" concepts emerge only through a sophisticated and complex processing of experience, unnamed assumptions, and hidden knowledge that the expert has cultivated. If the expert is ultimately unable to explain this background knowledge, you will have difficulty capturing the knowledge and creating the expert system.

Articulate experts are good with language, have a high degree of self-awareness, and find the give and take of knowledge engineering interesting and challenging. They are usually intelligent and can "think about thinking." They display some degree of patience, acknowledge the depth of the background knowledge they take for granted, and can "bracket" these assumptions, getting back to first principles and basic knowledge. Experts must take a personal interest in educating the knowledge engineer. Their role is not only to explain reasoning, but to teach and test the knowledge engineer.

The expert must be committed to the project. This is a factor that is often ignored because of its mundane nature. In practice, it is crucial to the project's success. Experts are scarce. They are in demand. They may be managers, they may travel, and they may have an appetite for high-level, challenging activity. They may enthusiastically endorse the effort to develop an expert system.

Then reality sets in. They assume they can fit the knowledge engineering activity into several one-hour appointments. They underestimate the amount of detail the interviewing process requires. They become impatient with the slow pace. They fail to budget adequate time for evaluating the software prototype throughout the development cycle. They lose interest as the aura wears off. It becomes difficult to meet next week's progress goals when the expert whose knowledge makes up the system refuses to see you until the week after next.

Experts must be personally committed to the long-term success of the project. They must see it as a personal win, in their own interest as well as the organization. For the project to be successful, the project must rise high on the priority list. Depending on the scope and ambition of the project, significant chunks of time must be allotted for initial interviewing, follow-up sessions, prototype evaluation, and maintenance.

Why should the expert see the success of the system as a personal win? Because it propagates the expert's influence throughout the organization. Because the role of expert becomes even more critical in creating and maintaining the expert system. The software is not a threat to replace the expert, but a screen from the trivial time-wasting jobs that tax experts, so that they may concentrate on the truly challenging applications of their knowledge. Experts are always needed, because expertise evolves.

Get the Organization Sufficiently Committed. Company management must also be committed to the project. Like the expert, it is easy for management to endorse the *concept* of creating an expert system. They may be less enthusiastic when conflicts arise between putting the expert in the field and consigning him or her to another day on the project. The organization must see the commitment in terms of investing in the short-term in order to win long-term gains.

The success of any technology ultimately depends on the perceptions and attitudes of the humans who create and use it. Without the commitment from

Table 2.5.   Organizational Issues to Consider in Choosing an Expert Systems Topic.

Can you get organizational commitment to learn and explore?

Are expectations reasonable?

Have you established a realistic role for the expert system?

Is the expert suitable?

Is the expert committed?

Will management support the diversion of the expert's time?

both the organization and the expert, you may find yourself waiting in line for a quick dose of expertise. This will probably be insufficient for understanding the domain well enough to encode it.

THE TRAIN AND THE CAR

To answer the questions this chapter raises, you must dig deeply into the domain. You will spend considerable time with the expert. Significant interviewing time is absolutely essential to get a handle on the risk factors of the project. Since you most likely aren't an expert in the proposed domain, this means a willingness to dig into the content of the expertise in order to answer the important questions of this chapter.[3] Once you have done this, you may find surprises—both desirable and undesirable—along the way.

Expert systems projects require an acknowledgment and acceptance of a certain amount of risk. With conventional software, we are used to building software in much the same way as a railway is built. First, you survey the land. Then, the route is planned from beginning to end. The site is excavated. Track is laid down. Once the track is laid, there are no changing traffic conditions or other interruptions for the train. The path has been decided. There is little that is unknown for the train engineer.

Expert systems development is more like driving a car to a place about whose whereabouts you have only approximate knowledge. Before you drive, you look at the map and ask for directions. Then you get in the car and go. You look out the windshield, and continually evaluate and adjust your direction. You may find unexpected obstacles not found on the map. You swerve to avoid the dog that runs into your path. You may hit dead ends, or have to back up and detour. You encounter road construction. It is even possible that the road will be blocked, and cannot get you where you thought you wanted to go.

The risk of operating a railroad is borne during the planning stages. Once the planning is done, the construction is a workmanlike job. The risk of driving the car is in the process of driving. Road conditions change so you don't have the *complete* picture of what you should expect—no matter how carefully you read the map. Similarly, problems of human knowledge are bottlenecked by the articulation of the expert's knowledge. You won't be able to flush out every relevant factor before you start. Therefore, be prepared to adjust your course, and revise definitions and goals as you go. If you ignore the questions discussed here, you may have to turn around and go home.

Use the guidelines of this chapter as your map. When you do the work to answer the questions it raises, you've surveyed the road as best you can. You

---

[3]We cover interviewing the expert and what information you need to gather in Chapters 10 and 11.

will have lowered the risk to a level in which the benefits of the expert systems project should outweigh whatever risk of adjustment remains. Now stay flexible and drive. Make sure the organization knows the type of vehicle you're driving.

SUMMARY

The seeds of success are sown in the choosing, formulating, and expectation-setting stages of the development cycle. No amount of technical competence can turn a poorly defined domain into one that is well-defined. Knowledge cannot be properly acquired from an uninterested expert. No amount of programming skill will win over negative, resistant users. Therefore, developers and their managers will do well to address the issues of this chapter carefully.

Rule-based expert systems are one of the most widely used paradigms for representing knowledge. But they have limitations that preclude their exclusive use in some applications. To use a rule-based shell, it is important to choose problems that rule-based shells can address. By using the guidelines in this chapter, you will increase your chances of choosing problems that work within the capacity, performance, and representational constraints that rule-based expert systems have.

3 | *Understanding the Basics*

In this chapter, we explain the basic building blocks of rule-based systems. We look at the differences between conventional programming variables and their expert systems counterparts: attributes. We discuss attribute properties and show those that are most commonly used. We look at the component parts of rules and show some common forms and variations.

RULE-BASED EXPERT SYSTEMS

We broadly define expert systems by their ability to provide humanlike interaction. This book, however, has a narrower gaze, focusing on expert systems developed with rule-based expert systems shells. This represents a major portion of expert systems development today, especially for new developers. It also represents both the easiest way to get started developing expert systems and the one that deals with useful expert systems types like diagnostic, selection, and classification systems.

Technically, rule-based expert systems can be thought of as having three components: a knowledge base, an inference engine, and a user interface (Figure 3.1). The "knowledge base" is the portion of the expert system which contains the knowledge. This knowledge is expressed as a collection of IF/THEN rules. The "inference engine" is a software module programmed to process these rules. The "user interface" provides the means by which users interact with the expert system. The user interface accepts entries, displays data to the user, and may provide graphics, rule editing, and other capabilities to help you create and improve the quality of the knowledge base and its interaction with users. User interface facilities may include windowing, graphics, query features, and others.

Expert systems shells are software products designed to enable the development of expert systems. They are called "shells" because they don't contain

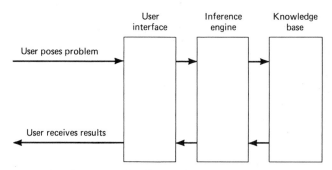

Figure 3.1 Structure of an Expert System.

knowledge about anything—they are a shell of an expert system, an expert system without knowledge. Accordingly, the shell has two of the three components of an expert system: the user interface and the inference engine.

The inference engine is the part of the shell that is already programmed for you. It has been written by the vendor to interpret the knowledge bases you create. This is one of the major advantages of shells—you don't have to write this program yourself. Moreover, the inference engine is general enough that it can interpret any knowledge base that is created in accordance with the specifications of the product. Therefore, it is reusable over many different topics.

The inference engine chooses which rule to consider, "knows" where to look to find data when they are needed, and recognizes when it is through working on a problem. Thus the developer's job is focused on the reverse of the issue that concerns the conventional programmer. The knowledge base developer works at creating the data—that is, the knowledge base—that the inference engine processes. In conventional programming, developers work at telling the computer what to do. Instead, you focus on telling the computer *what* to *know*. You do this by using rules.

ATTRIBUTES

Attributes are symbols you use in expert systems to represent knowledge. They are also called parameters, variables, factors, conditions, facts, or expressions depending on the expert systems shell you use. If you have ever programmed in BASIC or other "conventional" languages, the closest analogy to an attribute is the *variable*. Keep in mind, however, that there are important differences between expert systems attributes and the conventional variable. We'll look at these as we go.

In an expert system that advises on the topic of car-buying, you may have attributes like "desired_car," "advice," "budget," and "prestige." The values these attributes may have can be limited or *constrained*. For example:

Desired_car: (Truck, van, sedan, sports_coupe)
Budget: numeric
Advice: "I recommend you consider buying . . . "
Prestige: (yes, no)

Each of the above examples contains different value types. The attribute *budget* may contain only numeric information. *Prestige* represents whether or not the buyer values prestige. It is a "boolean" value, that is, it may have the values yes or no. *Advice* contains a text string. *Desired_car* contains "symbolic" values; in this case, various kinds of cars. The values that *desired_car* may have are preenumerated, that is, all its possible values are known.

Whenever the expert system "assigns" a value to an attribute, we say that value is "bound" or "instantiated" to the attribute. Attributes become bound to values from knowledge sources which may include rules, keyboard entries, external programs, and data files. The result is often referred to as an "attribute-value" or "a-v" pair. This means that the attribute used to represent something is bound to one or more values. *Desired_car = van* is an example of an a-v pair.

One important way in which expert systems attributes differ from variables in conventional programming is that attributes symbolically represent the concepts and things about which the expert reasons, while variables represent memory locations. For example, the assignment statement

color = red

has the following meaning in an expert system:

The symbol *color* is given the value *red.*

It would have the following meaning in a conventional program:

Replace the value stored in the memory location represented by the name *color* with the value stored in the memory location represented by the name *red.*

In conventional programming languages, *color* and *red* would play the role of an easy-to-read shorthand for accessing memory locations.

Expert systems programming focuses instead on representing knowledge. Here *red* means nothing more than the characters r-e-d that we've associated with a symbol *color.* It has meaning insofar as we, as intelligent life, believe there is a relationship between the two. We should draw no conclusion about how the expert system represents this internally, nor what the computer will do with this knowledge. The expression *color* = *red* does not direct the computer to "do" anything. Likewise, most expert systems shells will treat

budget = 10

as representing that the attribute *budget* should be bound to the characters "1 and 0," not some binary or floating point representation of the number ten. If later you want to perform some arithmetic operation with the number "ten," you may or may not be able to do this in the particular expert systems shell you use. If you can, you may need to follow special syntax rules to distinguish between the value consisting of the characters "1 and 0," and the number *ten*. In this book, we make this distinction by enclosing the latter in parentheses:

budget = (10)

When assigned in this manner, budget may be arithmetically manipulated like a conventional numeric variable. This distinction between symbolic and numeric values highlights one of the traditionally important differences between expert systems and conventional programming. Expert systems excel in representing and manipulating nonnumeric symbolic knowledge. Conventional programs excel in handling numeric symbols. In expert systems, you should pay special attention to how you express arithmetic operations in the shell.

Another difference between attributes and variables is that attributes may have *properties*. Properties are traits that belong to an attribute that influence how the expert systems shell processes it. For ease of reading, we organize these traits into an *attribute property list* for each attribute. Each item in the list names a certain attribute property and provides a value for it. We've already seen one property: "**type**." The attribute property list for *desired_car* and *prestige* look like this:

NAME: desired_car
TYPE: symbol
EXPECT: (Truck, van, sedan, sports_coupe)
PROMPT: "What kind of vehicle do you prefer?"

NAME: prestige
TYPE: boolean
EXPECT: (yes, no)

The attribute names are *desired_car* and *prestige*. As we have seen, the TYPE constrains the kind of value each attribute may have. The TYPE of *desired_car* is "symbol" and the type of *prestige* is "boolean." The "EXPECT" property names the particular values that the attribute is permitted to have.

Only preenumerated attributes have EXPECT properties. Finally, the "PROMPT" property contains a question that the inference engine may use to ask the user for a value for that attribute.

Multivalued Attributes

Another property that separates conventional variables and expert systems attributes is that of *multiple values*. Because variables represent a memory location, and memory locations can only hold one value at a time, variables can only represent one value at a time.

The problems which humans solve may have more than cause. Human advice may contain more than one suggestion. For example, if the expert systems user stipulates that he or she required an above-average amount of space in the car about to be bought, it would be perfectly reasonable for an expert system to recommend that the client consider both a truck *and* a van. Because attributes represent symbols, and symbols may plausibly have more than one value, most shells let you bind more than one value to an attribute.

Our updated property lists look like this:

```
NAME:    desired_car
TYPE:    symbol
EXPECT: (Truck, van, sedan, sports_coupe)
PROMPT: "What kind of vehicle do you prefer?"
MULTI:   yes


NAME:    prestige
TYPE:    boolean
EXPECT: (yes, no)
MULTI:   no
```

As we progress through this book, we will add categories to the attribute property list. In the glossary, you will find how the attribute property list translates into the syntax used by various popular expert systems development tools.

RULES

Data turn into knowledge when we understand the relationships that exist among those data. You represent the data—the things and ideas of the domain—using attributes. You represent the relationships among those attributes using rules.

What Are Rules?

Rules are the basic building blocks of rule-based expert systems. Rules consist of a *premise* and a *conclusion*. The action specified in the conclusion is taken when the rule is considered and the expression in the premise is found to be true.

RULE 1
IF   color = yellow
THEN fruit = banana

Rule 1 is an example of a rule. It consists of a premise containing one clause (a *simple* premise) and a conclusion. *Rule 1* binds the value *banana* to the attribute named *fruit* when it is determined that the value *yellow* is currently bound to the attribute *color*. When the conclusion of a rule is executed, we say that the rule "fires." In expert systems terms, the attribute *fruit* is instantiated or bound to the value *banana*. This means that the value *banana* is assigned to the attribute *fruit*.

Note four syntactical points about the rule. The rule has a name which follows the keyword RULE (in this case, the number "1"). The premise starts immediately following the keyword IF. Conclusions appear directly after THEN. All three structures appear in all rule-based shells. Most use exactly these keywords. The particulars for most shells are spelled out in the glossary.

Also, the equal sign appears twice in *Rule 1*, but plays two different roles. In the premise, the equal sign tests whether the attribute named on the left side of the expression is currently bound to the value named on the right side. In the conclusion, the equal sign serves as an assignment operator. The value *banana* is bound to attribute *fruit* if the premise is found to be true. These two uses of the equal sign are analogous to the two different operators in the C language: " = = " and " = ."

Why Rules? Why do we use rules to represent knowledge? There are many reasons why rules are useful. Well-written rules are *transparent,* that is, they allow you to see through the syntax to the meaning. They are therefore easy to read and understand. A rule-based expert system can provide a clear record of the knowledge within a domain and make it easier to understand than conventional programming. This makes the knowledge more accessible, eases development and maintenance of the expert system, and in general increases the productivity of those who do the development.

The IF/THEN form that rules take is often a natural way to represent a reasoning process. Rules are easy to construct and modify. Because well-written rules are relatively independent, they can usually be changed without affecting other parts of the knowledge base.[1] Rules allow you to quickly create

---

[1] We discuss the notion of well-written rules in Chapters 12 and 14.

prototypes to test ideas and prove feasibility. They encourage you to begin testing early in the development process—essential for a good result.

Rules Are Your Reasoning Building Blocks. A rule is an autonomous, self-standing entity. Each should clearly reflect its own bit of knowledge. One of the most difficult tasks for novice developers is getting in the habit of thinking about rules as independent units that are not procedurally linked to other rules. If you have programmed in other languages, you may think of the IF/THEN structure as one that determines branching and control transfer. Here are three different simple examples taken from the programming languages COBOL, C, and BASIC:

COBOL:

```
    200-MOVE-AND-WRITE.
    MOVE SPACES TO RECORD-IN
    TAPE-INFO.
    READ INPUT-FILE INTO RECORD-IN
    AT END
        GO TO 209-EXIT.
    IF SUPPRESS-RECORD = "X" AND
    (CONTROL-SORT-CODE = "T" OR
    CONTROL-SORT-CODE = "C")
        GO TO 200-MOVE-AND-WRITE
    ELSE
        PERFORM 210-TITLE-REPORT THRU 229-EXIT.
    209-EXIT.
    EXIT.
```

C:

```
main()
{
    float x;

    while ((c = getchar())-'0')
        if (isdigit(c)){
```

```
        x = multiple();      /* call function "multiple()" */
        printf("The current value of x is %g\n", x);
    }
    else
        printf("The character is ignored");


}
```

BASIC:

```
4240 IF SCR% = 0 THEN 4398
     IF SCR% < = NRVALS% THEN
        CALL CSAVE(SCR%, V, I%)
     ELSE
        CALL FIXGET(SCR%, V$)
        CALL EVALU8
        IF E% < > 0 THEN
            I% = BITSERROR%
        ELSE
            I% = 0
        END IF
     END IF
```

Notice that in each of these examples the IF/THEN structure is just as likely to transfer control to other parts of the program as it is to assign values. In these languages, the programmer is concerned with detailing a lockstep procedural script for each step the program will execute. This is a major difference between conventional programming languages like C, COBOL, and BASIC, and expert systems programming. Control transfer among statements and software modules plays an important and explicit role in the former. In expert systems, however, control transfer plays a much smaller role. As the expert systems developer, you focus more of your attention on identifying and codifying individual pieces of nonprocedural knowledge as rules.

Rules Are Like Data Base Records. Conventional program statements have meaning insofar as they are properly positioned in relation to other statements in the program. Any one statement tells you nothing about the overall func-

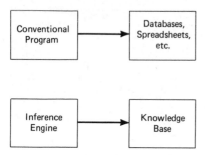

Figure 3.2. The inference engine plays the role of the conventional program.

tionality of the program. The program is an instruction script telling the computer what to do.

On the other hand, each rule documents something about the domain. There is little or no necessary rule order for most knowledge bases to properly represent this "something." While we will later examine techniques that help you fine-tune the processing of the knowledge base, *rule order usually should not affect whether a knowledge base ultimately provides correct results.*

This important difference between conventional and expert systems programming is illustrated in Figure 3.2. The conventional program specifies a series of instructions that act on various resources: computer memory, disk drives, external data bases, printers. The knowledge base, however, is more like a data base. It consists of a series of logically organized components (rules) that are in many ways similar to records. Like a record, a rule is not procedurally linked to other rules. Like a record, the information it contains is logically related. When you create a data base, you create nonprocedural, independent units of data. When you create rules, you create independent units of knowledge which express the relationship among certain factors.

How are rules used? Like data bases, they are accessed and processed by a program. The data base is processed using a data base manager. The knowledge base is processed by an inference engine. The inference engine uses one of several methods of "inferencing" to select which rule in the knowledge base to process. The data base manager uses an algorithm to choose which record to process.

To summarize, the knowledge base is a data base of knowledge. Your most important task is to accurately represent this knowledge. This highlights a key difference between conventional and expert systems programming: when you create a knowledge base, you create "data," not a script of instructions telling the computer what to do.

There Is No Right or Wrong Size for a Rule. Rules are autonomous, self-standing entities. Each should clearly reflect its own independent bit of knowledge. The size and complexity of a rule should be decided by the complexity of the knowledge. There is no arbitrary "right" or "wrong" size. Rules may contain a single premise clause or twenty clauses. Let the knowledge dictate the rule's size.

Premises

The example *Rule 1* examined above contains a simple premise. A simple premise is one that contains a single premise clause. A premise clause tests the relationship between one attribute and a potential value. Simple premises don't provide enough expressive potential to encode more complex reasoning. To help you express more sophisticated knowledge, premises may contain more than one clause. You accomplish this using the keywords *OR* and *AND*. For example:

RULE 2
IF   color = red
AND   size = like_a_rubber_ball
THEN fruit = apple

The premise of *Rule 2* contains two clauses connected by AND. This is called a "conjunction." Conjunctions require that all premise clauses connected by AND be true for the rule to fire. In this example, this means that *color = red* and *size = like_a_rubber_ball* must both be true in order to fire *Rule 2* and infer *fruit = apple*.

Disjunctions are groups of premise clauses connected by the keyword OR. Only one clause among many connected by OR need be true for the overall premise, and therefore the rule, to be true. *Rule 3's* premise is a disjunction. If either clause is true, the entire premise is considered true and the rule fires.

RULE 3
IF   color = orange
OR   juice = orange_juice
THEN fruit = orange

Several expert systems shells don't support disjunctions. You can overcome this limitation by splitting the knowledge item into separate rules with simple premises. Write one rule for each OR clause in the original rule. For example, *Rule 3* could be rewritten

RULE 3a
IF   color = orange
THEN fruit = orange

RULE 3b
IF   juice = orange_juice
THEN fruit = orange

If either of the two rules is true, attribute *fruit* is instantiated to *orange*. *Rule 3* is functionally equivalent to *Rule 3a* and *Rule 3b* insofar as they both conclude the proper values.

Conjunctions and disjunctions may contain more than two clauses. This enables you to express knowledge in which many factors must be considered in a single rule. For example:

RULE 4
IF   desired_car = sports_coupe
OR   delivery = now
OR   prestige = high
OR   price = low
THEN recommendation = buy

RULE 5
IF   color = red
AND   size = small
AND   grows_on = bush
AND   taste = sweet
THEN fruit = strawberry

If any one of the four premise clauses in *Rule 4* is true, *Rule 4* will fire. For `Rule 5* to fire, all four premise clauses must be true.

Rules may also contain both AND and OR in the premise.

RULE 6
IF   desired_car = van
OR   desired_car = truck
AND   amount = high
OR   amount = medium
AND   prestige = low
THEN advice = "Don't buy a sedan"

This rule is easier to evaluate than it may at first seem. First, group clauses connected by OR together and evaluate whether any one clause of that group is true. If so, that entire group is true because each group is treated as a disjunction. Do this for each group of clauses connected by OR. Then evaluate the logical outcome of each evaluation as clauses that are connected by AND. You can do this by imagining that parentheses surround the clauses connected by OR.

RULE 6
IF   (desired_car = van   *Group 1*
      OR desired_car = truck)
AND   (amount = high   *Group 2*
      OR amount = medium)
AND   prestige = low   *Group 3*
THEN advice = "Don't buy a sedan"

Rule 6 fires if all three of the following conditions are true:

- One or both of the two clauses in "Group 1" are true.
- One or both of the two clauses in "Group 2" are true.
- The clause in "Group 3" is true.

The AND operator takes precedence over OR. Whenever AND operators are present, every group of clauses connected by AND must be true for the rule to fire.

Conclusions

Rule conclusions are usually identified by the keyword THEN. This is the part of the rule in which one or more values are bound to attributes. In conventional programs, the action in an IF/THEN construction may be a subroutine call or control transfer. But since rules are declarations of knowledge, their conclusions almost always instantiate an attribute.

Some expert systems shells offer ELSE rule constructs. For example:

RULE 7
IF   color = red
AND size = like_a_rubber_ball
THEN fruit = apple
ELSE fruit = strawberry

The ELSE construction should be used with caution. It should only be applied to binary conclusions—those that can have only two values. Rules containing ELSE have a dangerous trait: they always fire. If the premise is true, the clause following THEN is executed (*fruit* is instantiated to *apple*). If the premise is not true, the clause following ELSE is executed (*fruit* gets the value *strawberry*). Such rules may add an undesirable procedural character to rule sets containing them. As we will see later, the relative position of a rule containing an ELSE clause can dramatically affect the results of a knowledge base. Knowledge bases created with many rules containing ELSE may behave more like programs written in conventional languages. We look in greater depth at ELSE clauses in Chapter 12.

Multiple Conclusions

Most shells allow you to conclude more than one value in a conclusion. This gives flexibility in representing knowledge in which one condition implies several consequences. For example:

RULE 10
IF   prestige = high
THEN candidate = R_R
       candidate = M_B
       candidate = B_W

Here the fact that *prestige* is *high* means that three cars should be inferred. Many shells also support the conclusion of values for different attributes:

RULE 11
IF   barometer = rising
THEN chance_of_rain = lower
       chance_of_sun = higher
       chance_of_clouds = lower;

Because the value of *barometer* implies more than one fact, it may seem useful to represent this in one rule. However, just because the shell gives you this ability does not mean you should automatically use it. It's probably better to split *Rule 11* into three different rules.

RULE 11a
IF   barometer = rising
THEN chance_of_rain = lower

RULE 11b
IF   barometer = rising
THEN chance_of_sun = higher

RULE 11c
IF   barometer = rising
THEN chance_of_clouds = lower

The splitting method may seem more cumbersome, but it avoids some difficult problems relating to the testing and verifying of the knowledge base. We look at these issues and offer guidelines for deciding which of the two approaches is better in Chapter 14.

SUMMARY

This chapter has surveyed the basics of attributes and rules. We've seen how attributes represent the things in the problem domain. While they have similarities to conventional variables, there are important differences. We've seen how rules are independent units that represent knowledge. Your ultimate concern as an expert systems developer is to create a data base of knowledge. This is much more important than trying to control how the inference engine processes those rules.

To better understand the workings of the expert system, you need to understand what happens to the knowledge data base when it is processed by the inference engine. Chapter 4 looks at how the inference engine works.

4 | The Inference Process: Backward Chaining

In the previous chapter, we drew a comparison between data bases and knowledge bases. The expert systems developer's job is to seek out and encode knowledge. This knowledge is expressed as rules, nonprocedural representation structures.

In conventional data processing, developers sometimes write programs which process outside data bases. They use techniques that make the retrieval and manipulation of these sources fast and efficient. The program may use an indexed key to speed data base searches. It may organize data into a data structure to ease their manipulation. Approaches are determined by the needs of the task at hand.

In expert systems programming, the inference engine is the program that processes the knowledge data base. The fact that the inference engine already exists in the shell is one of the benefits that comes with using a shell—you don't have to write this program. This is similar to the benefits of using a relational data base manager like Ashton-Tate's dBASE® software. The program already has the procedures and algorithms necessary for creating and manipulating data. Likewise, the inference engine is already programmed to access and process knowledge bases you create.

SEARCH STRATEGIES

Just as a conventional program uses algorithms to organize data files and choose data records, inference engines also use special strategies for selecting which rules to process. These techniques are called "search strategies." It is essential that you understand these processes in order to create expert systems that run efficiently.

Rule-based expert systems shells commonly offer one or both of two search strategies for processing knowledge bases. These are called "backward chaining" (also "back chaining," "reverse reasoning," and "goal-directed reasoning") and "forward chaining." These search strategies control how the inference engine determines when rules are needed, which rules to select, and how rules should be processed. Almost every rule-based shell offers backward chaining. Some also offer forward chaining. Because the main emphasis of this book is on backward chaining systems, we look at backward chaining now. We'll look at forward chaining in a later chapter.

MEET THE EXPERT

Let's look at an example. Sue, the computer center consultant, is an expert at recommending personal computer configurations for desktop publishing. She is busy and much in demand. She saves her company money by avoiding costly mistakes, increasing worker productivity, and by putting the right tool in the hands of those who need it. She does so without buying unneeded hardware and software.

Two Kinds of Expertise

Knowledge about the Domain. How do we know Sue is an expert? She is an expert because she performs substantially better than her peers. Those around her don't have the experience, information, or aptitude to fully duplicate Sue's results. The nature of Sue's expertise is such that she cannot comprehensively explain it to her less able compatriots. Thus her status as an expert is not reached by examining *how* she reaches a conclusion. Instead, she's an expert *because* she reaches the right conclusion.

If you ask Sue why her performance is so far above her peers, she may have difficulty answering. Sue believes that her success lies in part because she has identified patterns that remove less promising options and thus narrow the choices she must weigh in making a recommendation. She has developed rules of thumb (heuristics) that help her effectively generalize common scenarios.

While the rules of thumb don't hold up in every case, Sue has a good "feel" for when a particular rule of thumb applies. Sue has accumulated a large number of these useful generalizations. Sue can express many of these "useful generalizations," "identifiable patterns," and "rules of thumb" in an IF/THEN form. Given some prodding, Sue can articulate that for some particular set of states, a certain conclusion should be inferred.

Knowledge about Using the Knowledge. There is second aspect to Sue's expertise that is not unique to Sue, but belongs to all experts. This is the ability

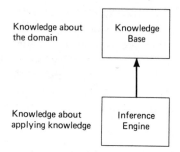

Figure 4.1. Division of Labor between Backward Chaining Inference Engine and Knowledge Base.

to ask the right question and apply the knowledge that best fits the situation. By comparing experts' performance against that of nonexperts, you find that experts ask questions that provide more useful information for making good decisions, whereas nonexperts may ask less incisive or probing questions. Nonexperts may know some of the rules of thumb that experts use, but are less effective at knowing when to apply them. Aside from the specific knowledge they have about their field, experts ask good questions and can recognize when they have enough information to make recommendations.

Thus experts have two kinds of knowledge: knowledge about the problem domain, and general knowledge about how and when to apply that knowledge (Figure 4.1). These two parts correspond to the two parts of the expert system we have discussed. Knowledge about the problem domain is encoded by the developer into a knowledge base. Knowledge about seeking, choosing, and processing rules already resides in the inference engine.

CONSULTATIONS

Sue provides advice by engaging in consultations. Consultations are the question-and-answer sessions in which the expert engages with those who hope to benefit from the expert's knowledge. When users interact with an expert system, they are said to "consult" the expert system. The dialog between user and expert system is also called a consultation.

Goals

The Expert: Sue begins each consultation by establishing its *goal*. The goal is the consultation's desired end result. In some cases, people may come to Sue to ask if a decision that has already been made was correct. In others, they may ask for a recommendation for some particular component of their desktop publishing system. Because of the high quality and importance of Sue's expertise, she spends most of her time recommending complete systems. This is the case with our example. Sue establishes this goal by listening to the client say, "I need help configuring a system I'm trying to put together."

The Expert System: Like Sue, backward chaining expert systems need a goal. By fixing a goal, you help the inference engine determine which rules will be useful for solving the problem. Some rules may infer conclusions not relevant to the problem at hand. Other rules are directly germane to a goal, "recommending a desktop publishing system." By establishing the goal, you help the inference engine process only those rules that contribute to the problem at hand (Figure 4.2).

The Expert: Having determined that the client is interested in configuring a desktop publishing system, Sue engages in a reasoning process. The first thing that Sue might do is determine, "Do I know anything about desktop publishing systems?"

The Expert System: This is what the inference engine does when the goal is established. It begins the backward chaining process by scanning the knowledge base for rules that conclude the goal. In Figure 4.3, you can see that the inference engine has identified two rules (in boldface) that conclude the current goal.

Backward chaining is sometimes called "goal-directed" reasoning because it considers only those facts and rules that contribute directly to the problem's solution. Even though the example knowledge base fragment contains six rules, right now the inference engine only "cares" about two of them—those that conclude the goal.

The Expert: Having determined that she does have some knowledge about desktop publishing, Sue determines what information she needs. Through some conscious or unconscious decision process, she begins applying her past experience against aspects of this problem she recognizes. She tries to get information she believes will help solve the problem.

The Expert System: The inference engine's next step is the same. Having identified those rules that conclude the goal, it selects one. Because it occurs first in the rule set, *Rule 1* is selected first.

RULE 1
IF   budget_considerations = ok
AND   hardware = found
THEN find_rec = ok

If *Rule 1* fires, then *find_rec* will be instantiated to "ok," and the goal attribute gets a value. This is how the backward chaining process ends. When

Inference Engine

ACTIONS Script   GOAL Information
What is the goal? find_rec   Current Goal: find_rec
                                  Goal Backlog: _____

Knowledge Base: Desktop Publishing expert

Goal: find_rec

RULES

RULE 1
IF   budget_considerations = ok
AND   hardware = found
THEN find_rec = ok

RULE 2
IF   budget_ceiling = high
OR   budget > (1000)
THEN budget_considerations = ok

RULE 3
IF   hardware NOT = found
THEN find_rec = not_ok

RULE 4
IF   find_rec = not_ok
THEN advice = "There's a problem with
         your configuration"

RULE 5
IF   budget_considerations = not_ok
THEN advice = "Can't afford desktop
         publishing";

RULE 6
IF   printer = KNOWN
AND   monitor = KNOWN
AND   computer = KNOWN
THEN hardware = found

Figure 4.2. The First Inference Engine Act: What Is the Goal?

the inference engine finds a value for the goal or determines that no value can be found, the consultation is over. If *Rule 1* fires, the consultation ends successfully.

In order for *Rule 1* to fire, however, the premise must be true. The premise is a conjunction—its two clauses are connected by AND. For the overall rule to be true, both premise clauses must be true. The inference engine starts by considering the first premise clause.

Inference Engine

ACTIONS Script		*GOAL Information*	
Action 1:	What is the goal? find_rec	Current Goal: find_rec	
Action 2:	**Which rules conclude the current goal? Consider first rule: Rule 1.**	Goal Backlog:	

Knowledge Base: Desktop Publishing expert

Goal: find_rec

RULES

RULE 1
IF budget_considerations = ok
AND hardware = found
THEN find_rec = ok

RULE 2
IF budget_ceiling = high
OR budget > (1000)
THEN budget_considerations = ok

RULE 3
IF hardware NOT = found
THEN find_rec = not_ok

RULE 4
IF find_rec = not_ok
THEN advice = "There's a problem with your
   configuration"

RULE 5
IF budget_considerations = not_ok
THEN advice = "Can't afford desktop publishing";

RULE 6
IF printer = KNOWN
AND monitor = KNOWN
AND computer = KNOWN
THEN hardware = found

Figure 4.3. Two rules conclude the goal.

IF   budget_considerations = ok

The Expert: This reflects Sue's expertise in desktop publishing. She has found
the most crucial factor for configuring desktop publishing systems is the
client's budget constraints. Many of her clients underestimate the investment
needed to get involved with desktop publishing. Also, the *kind* of system she
can recommend is closely tied to budget matters. Therefore she considers this
factor first.

Sue quickly checks what she knows about the client's budget constraints. Since the consultation has just begun, she concludes that more information about the client's budgetary constraints is necessary. She must gather data.

The Expert System: The inference engine undergoes a similar operation. It tries to evaluate the first premise clause of *Rule 1*. It does this by checking its working memory for a value for *budget_considerations*. Because the consultation has just started, no such value yet exists.

Now something important happens. Because it doesn't know the value of *budget_considerations,* the inference engine "realizes" that it doesn't have enough information to evaluate *Rule 1*. Yet it must evaluate *Rule 1* since that rule concludes the knowledge base goal. So this is what the inference engine does: it temporarily makes *budget_considerations* the current goal and seeks other sources that might conclude a value for it (Figure 4.4). The original goal, *find_rec,* is put aside while a value for *budget_considerations* is sought. When the search for *budget_considerations* ends, *find_rec* will be restored as the current goal. Notice the goal-directed nature of backward chaining. The inference engine methodically tracks down each piece of information it needs to conclude the goal by making each element a temporary goal.

The Expert: Realizing she needs more information, Sue undertakes a reasoning process to conclude a value for the client's budget considerations. If she can infer that the client's budget ceiling is *high,* she feels comfortable that the client's budgetary constraints are adequate (*ok*). As an alternative to this, if she cannot determine the budget, she checks whether the client is planning to spend at least one thousand dollars. She knows that she can recommend some kind of system if the client is able to invest at least this much.

The Expert System: Like Sue, the inference engine seeks ways in which it can conclude a value for its temporary goal *budget_considerations*. It searches the knowledge base from the start, looking for rules that conclude *budget_considerations*. *Rule 2* satisfies this condition. So the inference engine undertakes evaluating *Rule 2:*

RULE 2
IF   budget_ceiling = high
OR   budget > (1000)
THEN budget_considerations = ok

The first premise clause tests whether the attribute *budget_ceiling* has a value of *high.* The inference engine checks working memory to determine whether it has a value for *budget_ceiling*. Again, it comes up empty. Because a value for the attribute *budget_ceiling* is needed to evaluate *Rule 2*'s premise, *budget_ceiling* is made the current goal and *budget_considerations* is itself temporarily put aside on the goal backlog (Figure 4.5).

Inference Engine

ACTIONS Script

Action 1:   What is the goal? find_rec
Action 2:   Which rules conclude the current
             goal? Consider first rule: Rule 1.
Action 3:   Find value for
             budget_considerations.
**Action 4:   Find rules concluding
             budget_considerations (Rule 2).**

GOAL Information

Current Goal: budget_considerations
Goal Backlog: find_rec

Knowledge Base: Desktop Publishing expert

Goal: find_rec

RULES

RULE 1
IF   budget_considerations = ok
AND   hardware = found
THEN find_rec = ok

**RULE 2
IF   budget_ceiling = high
OR   budget > (1000)
THEN budget_considerations = ok**

RULE 3
IF   hardware NOT = found
THEN find_rec = not_ok

RULE 4
IF   find_rec = not_ok
THEN advice = "There's a problem with your
             configuration"

RULE 5
IF   budget_considerations = not_ok
THEN advice = "Can't afford desktop publishing";

RULE 6
IF   printer = KNOWN
AND   monitor = KNOWN
AND   computer = KNOWN
THEN hardware = found

Figure 4.4. The inference engine establishes a subgoal.

The inference engine searches the knowledge base for rules that conclude a value for *budget_ceiling*, as it did before for *budget_considerations* and the original goal *find_rec*. But the knowledge base contains no rules that conclude *budget_ceiling*. What does the inference engine do now?

Inference Engine

ACTIONS Script

Action 1: What is the goal? find_rec
Action 2: Which rules condlude the current goal? Consider first rule: Rule 1.
Action 3: Find value for budget_considerations.
Action 4: Find rules concluding budget_ considerations (Rule 2).
Action 5: Consider first premise clause. Find value for budget_ceiling.
Action 6: Find rules concluding budget_ceiling. None found.

GOAL Information

Current Goal: budget_ceiling
Goal Backlog: budget_considerations
                find_rec

Knowledge Base: Desktop Publishing expert

Goal: find_rec

RULES

RULE 1
IF   budget_considerations = ok
AND   hardware = found
THEN find_rec = ok

RULE 2
IF   budget_ceiling = high
OR   budget > (1000)
THEN budget_considerations = ok

RULE 3
IF   hardware NOT = found
THEN find_rec = not_ok

RULE 4
IF   find_rec = not_ok
THEN advice = "There's a problem with your
      configuration"

RULE 5
IF   budget_considerations = not_ok
THEN advice = "Can't afford desktop publishing";

RULE 6
IF   printer = KNOWN
AND   monitor = KNOWN
AND   computer = KNOWN
THEN hardware = found

Figure 4.5.   Yet another chaining level is required.

The next step is to look at the attribute property list for *budget_ceiling*. We have not shown any attribute property lists in the examples so far. Here is the property list for *budget_ceiling*.

NAME: budget_ceiling
TYPE: symbolic
EXPECT: (high medium low)
PROMPT: none
MULTI: no

At this point, the inference engine is concerned with the property named "PROMPT." When the inference engine determines that no rules can conclude the current goal, it next tries to ask the user for a value. If it finds an entry in the current goal's PROMPT property, it will display this entry and await a response from the client. If *budget_ceiling*'s PROMPT value had been:

PROMPT: "Describe your budget ceiling as high, medium, or low."

the inference engine would display this prompt and wait for the client's response. The client entry would then become the value of *budget_ceiling*, and the first premise clause of *Rule 2* could be evaluated. However, the actual value of *budget_ceiling*'s PROMPT property is "none," meaning that there is no PROMPT property for that attribute. This prevents the inference engine from asking the client for the value of *budget_ceiling*.

The inference engine can find no value in working memory and no rules that conclude *budget_ceiling*. The attribute has no PROMPT property and therefore the value cannot be obtained from the client. Since there is no knowledge source that provides a value for *budget_ceiling*, the inference engine ends its search. *Budget_ceiling*'s value remains unknown.

Because its value is unknown, the premise clause containing *budget_ceiling* cannot be evaluated. While the inference engine has not found evidence that the expression is false, the inference engine treats the clause as such because it cannot confirm that the clause is true. Therefore, the first premise clause of *Rule 2* fails. *Budget_ceiling* is removed as the current goal, and as the most recent entry on the goal backlog, *budget_considerations* once again becomes the current goal. The inference engine returns to the rule it was considering at the time it put *budget_considerations* on the goal backlog.

RULE 2
IF   budget_ceiling = high
OR   budget > (1000)
THEN budget_considerations = ok

The fact that *Rule 2*'s first premise clause fails does not cause the entire rule to fail because *Rule 2*'s premise is a disjunction (that is, its premise clauses are connected by OR). A rule whose premise clauses are connected by OR is true if any one of those clauses are true. Therefore, if *Rule 2's* second premise clause is found to be true, the rule will nevertheless fire even though the first clause failed. Since this rule still holds the chance of concluding the current goal, the inference engine tries to evaluate the second clause of *Rule 2's* premise (Figure 4.6):

OR   budget > (1000)

This clause tests whether the attribute *budget* has a value greater than the number 1000. (The expression on the right hand side of the equals sign is enclosed within parentheses to denote that we are testing the numeric value of the attribute.) The inference engine checks working memory to ascertain whether it has a value for *budget*. It does not. *Budget* becomes the current goal and the inference engine seeks rules that conclude it. No such rules exist. The inference engine next checks for a PROMPT property for *budget*.

NAME: budget
TYPE: numeric
EXPECT: positive integer
PROMPT: "How much money can you spend?"
MULTI: no

This time the attribute does have a PROMPT property. The inference engine displays the PROMPT to the client and awaits a response. The client enters the number *2000*. This value is bound (assigned) to the attribute *budget*. Since the value has now been obtained, *budget* is replaced as the current goal by *budget _considerations* and the premise clause is evaluated.

Because *budget's* value is indeed greater than 1000, the second premise clause is true. Premises whose clauses are connected by OR are true if any one clause is true. Therefore, the rule fires and *budget_considerations* is instantiated to *ok*.

Having obtained a value for *budget_considerations,* the inference engine has fulfilled its mission of establishing a value for the current goal. It is therefore through seeking values for *budget_considerations,* and removes *find_rec* from the goal backlog to make it the current goal. The inference engine returns to *Rule 1* which can now be processed further because the value for *budget_ considerations* finally has been obtained.

The inference engine can now determine that the first premise clause of the rule is true. The rule cannot yet be fired, however, because the premise is a conjunction—its two clauses are connected by AND. All clauses connected by AND must be true in order for the rule to fire. The engine therefore moves to the second premise clause of *Rule 1* so it can finish evaluating the rule.

Inference Engine

ACTIONS Script

Action 3: Find value for
budget_considerations.
Action 4: Find rules concluding
budget_considerations (Rule 2).
Action 5: Consider first premise clause. Find
value for budget_ceiling.
Action 6: Find rules concluding
budget_ceiling. None found.
Action 7: Is there a prompt for
budget_ceiling? No.
Action 8: Budget_ceiling is *unknown*. First
premise clause fails.
**Action 9: Consider second premise clause.
Find value for budget.**

GOAL Information

Current Goal: budget
Goal Backlog: budget_considerations
find_rec

Knowledge Base: Desktop Publishing expert

Goal: find_rec

RULES

RULE 1
IF   budget_considerations = ok
AND   hardware = found
THEN find_rec = ok

RULE 2
IF   budget_ceiling = high
OR   budget > (1000)
THEN budget_considerations = ok

RULE 3
IF   hardware NOT = found
THEN find_rec = not_ok

RULE 4
IF   find_rec = not_ok
THEN advice = "There's a problem with your
configuration"

RULE 5
IF   budget_considerations = not_ok
THEN advice = "Can't afford desktop publishing";

RULE 6
IF   printer = KNOWN
AND   monitor = KNOWN
AND   computer = KNOWN
THEN hardware = found

Figure 4.6. The inference engine fails *Rule 2*'s first premise clause. It considers the next clause.

RULE 1
IF   budget_considerations = ok
AND   hardware = found
THEN find_rec = ok

The Expert: Sue has determined that the client's financial resources are adequate to configure a desktop publishing system. She now realizes that the next step is to determine exactly what kind of hardware the client requires. In Sue's way of thinking about the problem, there are three key components she must determine: the printer, the monitor, and the computer. Each component is determined by various budgetary constraints and client needs. While she may not be able to recommend everything the client wants, she knows that any recommendation must include these three components. Therefore, she now begins thinking about the hardware recommendation.

The Expert System: The inference engine repeats the process that it used in the first premise clause. It first checks working memory to determine whether it already has a value for *hardware*. Since it does not, it makes *hardware* the current goal. The inference engine places *find_rec* on the goal backlog. The engine seeks rules that conclude *hardware*. *Rule 6* meets this condition (Figure 4.7).

RULE 6
IF   printer = KNOWN
AND   monitor = KNOWN
AND   computer = KNOWN
THEN hardware = found

Notice that each of the three premise clauses in *Rule 6* is evaluated against the value **KNOWN**. The value is written in capital letters. **KNOWN** here is a keyword used to test whether *any* value exists for the attribute named on the left hand side of the expression.[1] Study the first clause:

IF   printer = KNOWN

The expression evaluates whether *any* value for *printer* has been established. It does not test whether the attribute *printer* is equal to the symbol "K-N-O-W-N." The premise clause is true when the search for printer ends and some value has been instantiated. If no value exists, the clause fails, and *printer* remains unknown.

In processing the rule, the inference engine first examines working memory. Having determined that no value currently exists, it establishes *printer* as

---

[1]Some tools provide the ability to test for UNKNOWN instead of KNOWN. For these, write the rules using the negation; e.g., *IF printer NOT = UNKNOWN*. See Chapter 6 for more information.

Inference Engine

ACTIONS Script

Action 8: Budget_ceiling is *unknown*. First premise clause fails.

Action 9: Consider second premise clause. Find value for budget.

Action 10: Value obtained from user. Evaluate premise clause.

Action 11: Premise clause is true, therefore rule is true. Fire *Rule 2*.

Action 12: Restore find_rec as goal. Evaluate first premise clause of *Rule 1*. Clause is true.

Action 13: Consider second premise clause. Find value for hardware.

Action 14: Find rules concluding hardware. Rule 6.

GOAL Information

Current Goal: hardware
Goal Backlog: find_rec

Knowledge Base: Desktop Publishing expert

Goal: find_rec

RULES

RULE 1
IF   budget_considerations = ok
AND   hardware = found
THEN find_rec = ok

RULE 2
IF   budget_ceiling = high
OR   budget > (1000)
THEN budget_considerations = ok

RULE 3
IF   hardware NOT = found
THEN find_rec = not_ok

RULE 4
IF   find_rec = not_ok
THEN advice = "There's a problem with your configuration"

RULE 5
IF   budget_considerations = not_ok
THEN advice = "Can't afford desktop publishing";

RULE 6
IF   printer = KNOWN
AND   monitor = KNOWN
AND   computer = KNOWN
THEN hardware = found

Figure 4.7. *Rule 6* declares a problem-solving strategy.

the current goal and seeks rules that conclude it. To simplify the example, we have omitted the rules that conclude *printer, monitor,* and *computer.* The rules that instantiate these attributes are in fact a significant part of Sue's expertise about desktop publishing configurations. The expertise is too involved to detail here. For now, simply note that these other rules do indeed conclude values for *printer, monitor,* and *computer.*

After concluding a value for *printer,* the inference engine restores *hardware* as the current goal and returns to evaluate the premise clause in which it appears. Because a value—any value—was established, the first premise clause is true. Because the three premise clauses within the rule are connected by AND, all three clauses must be true in order for the rule to fire. The process is therefore repeated for attributes *monitor* and *computer. Monitor* and *computer* each become temporary goals for which the inference engine tries to establish values. When these values are established, *Rule 6* fires and *hardware* is instantiated to the value *found.*

Having determined a value for *hardware,* the inference engine restores *find_ rec* as the current goal. It returns to *Rule 1* to evaluate the second premise clause of that rule. Because the attribute *hardware* has just been assigned the value *found,* the second clause is true. Because both clauses in *Rule 1* are true, the rule is true and *find_rec* is instantiated to the value *ok.* Since *find_rec's* value has been established, it is removed as the current goal. Since there are no more goals on the backlog, there are no more goals to seek, and the inference engine's job is complete. The consultation is done. The conclusion is conveyed to the client.

The Expert: Sue has determined that the client has the financial resources necessary for configuring a desktop publishing system. She has thought about the client's hardware needs, based on various rules of thumb she uses and the answers to questions she received. Sue has undergone a remarkable human process. The expert systems fragment we've looked at reflects Sue's reasoning process. The inference engine mimics Sue's reasoning process in a remarkably human way. While we cannot exactly say that the expert system reasons precisely as Sue does, its results and appearance are humanlike enough to give the impression of intelligent behavior. This is as much as we can ask of a computer-based expert system, based on our understanding of human knowledge and expert reasoning today.

SUMMARY

This example has demonstrated the efficient, goal-directed behavior of backward chaining. Only those rules that contribute to concluding a value to the current goal are used. For example, *Rule 4* and *Rule 5* were never processed by the inference engine because their conclusion, *advice,* never became the current goal.

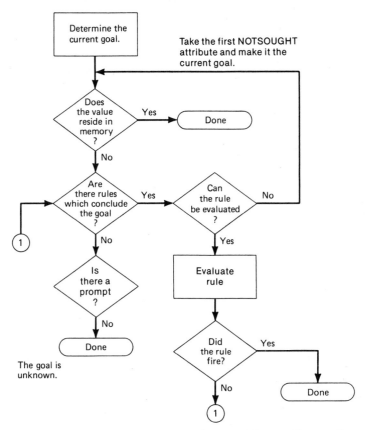

Figure 4.8. Basic Strategy Backward Chaining Inference Engines Use to Find an Attribute Value.

The backward chaining inference engine brings the rule-based knowledge data base to life. The inference engine mimics the step-by-step process of consideration a human expert might undergo in solving the problem. The method is remarkably simple. It is summarized in Figure 4.8. When the inference engine needs a value for an attribute, it first checks working memory to see if it already has a value for the attribute. If not, it makes that attribute the current goal. It seeks rules that conclude the attribute. If there are no rules, or those rules fail, the inference engine checks to see if the attribute has a PROMPT property. This technique is recursively applied each time a new current goal is established. The inference engine performs the minimum necessary processing to arrive at a conclusion. All inference engines go through these steps. Some, however, add or interpose other steps in the process. We will look at some of these steps as we proceed.

5 | *Forward and Mixed Chaining*

In this chapter, we examine forward chaining. We look at how it works and when you might use it. We also examine mixed chaining, which as the name suggests, is the blending of both backward and forward chaining strategies. We look at different ways of implementing mixed chaining in rule-based shells. First, in order to understand why you might want to use a search strategy other than backward chaining, we look at some general categories of expert systems and their defining characteristics.

TYPES OF EXPERT SYSTEMS PROBLEMS

A human expert is not likely to say that his or her domain is a selection problem which matches proposed solutions to the features of the problem until a successful fit is found. Humans don't usually distinguish the problems they solve by type. Therefore, any discussion about expert systems types is one that must immediately acknowledge that any given problem may not fit neatly into one category, and may contain aspects of more than one type.

Nevertheless, identifying types is useful. Some problems often do share traits that suggest general approaches to representation and search strategy. The list of types below is more illustrative than exhaustive. Our goal here is to discuss generally what types of characteristics indicate good candidates for the novice developer, and what these traits may tell you about choosing a search strategy.[1]

---

[1]The definitions for *diagnostic, design, interpretation,* and *planning* systems (in quotation marks and italics on the following pages) are taken from the book edited by Frederick Hayes-Roth, Donald A. Waterman, and Douglas B. Lenat, *Building Expert Systems* (Reading, MA: Addison-Wesley, 1983), 13–15. We refer the reader to this source for information on other expert systems types.

Classification

Classification problems are those in which the expert tries to establish membership of an object or concept into one or more known groups or classes. There may be many classes, although they are usually preenumerated. The gist of the problem-solving method can be seen as recognizing in real-world cases those essential traits that define membership in a particular class. The expert's talent is making subtle distinctions among cases.

Selection

Selection expertise chooses one or more options from a group of competing candidates. The criteria and candidates may be known in advance or change from case to case.

Selection problems must often select from among a group of qualified candidates based on picking one that is relatively "better." For example, given three employees who meet basic promotion criteria competing for one available position, which is "best" qualified and should get the appointment?

Selection problems differ from classification problems in two ways. A classification problem's decision criteria come from a constant set of traits that define the class to which it is being compared. A selection problem's criteria may be identified or inferred during the consultation, depending on the circumstances of the particular case. Also, classification problems generally deal with one object at a time. The task in a selection problem is to choose among several competing candidates.

Diagnosis

"*Diagnostic problems infer system malfunctions from observables.*" There are two basic types of diagnostic systems. The type we are most concerned with uses rules to infer associations among the symptoms of the problem and its causes. The second—and often more sophisticated—uses a model of the system and its potential problems to generate possible causes that fit the symptoms. These are then evaluated.

The first type of diagnostic system is readily built using rules. The so-called "help desk" expert system, which assists users of some systems to resolve problems, is a popular and (usually) technically feasible type. In its most common form, help desk systems function much like selection problems. The system has a knowledge of what kinds of things can go wrong. The user's answers to questions about system malfunctions act as selection criteria.

When the problem description matches that of a cause the system "knows" about, the diagnosis is made.

Design and Planning

"Design systems develop configurations of objects that satisfy the constraints of the design problem." "Planning systems design actions." Both these types usually contain representations of the operative objects or mechanisms in the domain. For this reason, a rules-only approach is often insufficient to solve the problem.

Because the solutions for design and planning systems arise out of the interactions of the objects of the system, there may be hundreds or even thousands of legitimate plans or designs. Therefore, the solutions in these types of expert systems are often not preenumerated. Much of the knowledge of such expert systems revolves around meeting the goals of the system while satisfying whatever constraints have been imposed. The technical challenge arises from producing adequate solutions while avoiding the impractical task of considering every possible solution.

Interpretation

"Interpretation systems infer situation descriptions from observables." This means that the system accepts certain data, evaluates them, and assigns to them some type of meaning. This "meaning" takes the form of plausible and coherent explanations of those data.

SHORTCOMINGS OF BACKWARD CHAINING

Backward chaining is a powerful strategy for processing knowledge because of its efficient, goal-directed nature. The inference engine asks only for information that helps solve the problem. This leads to short, focused consultations. However, backward chaining is not the right choice for every expert systems problem.

One of the most important weaknesses of backward chaining is its inability to flush out the implications of facts whose significance is not immediately known. For example, interpretation problems begin with a series of facts or circumstances. Intepretation expert systems try to build reasonable explications of those facts. Backward chaining may not be the right approach to accomplish this goal because there may be no way to determine which facts are important. Similarly, design and planning problems may require complex reasoning to determine when a plan or design is completed and adequate. The very notion of a goal in such circumstances can be quite different from the more readily identifiable goal of a classification, selection or diagnostic problem.

While the notion of a goal may be complex for some problems, other problems don't even have a goal. Therefore the strategy of firing only those rules that contribute to the solution of the problem may be meaningless. Some problems require understanding the implications of some data or decision. For example, making a design decision may have subtle implications for the rest of the design. Once such a decision is made, it may be desirable to flush out any and all inferences that can be made. Only then might it be useful to evaluate what that decision means. Thus, some parts of a problem may require processing in which the concept of a goal is not helpful. For such problems, we need an alternative or supplement to backward chaining. One such alternative is called "forward chaining."

FORWARD CHAINING

Forward chaining, also called "data-driven" chaining or reasoning, is the general term used to describe a group of search strategies which start with known facts and try to infer the conclusions implied by those facts. Forward chaining attempts—often by building up a series of intermediate conclusions along the way—to infer the consequences built into a set of information.

Forward chaining is an imprecise term. The particulars of implementation differ among shells. Some shells claim to offer forward chaining, but really offer a form of mixed chaining (we'll look at this shortly). Therefore, we explore the general principles on which forward chaining is based. Also, we will look at when you should consider using forward chaining.

Differences between Forward and Backward Chaining

Forward chaining differs from backward chaining in three major ways. First, forward chaining starts by examining rules' premises, and fires those rules that immediately can be concluded. The new knowledge garnered from these conclusions is used to evaluate other rule premises. In this manner, conclusions get "built up," starting with low-level facts that are used to infer higher abstraction levels. Contrast this to backward chaining, which begins with the highest level abstraction—the goal—and works backward to lower-level detail by looking at rule conclusions.

Second, the inference engine considers rules in the order in which they appear in the knowledge base. Backward chaining considers only those rules which conclude the current goal. Since the job of forward chaining is simply to infer whatever it can, the concept of a goal may be irrelevant to a forward chaining inference engine.

Third, a forward chaining inference engine generally does not suspend one rule's consideration in order to seek values for attributes that have not yet been sought. In other words, backward chaining seeks all the values it needs in order to evaluate a rule right away by seeking the subgoals the rule depends on. Forward chaining just "puts aside" rules it can't evaluate right away. It goes on to consider other rules, and comes back later to try again.

The implications of this approach help shed light on the types of applications that forward and backward chaining best address. Backward chaining gives each factor immediate consideration, fully pursuing that factor's values. It does this because it only considers those rules contributing to the goal's solution in the first place. The inference engine "knows" that rules concluding the goal are important. Backward chaining ensures that each is evaluated as soon as possible. Each is either fired or failed at the time of consideration.

Forward chaining is driven by data. There is less bias about what is important. Since the concept of a goal or desirable outcome may be irrelevant, there is no prior assumption about which rules actually contribute to a final conclusion. Thus it makes sense for the inference engine to try *every* rule. Rules are considered in order of appearance. If the inference engine does not have enough information to evaluate the rule, it moves on to the next rule. It comes back later when it may have made enough inferences to evaluate those rules that it couldn't deal with earlier in the consultation.

An Example

Consider the knowledge base fragment shown in Figure 5.1. It contains knowledge concluding what type of car should be bought.

The consultation begins begins with a series of given facts:

Family_members = (6)
budget = moderate
Mileage = moderate
move_often = yes

These assertions are simply given in some way at the start of the consultation. They may come from users, data bases, knowledge base assertions, or other knowledge sources. In the context of the domain, these facts are details. Nonexperts may have a difficult time figuring out what they mean. The expert in this particular domain is skilled at using these facts to produce recommendations about what kind of car is right for a family possessing the traits described by these facts.

Family_members = (6)
budget = moderate
Mileage = moderate
move_often = yes

RULE   rec_mini_van
IF   family_size = large
AND   budget = moderate
AND   workload = normal
THEN   car = minivan

RULE   rec_van
IF   family_size = large
AND   workload = high
AND   budget = moderate
OR   budget = high
THEN   car = van

RULE   rec_sedan
IF   family_size = small
OR   family_size = medium
AND·   budget = low
OR   budget = moderate
AND   workload = normal
THEN   car = sedan

RULE   rec_pickup
IF   family_size = small
AND   heavy_pulling = yes
THEN   car = pickup

RULE   workload_high
IF   mileage = high
OR   heavy_pulling = yes
THEN   workload = high

RULE   heavy_family
IF   mileage = moderate
AND   family_size = large
THEN   workload = high

RULE   workload_normal
IF   heavy_pulling = no
AND   mileage NOT = high
AND   family_size = small
OR   family_size = medium
THEN   workload = normal

RULE   family_small
IF   family_members < (4)
THEN   family_size = small

RULE   family_medium
IF   family_members < (6)
THEN   family_size = medium

RULE   family_large
IF   family_members > = (6)
THEN   family_size = large

Figure 5.1. Sample Knowledge Base for Selecting a Car.

Using forward chaining, the inference engine considers each rule in order of appearance. It first considers *Rule rec_mini_van.*

RULE rec_mini_van
IF   family_size = large
AND budget = moderate
AND workload = normal
THEN car = minivan

The first premise clause in the rule is *family_size = large.* The inference engine discovers that the attribute *family_size* does not yet have a value. The forward chaining inference engine "temporarily puts aside" the rule, and goes on to the next. If the inference engine had been processing the knowledge base using backward chaining, it would make *family_size* the current goal and seek rules that conclude it. The inference engine does not do that now.

"Temporarily puts aside" does not mean that the rule fails. The forward chaining inference engine only fails rules which can be evaluated. Since *Rule rec_mini_van's* first premise clause cannot yet be evaluated *(family_size's* value is not available), the rule can't be evaluated. Instead the inference engine leaves the rule available for future consideration. Contrast this to a failed rule in which enough is known to judge the rule. In such a case, the rule is removed from consideration once and for all.

So, in our example, the inference engine "temporarily puts aside" the first rule and moves on to the next rule it encounters: *Rule rec_van. Rec_van's* first premise clause also depends on evaluating the value of *family_size.* This clause, too, cannot be evaluated because *family_size* is not yet known. *Rule rec _van* is temporarily put aside. The next two rules, *rec_sedan* and *rec_pickup,* also cannot be evaluated because of the lack of value for *family_size.*

The fifth rule considered is *Rule workload_high. Mileage,* the attribute in its first premise clause, is KNOWN. However, the value tested in the premise— *mileage = high*—does not match the actual binding *mileage = moderate.* Thus the first clause fails. Since the rule is a disjunction, the rule could nevertheless succeed if the second premise clause is true. The inference engine evaluates the second clause *(heavy_pulling = yes).* The value of *heavy_pulling* has not been established. Since the rule might yet be true, this rule too is temporarily put aside.

Rule heavy_family occurs next and its first premise clause is true. Because the rule is a conjunction, the second clause must also succeed in order to fire. The attribute *family_size* is required and does not yet have a value. Thus the rule is temporarily put aside. The next rule, *Rule workload_normal,* is similarly put aside because the value of *heavy_pulling* is required, but not available.

The next rule is *family_small:*

RULE family_small
IF   family_members < (4)
THEN family_size = small

This rule *can* be evaluated. Since the actual value of *family_members* is the numeric value of six, the rule fails. Note that since the rule is fully evaluated (fired or failed), *the rule is no longer available for future consideration.* This is different from the rules that were earlier "put aside" by the inference engine. Failed and fired rules are treated as in backward chaining. They are gone, and won't be considered again.

The next rule, *family_medium* fails in a similar manner. The last rule, *family _large,* also can be evaluated. Since the actual value of *family_members* indeed *is* greater than or equal to the value of six, the rule fires. Attribute *family_size* is instantiated to *large.*

The inference engine has processed the entire knowledge base. All ten rules have been considered. The inference engine did not have enough information to evaluate seven of those rules. Two rules failed. One fired and added a value to the knowledge base's known information. Since new knowledge has been added since the cycle began, the inference engine returns to the beginning and reconsiders all rules that were "temporarily put aside." It does this in order to evaluate whether the new conclusion can help evaluate rules that couldn't be evaluated before.

Beginning again from the top, the inference engine reconsiders the first rule, *rec_mini_van.* This time the engine has enough knowledge to evaluate and pass the first two premise clauses. However, it does not have enough to evaluate the third clause: *workload = normal.* The rule is again put aside. The next rule, *rec_van,* also depends on having the value of *workload,* and thus it, too, is put aside.

The first two premise clauses of the third rule, *Rule rec_sedan,* test the value of *family_size.* During the first cycle through the knowledge base, this information was not available. Now it is, and upon evaluating these premise clauses, the inference engine fails the first two clauses of the rule. Because the rule is a conjunction, this causes the rule to fail as a whole. The same happens with *Rule rec_pickup.* These two rules fail, and are removed from consideration for the remainder of this consultation.

Rule workload_high cannot be evaluated because *heavy_pulling*'s value is not available. *Rule heavy_family,* however, can be evaluated and it fires. The value *workload = high* is added to the consultation's knowledge. The inference engine does not have enough information to evaluate *Rule workload_normal.* The remaining rules have been all eliminated from consideration because they either failed or fired.

Consider the current status of the knowledge base in Figure 5.2. Two rules have fired, adding two new facts to what is known. Four rules have failed. The second forward chaining cycle added one new fact. Since something new was inferred, the inference engine starts again at the first eligible rule.

This time the first rule, *Rule rec_mini_van,* can be completely evaluated since previous cycles have determined the values of *family_size* and *workload.* The rule fails. Similarly the next rule, *Rule rec_van* can also be evaluated. It

Originally known
Family_members = (6)
budget = moderate
Mileage = moderate
move_often = yes

Inferred from rules
family_size = large
workload = high

RULE   rec_mini_van
IF   family_size = large
AND   budget = moderate
AND   workload = normal
THEN   car = minivan

RULE   rec_van
IF   family_size = large
AND   workload = high
AND   budget = moderate
OR   budget = high
THEN   car = van

RULE   rec_sedan   (failed)
IF   family_size = small
OR   family_size = medium
AND   budget = low
OR   budget = moderate
AND   workload = normal
THEN   car = sedan

RULE   rec_pickup   (failed)
IF   family_size = small
AND   heavy_pulling = yes
THEN   car = pickup

RULE   workload_high
IF   mileage = high
OR   heavy_pulling = yes
THEN   workload = high

RULE   heavy_family   (fired)
IF   mileage = moderate
AND   family_size = large
THEN   workload = high

RULE   workload_normal
IF   heavy_pulling = no
AND   mileage NOT = high
AND   family_size = small
OR   family_size = medium
THEN   workload = normal

RULE   family_small   (failed)
IF   family_members < (4)
THEN   family_size = small

RULE   family_medium   (failed)
IF   family_members < (6)
THEN   family_size = medium

RULE   family_large   (fired)
IF   family_members > = (6)
THEN   family_size = large

Figure 5.2. Partially Processed Example Knowledge Base.

fires and adds the value *car = van*. The next two rules have already failed, so the next rule to consider is *Rule workload_high*. Since the value of *heavy_ pulling* is still not known, the rule cannot be fired or failed. It is again put aside. The same thing happens with *Rule workload_normal*. No other rules are available for consideration.

The value of *car* was added in this cycle. Two rules remain that have not been fired or failed. The inference engine cycles a fourth time to see if the new value of *car* will help evaluate those rules. Since both are dependent on the value of *heavy_pulling*, and *heavy_pulling*'s value has not been determined, these rules are put aside. Thus this most recent cycle yields no new values. This is how the inference engine determines when to end knowledge base processing during forward chaining: a full processing cycle takes place in which no inferences are made. Thus the forward chaining inference engine ends the consultation.

Notice the character of this example. The inference engine churns through the knowledge base repeatedly, flushing out the implications of an initial set of data. Rules are considered until they are fired or failed. Unlike backward chaining, there is no attribute holding a special significance over others to guide which rules get tried. Instead, the inference engine concludes everything possible given a set of starting knowledge.

This simple knowledge base could have been processed using backward chaining by naming the goal as *car*. In this case, the consideration sequence would have been shorter and more efficient. Both chaining methods cause the appropriate inferences to be made. This is not always true, however. With more complex applications, the job may be to infer everything possible. Backward chaining can only do this if "everything" contributes in some way to the goal. Thus the choice of which to use is often made by determining whether you have one or several specific attributes whose value is especially significant (backward chaining) or whether you want all possible inferences the knowledge base contains to be flushed out (forward chaining).

We mentioned earlier that forward chaining is a loose term for the general principle of moving from known facts to the implications of those facts. It has many varieties. Depending on the forward chaining shell you use, there may be variations in how the knowledge base is processed. However, the general quality of forward chaining remains the same: start with a set of known facts, and infer the conclusions implied in those facts.

CHOOSING SEARCH STRATEGIES

It is important to remember that the most important decision you make regarding expert systems development is the choice of representation. When you work with a rule-based shell, you have already chosen rules as your primary way of representing knowledge. The choice of chaining strategies is important, but at this level either approach often will properly process a knowledge base. Backward chaining may process some knowledge bases more efficiently. Forward chaining may draw more inferences. If your shell offers both modes of operation, you may want to experiment between the two processing paradigms.

Table 5.1 summarizes important questions you should ask along with what their answers may imply with regard to chaining approach.

Backward chaining works best for domain types in which a goal has been fixed. It usually works well for problems in which the solution candidates are preenumerated, particularly when the problem-solving strategy is matching hypothesized solutions against the facts until a solution is found. Backward chaining usually works well for selection, classification, and diagnostic prob-

Table 5.1. Questions Relevant to Choosing between Forward and Backward Chaining.

Trait	Forward	Backward
Solutions are:	not preenumerated	preenumerated
The goal is:	not necessarily known	known
The objective is to:	flush out all facts	infer one key fact
Starting situation:	some facts known	few facts known
"Question and answer" type input required from user:[a]	no	yes
Percent of rules typically applying to one case:	relatively high	relatively low
Strategy:	build solution	detect solution
Problem type (assuming rules are appropriate):	configuration planning interpretation	classification selection diagnostic

[a]Most forward chaining shells don't prompt for data. However, several shells offer hybrid forward chaining modes that force the inference engine to ask users for input for the values of attributes that have been not yet sought.

lems. If your project falls into these categories, backward chaining is probably a good search strategy to use.

On the other hand, if the problem begins with a set of facts whose meaning is not readily apparent, forward chaining may be the best approach. Forward chaining is also a good approach if it is likely that a high percentage of the knowledge base's rules will apply. Why use the selective approach that backward chaining employs if most of the rules will be considered anyway?

If you have already chosen a shell, you may already have chosen a search strategy by default. If you suspect that forward chaining would benefit your work and the shell you now have does not offer it, keep reading. The next section of this chapter addresses how to combine the two approaches so you can "simulate" the effects of forward chaining.

MIXED CHAINING

Mixed chaining refers to the strategy of using both forward and backward chaining within a single knowledge base. There is good reason to do this. At the start of this chapter, we noted that dividing problems into "types" is somewhat arbitrary since many problems display properties of more than one type. Accordingly, some problems may benefit from a combination of backward and forward approaches. The distinctions we've made between forward and backward problems refer to technical processing differences. From the point of view of how an expert may solve a real-world problem, these differences may be artificial. Some problems may need *only* backward chaining or *only* forward chaining. However, these are coincidences occurring in a world rich with problems in which both techniques can be useful for addressing any one problem. Therefore, by being able to choose strategies that fit each problem aspect, you have a richer and more powerful toolkit for creating expert systems.

Moreover, mixed chaining techniques can help overcome some of the technical limitations of backward chaining. The primary one of these is the poor behavior visibility of a knowledge base—that is, the relative difficulty in predicting exactly when a given rule will be considered. This can make it difficult to display messages and to control when questions get asked. We will look at how mixed chaining techniques can help overcome these limitations in Chapter 14.

Most mixed chaining strategies begin with an assumption that backward chaining is the default search technique. When a situation arises in which forward chaining is needed, the inference engine is caused to process the knowledge base in a forward manner. When the need for forward chaining ceases, the inference engine is forced back into backward chaining. For this reason, the following techniques are useful both for creating mixed chaining *and* for adding forward chaining capability in shells that don't offer a solely forward chaining mode. Using the techniques that apply to your shell, you can create expert systems that give the character of mixed and forward chaining.

Forward Rules

Many shells allow you to temporarily override the backward search by letting you define a "forward" rule property that causes immediate consideration of the rule's premise under certain conditions. We call these *forward rules.*[2] For example:

GOAL REC

Attribute Property List:

NAME: job
TYPE: symbolic
EXPECT: (financial graphics expert_system other)
PROMPT: "What are the jobs to be done?:

RULE 1
IF   job = financial
THEN rec = "Use 1-2-3. It is the only financial package available. It runs only on micros."

RULE 9
IF   job = expert_systems
THEN rec = "Use an expert systems shell."

RULE 13
IF   job = other
AND experience = some_experience
THEN rec = "Use the C programming language for the task."

RULE 14
IF   job = other
AND experience = experienced
THEN rec = "Use Assembler language. It is only available on the mainframe however."

RULE 16
IF   job = other
AND experience = no_experience
THEN rec = "Use BASIC."

---

[2]See the Glossary for the terms various shells use to describe this type of rule.

RULE 17
IF   job = other
THEN DISPLAY "Since there are no prepackaged software, you will have to write your own program."
FORWARD: YES

RULE 18
IF   job = graphics
THEN rec = "No graphics programs are available. I can't make a recommendation for this area."

Except for *Rule 17,* the knowledge base is processed using backward chaining using the goal *REC. Rule 17* has the FORWARD property (FORWARD:YES). The inference engine does not backward chain on this rule. Instead, it immediately considers *Rule 17* whenever an attribute in that rule's premise becomes KNOWN. This is how the inference engine processes forward rules: it interrupts backward chaining whenever it infers a value for an attribute that appears in a forward rule's premise. The inference engine then immediately tries to evaluate the forward rule. If it can fire or fail the rule, it does so. If there is more than one attribute in the premise and the inference engine doesn't have values for them all, it "temporarily puts aside" the rule for later consideration. When the inference engine later concludes another attribute that also appears in the forward rule's premise, it tries again to evaluate the forward rule.

Thus the inference engine proceeds as follows:

1. Find the goal. The goal is *rec.*
2. Which rules conclude *rec? Rule 1* concludes *rec.*
3. Evaluate the premise. Is attribute *job* known? No.
4. Make *job* the current goal. Which rules conclude *job?* None.
5. *Job* has a PROMPT property. Prompt the user.
6. The user enters "*other.*"

The attribute *job* has just been instantiated. Normally, the backward chaining inference engine would finish processing *Rule 1.* However, because there is a FORWARD rule using *job* in its premise, the inference engine interrupts backward chaining.

7. Are there rules with the FORWARD property *job* in their premise? Yes, *Rule 17.*
8. Consider *Rule 17.* It is true. Fire the rule.
9. Are there other forward rules?
10. No. Resume backward chaining.

Had there been more than one forward rule with *job* in its premise, these rules also would have been considered in order of occurrence before backward chaining resumed. In this way, forward rules act as sets of forward chaining rules. As in forward chaining, if there is not enough information to evaluate the forward rule's premise, the rule is temporarily put aside. As in forward chaining, their consideration is not dependent on whether or not their conclusion contributes to the goal.

Note also that the forward search occurs immediately after the attribute instantiation takes place. The search for forward rules containing *job* in their premise occurred directly after *job* got its value. This forward search usually occurs even before the inference engine evaluates the backward chaining rule *(Rule 1)* that caused the prompt. Thus the forward search interrupts backward chaining. When the search and consideration of forward rules is done, backward processing then resumes.

Forward rules are useful for several reasons. First, they are useful in the same sense that any forward chaining is useful: it enables you to draw out the implications of some set of facts. When *job* is instantiated, the action possibly implies a set of direct implications. Forward rules allow the representation of this knowledge and give the inference engine a way to flush out these implications as soon as the causing inference is made. Forward rules are also useful for causing side effects. Note that the conclusion in *Rule 17* is a DISPLAY statement—an instruction to display some text to the user. Since backward chaining only fires rules that contribute to the goal, rules with only actions like DISPLAY in their conclusion would never win consideration in a backward chaining system since they don't infer anything. Forward rules give you a way to make these side effects happen.

Some shells have this forward processing feature built into their inference engine without explicitly defining rules as "FORWARD." One such product is AION's ADS®. While ADS' inference engine backward chains, it treats all rules as potential forward rules. Thus in our above example, *Rule 17* would not have a forward property. As soon as *job* is assigned, the inference engine looks at *all* rules to see if *job* resides in their premise. If so, it tries to fire those rules in the forward manner described above. The built-in tendency of its inference engine is to fire any rule it can based on new inferences made during backward chaining.

While forward rules give forward chaining-like capability, using them is not the same as using a forward chaining inference engine. Forward chaining is a mode that processes all rules in a similar manner. The "forward" tag, on the other hand, is a rule property. In a sense, forward rules are rules with procedural information implicitly telling the inference engine when to consider them. Thus, forward rules have a procedural quality that is different from the nonprocedural approach that a forward chaining inference engine uses. Nevertheless, forward rules provide a way to give a mixed chaining character to an expert system.

Demons

Demons are modules of code whose consideration is triggered by an inference in the knowledge base. In this sense, they resemble forward rules. However, demons are not rules and often have specific procedural programming capabilities. They are specifically designed to interrupt processing. Figure 5.3 shows a demon as found in the expert systems shell KES™.

Think of demons as independent agents. The backward chaining inference engine processes the knowledge base. Each demon "watches" the inference engine process the knowledge base. When *Balance Due* obtains a value, the demon *Refund Demon* interrupts the inference engine. The demon's *when* clause is evaluated. If it is found to be true, then the demon's action (specified by *then*) is executed. This *when* clause may contain multiple actions, IF/THEN expressions, and other procedural facilities that might be found in a conventional programming language. When the demon completes the actions specified in its *then* section, control is returned to the inference engine which resumes backward chaining where it left off.

Demons can be useful for accomplishing many of the same functions as forward rules. They help infer side effects. They can take care of updating screen displays. But demons differ from rules in that rules are limited to a strictly rule-based format while demons may contain commands that allow you to use them to write procedural programs. Forward rules are designed to enable forward inference. Demons usually let you do something more. Thus demons usually have more powerful capabilities than forward rules.

One particular kind of processing that demons are well suited for is exception processing. For example, there may be certain conditions that imply that the consultation should end immediately. Perhaps there is some major discovery that must be dealt with now. Demons give you the ability to grab control from the inference engine and do whatever is necessary. Whether you

Refund Demon:
\If the Balance Due to the government is negative, then the
\government owes you a refund
  when
    Balance Due llt 0
  then
    erase Refund.
    Refund = abs (Balance Due).
    message "".
    message combine ("Congratulations, you are due a refund of $", Refund,".").
    endwhen.

Figure 5.3. A Demon in KES.

display a warning and end the consultation or go through a series of procedural steps, demons are designed with this kind of processing in mind.

Procedural Control

Some shells have the equivalent of an ACTIONS section, a procedural module which controls goal selection, starts the inference process, and performs procedural operations. Figure 5.4 shows an ACTIONS section taken from VP-Expert.® The VP-Expert verb *find* establishes the goal and causes the inference engine to backward chain using the attribute *month* as its goal. After the inference engine completes its search for *month's* value, control returns to the ACTIONS section, and the commands beginning with the WKS verb are executed.[3]

Procedural modules are useful in that they give you direct control over the shell environment. They allow you to perform procedural actions before and after rule consideration takes place. Thus you can divide up the knowledge base into a series of smaller goals interspersed with procedural housekeeping between each step. After each step, control returns to the ACTIONS section where you then specify procedural actions.

What's the difference between demons and this ACTIONS facility? Shells that offer procedural control sections begin consultations by executing the ACTIONS section script. One of these script items is to begin backward chaining. On the other hand, demons usually *interrupt* the backward chaining inference engine to temporarily take over processing. Thus demons are one behavior that some inference systems provide. On the other hand, inference processing is one behavior that some procedural control systems offer. The difference is which of the two paradigms drive the system. With a little thought and experimentation, you can often simulate the effect of one with the other.

Can You Backward Chain in Forward Chaining Mode?

Some forward chaining shells offer processing modes that enable you to add backward chaining behavior to the inference engine. One such method is a forward chaining mode that treats each rule conclusion as the current goal. Like the forward chaining we examined earlier, the inference engine begins by

---

[3]In this example, *month* is used by the *WKS* verb to extract a column of data from a Lotus 1-2-3® worksheet beginning with the value contained in *month*. This column of data then is displayed to the console.

ACTIONS
find month
WKS detail, COLUMN = (months),sales
x = 1
display "The column month looks like this:"
WHILEKNOWN detail[x]
   display "{detail[x]}"
   x = (x + 1)
END;

Figure 5.4. An ACTIONS Section taken from VP-Expert

considering the first rule and sequentially considers each rule in order of appearance. During each consideration, however, the inference engine backward chains on attributes that have not yet been sought until each rule is completely evaluated. This sidesteps the process of putting aside rules. After the rule is fired or failed, processing continues with the next sequential rule as in standard forward chaining. That rule's conclusion then becomes the current goal and the process repeats.

Goal-terminated Forward Chaining

Some forward chaining shells let you specify when processing should stop by establishing a goal. The inference engine considers each rule in sequence (forward processing) until the goal attribute is instantiated (backward, goal-directed). If the goal cannot be instantiated and the inference engine cycles without making any inferences, consideration ceases (again, forward chaining behavior).

SUMMARY

Forward chaining is a loosely associated group of approaches to processing a knowledge base. Their common feature is that they enable you to consider all rules and flush out the implications of a starting set of facts. Not all expert systems shells offer forward chaining. Many vendors that do claim to offer it often use the term loosely. In some cases, the term is used so loosely that investigation is needed to really evaluate what the vendor means by it.

While the concept of forward chaining is easy to understand, the expert systems types it is often used to build can be more difficult than backward chaining systems. Therefore, it is especially important that you undergo the analysis process we cover in Chapter 2. While mixed chaining features are useful for supplementing backward chaining, solely forward systems often require more experience and the use of advanced capabilities not treated in this book. If the domain you are considering falls into one of the forward chaining categories (e.g., planning, design, and interpretation), proceed with caution. If you are just starting expert systems development, start with an application suitable for backward chaining.

P
A
R
T
#
T
W
O

Technical Topics

6 | Handling Unknown Information

One way in which expert systems display humanlike behavior is by reasoning in the face of unknown information. The expert system can inform the user when a problem cannot be solved. It can reason about whether a particular piece of information is known or unknown. It can accept unknown responses from users and pursue alternate lines of reasoning. These capabilities assume that the shell has a way of representing the concept of "unknown." In this chapter, we examine this capacity more fully, and show how you can use it to let your expert system capture and reason about unknown cases.

KNOWN, UNKNOWN, NOTSOUGHT

It is important to understand how the inference engine keeps track of an attribute's *status*. The inference engine keeps track of a status to evaluate whether attributes are KNOWN, UNKNOWN, or NOTSOUGHT. When you understand these distinctions, you can better understand exactly what it means for an attribute to be unknown and also how the inference engine controls its backward chaining.

An attribute becomes KNOWN when it is instantiated. The value can be symbolic, numeric, boolean, or any other valid type the attribute may contain. The value may come from any knowledge source: rules, assertions, external sources, the user. Once the assignment takes place, the inference engine "knows" the attribute.

An attribute is NOTSOUGHT when no attempt has yet been made to get a value. The first time the inference engine encounters a new attribute, its value is NOTSOUGHT. It has no value because the inference engine has *not* yet *sought* a value for that attribute. NOTSOUGHT is the default status of attributes when a consultation begins.

An attribute becomes UNKNOWN once the inference engine determines that the attribute cannot be instantiated. This usually means that no rule, user prompt, or other knowledge source could supply a value for the attribute. In other words, the inference engine looks for a value, but finds no source from which to get one. When it gives up, the inference engine changes the status of the attribute to UNKNOWN.

Because human experts must often reason in the face of incomplete information, most shells allow rules to test the status of attributes. Most shells also offer a way for the user of an expert system to answer a question by entering UNKNOWN. How this is done varies among shells. Some automatically add the selection UNKNOWN to menus. Others use a particular key, like the question mark ("?"), to signify UNKNOWN. Others require users to type in a keyword like UNKNOWN. Still others leave it to the developer to devise a scheme for entering UNKNOWN.

Remember that backward chaining inference engines treat NOTSOUGHT and UNKNOWN attributes in profoundly different ways. While both mean that the attribute has no value, NOTSOUGHT attributes simply haven't yet been tried. UNKNOWN attributes have exhausted the inference engine's resources for getting a value.

Here is a short knowledge base that summarizes attribute status:

RULE not sought
IF   attribute_not_yet_processed
THEN status = NOTSOUGHT

RULE known
IF   attribute_processed
AND   value = established
THEN status = KNOWN

RULE unknown
IF   attribute_processed
AND   value = not_established
THEN status = UNKNOWN

KNOWN/UNKNOWN STATUS AND INFERENCING

Understanding the distinction between NOTSOUGHT and UNKNOWN attributes is important in grasping how the backward chaining inference engine processes a knowledge base. Take the following simple example:

NAME: wet_outside
TYPE: boolean
EXPECT: (true, false)

NAME :   sunny
TYPE: boolean
EXPECT: (true, false)
PROMPT: "Is it sunny?"

GOAL: raining

RULE 1
IF   wet_outside = yes
THEN raining = yes

RULE 2
IF   sunny = yes
THEN raining = no

Raining is the goal. The inference engine checks to see whether or not *raining* is KNOWN. If *raining* is KNOWN, no further processing is needed. The goal of inferencing is to seek and find a value for the current goal. If that current goal already has a value, the inference engine's work is done.

Since the consultation is just starting, *raining* has no value. Since it has not yet been sought, its status is NOTSOUGHT. The fact that it is NOTSOUGHT causes the inference engine to try to establish a value for it with whatever knowledge sources are available. In this case, there are two rules that conclude *raining*.

Since it occurs first, *Rule 1* is considered first. The value of *wet_outside* is required to evaluate the rule. Since this is the inference engine's first encounter with *wet_outside*, its value is also NOTSOUGHT. This causes the inference engine to make *wet_outside* the current goal. The inference engine seeks values for *wet_outside*. None are found since there are no rules which conclude *wet_outside*. Neither does *wet_outside* have a PROMPT property. Nor are there any other apparent sources which might provide a value. Thus the inference engine has exhausted its options for getting a value for *wet_outside*. The inference engine thus changes *wet_outside*'s status to UNKNOWN.

Because *wet_outside* is UNKNOWN, *raining* is restored as the current goal. *Rule 1* is evaluated and fails. Since *raining* cannot be assigned a value by *Rule 1*, the inference engine checks to see if there are other sources that might conclude *raining*. *Rule 2* also concludes *raining*. The inference engine requires *sunny* to evaluate *Rule 2*. Because it hasn't before encountered *sunny*, *sunny*'s status is NOTSOUGHT. It becomes the current goal. The inference engine seeks sources for *sunny*. There are no rules concluding *sunny*, but *sunny* does have a PROMPT property. The inference engine displays the prompt "Is it sunny?" The user enters *true*. Now *sunny* has a value, so its status becomes KNOWN. Since it is KNOWN, *raining* is restored as the current goal, and the rule is evaluated. The rule fires and *raining* is instantiated. *Raining*'s value becomes KNOWN. Since it is KNOWN, the inference engine has finished its job and the consultation ends.

This example shows how the inference engine uses an attribute's status to determine when to start and finish inferencing. Note that when prompted for *sunny,* if the user had entered UNKNOWN (using the shell's UNKNOWN entry symbol), *Rule 2* would have failed since the response would cause *sunny* to be UNKNOWN and cause *Rule 2* to fail. Since all knowledge sources would then have been exhausted, the inference engine would have changed the status of the *raining* to UNKNOWN. The change from NOTSOUGHT to UNKNOWN means that all sources have been tried, no value has been gotten, and the inference engine has given up seeking values for that attribute.

TESTING STATUS IN RULES

Once the inference engine has tried to establish an attribute's value, the attribute's status is either KNOWN or UNKNOWN. Many shells enable you to test this within rules. This is a kind of *metaknowledge,* that is, "knowledge about knowledge." A rule testing an attribute's status does not directly contain information about the domain's knowledge. Yet the status may be useful for figuring out what to do next.

For example, an expert may conclude that if values for certain key attributes can't be established, the consultation should not proceed. The items may be so vital that no reasonable recommendation can be given without them. In this case, you may want the expert system to test whether the attribute is KNOWN or UNKNOWN so that you can immediately terminate processing instead of letting users run through a consultation when there is no hope of producing a recommendation. The expert system might instead instruct users to get the required information and try again.

    RULE end_if_unknown
    IF   economic_return = UNKNOWN
    THEN rec = "I cannot evaluate this domain without knowing its economic
           impact. Please find the answer to these questions and try again."

Other attributes may be less critical, but if too many in the aggregate are unknown, you may choose to end the consultation.

    RULE end_if_all_are_unknown
    IF   maintenance_plan = UNKNOWN
    AND   domain_well_defined = UNKNOWN
    AND   domain_expert_quality = UNKNOWN
    AND   organization_commitment = UNKNOWN
    THEN rec = "There is not enough information to make an evaluation."

In other cases the expert might complete a full consultation in the face of unknown data. Only then does he or she consider the implications of the unknown portions. The status of key attributes is then figured into the final recommendation. For example:

RULE good_domain_but_expert_need_unknown
IF   economic_return = established
AND expert_need = UNKNOWN
AND suitability = high
THEN rec = "The domain is tentatively recommended. However we suggest you determine whether there is a shortage of experts before starting."

You can see how testing the status of attributes helps you reason about more than their value. It allows you to create rules that reflect the expert's judgment about how much information is necessary to form a conclusion. In addition, it also enables the expert system to determine the strength or weakness of certain beliefs by examining how much information is UN-KNOWN. It aids you in refining the expert system and letting it distinguish between cases in which rules fail because the attribute's value is wrong from cases in which *no* value could be obtained.

Does the Inference Engine Chain on KNOWN and UNKNOWN?

There is an important question you need to answer to find out how using your shell's KNOWN and UNKNOWN testing functions causes the inference engine to act. Does the inference engine backward chain on NOTSOUGHT attributes whose status is being tested? For example, reconsider this rule:

RULE end_if_all_are_unknown
IF   maintenance_plan = UNKNOWN
AND domain_well_defined = UNKNOWN
AND domain_expert_quality = UNKNOWN
AND organization_commitment = UNKNOWN
THEN rec = "There is not enough information to make an evaluation."

Imagine that this rule is the first rule considered in the knowledge base. Because it is the first rule, the values of *maintenance_plan, domain_well_defined, domain_expert_quality,* and *organization_commitment* are all NOT-SOUGHT since the consultation is just beginning. The question is this: does the inference engine immediately evaluate the current status of each attribute or does it make each attribute the current goal and try to establish values for each?

In the former case, the inference engine does not distinguish between NOTSOUGHT and UNKNOWN and fires each premise clause since each attribute has no value. This can be useful when the rule is placed in such a way that you really are testing where you stand so far in the consultation. Thus the implicit meaning of the rule is that, "I've done some reasoning so far. Now this rule tests whether I've established values for important factors. If not, the consultation doesn't have enough information to continue. Let's quit." This is not the most common use for testing UNKNOWN. Usually, you want the inference engine to seek values for those attributes before testing their status. Most shells that test UNKNOWN this way offer a verb like FIND that you can put in a premise. This allows you to force backward chaining before making the test. Thus your rule might look something like this:

```
RULE  end_if_all_are_unknown
IF     find maintenance_plan
AND    maintenance_plan = UNKNOWN
AND    find domain_well_defined
AND    domain_well_defined = UNKNOWN
AND    find domain_expert_quality
AND    domain_expert_quality = UNKNOWN
THEN rec = "There is not enough information to make an evaluation."
```

The revised rule instructs the inference engine to first *find* each attribute before testing its status. This guarantees that the status will be either KNOWN or UNKNOWN.

The latter of the two cases of how UNKNOWN in premises is treated has the inference engine backward chain to establish a value when testing attribute status. If a value *is* established, the attribute is KNOWN and the premise clause fails. If no value is found, then the attribute's status becomes truly UNKNOWN and the premise clause succeeds. Thus the testing of the attribute's status causes the inference engine to make the attribute the current goal if its current status is NOTSOUGHT.

Many shells differ in how they handle UNKNOWN and KNOWN testing. The Appendix discusses how various popular shells let you test attribute status, and provides a sample knowledge base that lets you test how other shells operate with regard to the above discussion.

Be Careful with Syntax

Make sure you understand how your shell handles UNKNOWN, and what reserved words it uses to signify KNOWN and UNKNOWN. This is important so that you can avoid making a common error that emerges from how many shells allow you to test attribute status. For example:

NAME: color
TYPE: symbol
EXPECT: (red, blue, unknown)
PROMPT: "What is the color?"

GOAL: bird

RULE pigeon
IF   color = UNKNOWN
THEN bird = pigeon CF 20

Assume that the inference engine causes chaining on all NOTSOUGHT attributes, even if the rule is testing the attribute's UNKNOWN status. In evaluating *Rule pigeon,* the inference engine requires color and uses the PROMPT property to ask the user. The user selects the value "unknown." How does the inference engine evaluate the rule? The answer is that we don't know for sure without knowing the particular shell you are using. In some shells the value "unknown" has the same status as the values "red" and "blue," that is, it causes *color* to become KNOWN, bound to a symbol spelled u-n-k-n-o-w-n. In other shells, the selection would have caused the inference engine to interpret the user response as meaning, "The status of *color* is UNKNOWN." No value would be bound to *color,* and it would be regarded as UNKNOWN.

The Appendix discusses how particular inference engines treat the concept of UNKNOWN. If your domain requires reasoning about an attribute's UN-KNOWN and KNOWN status, you would do well to familiarize yourself with your inference engine's behavior in this area.

ADVANCED USES OF UNKNOWN

Here are two more tactics in which testing the status of an attribute can help you refine how you represent knowledge.

Screening Complex Paths

Sometimes a reasoning path has an easy road and a complex road. The complex road means that many questions or inferences must be processed in order to reach the conclusion. Sometimes there is an easier road dependent on the user's knowing some particular piece of information that allows you to end run the more complex path.

A typical scenario is that you expect some users of the expert system to be more knowledgeable than others. You may be able to ask knowledgeable users for certain *conclusions* directly. This saves the sophisticated user from answering questions that he or she may find time-consuming and obvious. This also saves the inference engine from processing extra or costly lines of reasoning. For less knowledgeable users, the expert system will instead ask for facts, and itself infer the conclusions implied by those facts.

For example, consider an expert system that diagnoses printer problems. The first bit of data the expert system needs to know is what kind of printer is being addressed. Knowledgeable users may know what type of printer they have. A novice may not. Thus the expert system first asks, "What kind of printer do you have?" "*Unknown*" is one of the selections. If the user responds with "unknown," the inference engine then asks questions like, "Does the printer have a paper spindle?", "Does the printer label say 'LaserJet series II'?", "Does the print appear to have a typeset quality to it?", and so on.

A fragment of the rules that represent this reasoning might look like this:

GOAL: printer

NAME: printer_type_from_user
TYPE: symbol
EXPECT: (dot_matrix, daisy_wheel, laser, unknown)
PROMPT: "What kind of printer do you have?"

RULE 1
IF   printer_type = dot_matrix
OR   printer_type = daisy_wheel
OR   printer_type = laser
THEN printer = found;

RULE 2
IF   printer_type_from_user = dot_matrix
THEN printer_type = dot_matrix

RULE 3
IF   printer_type_from_user = daisy_wheel
THEN printer_type = daisy_wheel

RULE 4
IF   printer_type_from_user = laser
THEN printer_type = laser

RULE 5
IF   printer_type_from_user = UNKNOWN
AND   printer_name = "Laser_Jet"
THEN printer_type = laser

RULE 6
IF   printer_type_from_user = UNKNOWN
AND   printer_quality = typeset
THEN printer_type = laser

RULE 7
IF   printer_type_from_user = UNKNOWN
AND printer_speed = slow
AND printer_sound = loud
THEN printer_type = daisy_wheel

The inference engine considers the first rule because it concludes the current goal *printer.* Because it requires a value for the attribute *printer_type,* the inference engine goes after rules concluding *printer_type.* The first rules it encounters are those that test the attribute *printer_type_from_user.* As you can see in the attribute property list for that attribute, *printer_type_from_user* has both 'prompt' and 'expects' lists, which are used since no rules conclude it. The user is then prompted for which kind of printer is being considered.

Prompt: "What kind of printer do you have?"

Dot_matrix   daisy_wheel   laser   unknown

The user selects one. If one of the first three options are chosen, the appropriate rule fires and causes *printer_type* and *printer* to be found. This ends this part of the consultation. If the user instead selects the choice "unknown," the inference engine then considers those rules concluding *printer_type* that start with the clause:

IF printer_type_from_user = UNKNOWN

These rules then generate additional prompts (not listed) that ask about print quality, speed, labels, and so on. The answers to these questions allow the inference engine to infer *printer_type.* This approach lets the more knowledgeable users answer one question, if they know the answer. If they don't, the inference engine infers the answer by asking for the facts necessary to make that conclusion. Placing the premise clause *printer_type_from_user = UNKNOWN* as the first clause in these rules guarantees that the rules are only considered when the user selects the choice UNKNOWN.

This strategy has one drawback. Users may feel uncomfortable answering UNKNOWN to a user prompt. Sometimes they guess to avoid answering UNKNOWN. Make sure the wording of the prompt makes clear that UNKNOWN *should* be selected if there is any doubt in the user's mind about the correct answer. This helps avoid responses in which users guess because they don't want to appear unknowledgeable

Multiple Paths

Sometimes there is more than one way to infer some conclusion. By encoding all of the reasoning lines for the same conclusion, you increase the likelihood of getting a value.

Consider an example. Company xyz's expert system recommends a software language depending on certain decision factors. The variables we're concerned with here can be summarized in this table:

Recommendation	Experience Needed	Budget	Environment
BAL	much	high	mainframe
COBOL	some	high	mainframe
BASIC	little	low	micro
C	much	low	micro

Only two of the three categories are significant for purposes of producing a unique recommendation. For example:

RULE 1
IF   budget = low
AND   experience = much
THEN rec = C

RULE 2
IF   budget = low
AND   experience = little
THEN rec = BASIC

RULE 3
IF   budget = high
AND   experience = some
THEN rec = COBOL

RULE 4
IF   budget = high
AND   experience = much
THEN rec = BAL

The weakness of this example is that if the user enters "UNKNOWN" to *budget* or *experience,* all four rules will fail. While there is nothing we can do to alleviate this problem for the attribute *experience,* we can add rules that buffer us from failure if *budget = UNKNOWN.*

RULE 5
IF   environment = micro
AND   experience = much
THEN rec = C

RULE 6
IF   environment = micro
AND   experience = little
THEN rec = BASIC

RULE 7
IF   environment = mainframe
AND   experience = some
THEN rec = COBOL

RULE 8
IF   environment = mainframe
AND   experience = much
THEN rec = BAL

Now, if *budget = unknown,* the inference engine will still consider *Rule 5* through *Rule 8* and test the values for *environment.* If these can be established, the conclusion can be produced in the face of the initial unknown data. These rules could be condensed further if desired:

RULE 1
IF   budget = low
OR   environment = micro
AND   experience = much
THEN rec = C

RULE 2
IF   budget = low
OR   environment = micro
AND   experience = little
THEN rec = BASIC

RULE 3
IF   budget = high
OR   environment = mainframe
AND   experience = some
THEN rec = COBOL

RULE 4
IF   budget = high
OR   environment = mainframe
AND   experience = much
THEN rec = BAL

Remember, it is not redundant to encode overlapping lines of reasoning. When you do this, you allow the inference engine to continue reasoning in the face of UNKNOWN information.

FORGETTING

Some domains benefit from the ability to change the status of attributes from KNOWN to NOTSOUGHT. Such uses may include:

* Monitoring applications in which data must be "freshly" analyzed over and over again.
* Systems in which "what-if" processing is desired by selectively changing one or more system parameters.
* Process and control problems.

Many shells offer the ability to *reset* or *forget* whatever values have been bound to them. The resetting operation changes the status of the attribute to NOTSOUGHT. Such operations are performed from within rules, or from the procedural control section of the expert system if it has one.

Recall that when attributes become KNOWN or UNKNOWN, the inference engine stops looking for values for them. When rules test such attributes in rules, the inference engine just looks up their value in memory or notes that they are UNKNOWN. Changing attribute status to NOTSOUGHT enables the knowledge base to "rethink" certain aspects of its knowledge that depend on these attributes. The change to NOTSOUGHT status induces the inference engine to treat the attribute as if it had never been considered before. This can make the inference engine reconsider rules it had previously tried. If new information has become available during the consultation, this new status may allow the inference engine to conclude new results or change old conclusions.

A classic use for this technique is in monitoring and control applications in which the expert system monitors and perhaps provides feedback to some equipment. Typically, the equipment provides a stream of data at some acceptable rate within the processing capability of the shell. Such expert systems typically have attributes representing "long-term" memory (LTM) and "short-term" memory (STM). STM is used for inferences and conclusions occurring from data received from the current input cycle. LTM is used for maintaining values that keep track of relevant performance characteristics over a larger period of time. The reasoning on which the ultimate feedback or conclusion is based may be comparisons of STM to LTM in order to evaluate changes from desired targets or performance goals. Such applications require that, after each short-term cycle is complete, its parameters be reset. Using your shell's features for resetting those attributes that represent STM to

NOTSOUGHT after each cycle enables the relevant short-term inferencing to occur each time the cycle is repeated.

Another use for "forgetting" attributes is to restart a consultation. By resetting all consultation parameters, and establishing the goal, the consultation starts over as if running for the first time. This can be a handy way to restart a help desk or other expert system that is used over and over again, in which users make a mistake, change their minds, or just want to run another consultation.

SUMMARY

The inference engine's ability to conveniently handle the concept of the unknown is one of the ways in which expert systems differ from conventional programming. It is essential to understand how differences in attribute status affect inference engine behavior. Most inference engines also let you test attribute status in rules. This allows you to write rules that reason in the face of incomplete information. Moreover, by testing attribute status, you can represent multiple reasoning paths, questioning sequences that account for differences in user know-how and knowledge in which preliminary conclusions must be retracted.

7 | Handling Multivalued Information

One of the traits of real-world problems is that their causes and solutions can have more than one plausible value. A key benefit of expert systems shells is their ability to represent multivalued information and process those multiple values without programming logic supplied from the developer. In this chapter, we examine this aspect of expert systems development.

AN EXAMPLE

Consider the example of Acme Ping-Pong Ball Manufacturing. The company has experienced serious sales force turnover and lost 25 percent of its force in one year to Better Bounces, Inc. The gravity of this problem is underscored by the fact that former Acme sales staff are taking major accounts from Acme when they leave. The president of the company has decided to hire a consultant to develop recommendations to stem the tide of defections.

The consultant has broad experience in these matters. She has helped save sales forces of 50 companies, using 43 different techniques she learned, discovered, or developed in similar situations. When the consultant arrives at the president's office, the president says, "Hello, how are you? Would you like a cup of coffee? My sales force is defecting; what should I do?"

Without any more information about Acme's problem, any one of the consultant's 43 solutions might apply. At this stage of the consultation, the consultant might list every possible solution. Given that most of the factors are unknown, the problem could have many solutions.

Of course, the consultant asks questions. She asks about Acme's annual turnover in previous years, the sales force's compensation plan, changes made in the past 18 months, changes in the marketplace, and overall company performance. When asked about his opinion about what the sales force problem is, the president makes two guesses and says that he believes the second guess is more likely than the first. The consultant notes these possibilities and continues asking questions.

Sometimes the president cannot provide clear answers to the consultant's questions. For example, the president doesn't know whether or not expense money has been consistently reimbursed on time. In response to whether the last national sales meeting was held within the last year, the president "believes" it was, but is not sure.

Ultimately, the consultant finishes gathering information, and tells the president, "There are four ways to solve your problem. . . ." She explains each option. The consultation is over. A decision is made and a new program put into place to address the problem.

Some of the characteristics of this scenario occur in knowledge-based problems. During the consultation, the consultant discovers several causes: pay was cut by 25 percent, territories were narrowed by half. Some problems have more than one contributing cause.

In our example, the president suggests several possible causes because he is uncertain about which actually causes the problem. He rates them in order of likelihood according to his best guess. Subsequent reasoning with these guesses must factor in uncertainty. The final conclusion may have several values each with some degree of uncertainty.

Sometimes more than one solution is provided because certain important factors are unknown. The data that are missing might narrow the number of solutions if they were known. Since they are not, more than one recommendation appears.

Finally, there may simply be more than one way to solve the problem. Solutions can be chosen among a set of known alternatives, or can be built up to meet objectives or satisfy constraints through a reasoning path. The path that is chosen may depend on personal style, preference, cost, or other subjective conditions not included in the domain. Therefore, the expert system may be required to give a set of possible solutions from which a human ultimately selects the best, given subjective factors outside the scope of the expert system.

HOW MULTIVALUED DEFINITIONS AFFECT INFERENCING

Attributes that can have more than one value are called "multivalued" attributes. We represent an attribute's ability to hold more than one value using an attribute property. An example follows of the property list for an attribute describing the kind of vehicle a potential buyer might want to consider:

```
NAME:    car_type
TYPE:    symbol
EXPECT: (Truck, van, sedan, sports_coupe)
PROMPT: "What kind of vehicle do you prefer?"
MULTI:   yes
```

The attribute *car_type* is a symbolic attribute with four allowable values (truck, van, sedan, sports_coupe). It has a prompt and the ability to bind multiple values if necessary.

The exact syntax for declaring attributes "multivalued" varies among shells. Many require an explicit declaration within the knowledge base like

multivalued(car_type)

or

PLURAL: car_type;

Other shells assume that *all* attributes can be multivalued. Developers denote distinctions between multi- and singlevalued assignments through the assignment operator they choose when binding values. The following example comes from the expert systems shell Guru™:

color = red; *replace any previous values bound to color with the value red.*
color + = red; *add the value red to any values that already exist for attribute color.*
color − = red; *remove the value red from any values that already exist for attribute color.*

In most expert systems shells, the inference engine usually treats multi-valued attributes differently from singlevalued. The following knowledge base fragment shows how a multivalued goal is handled.

GOAL: rec

Attribute Property List

NAME: rec
TYPE: text
MULTI: yes

NAME: 495ok
TYPE: boolean
EXPECT: (yes, no)
PROMPT: "Can you spend $495 for the software tool?"
MULTI: no

NAME: experience
TYPE: symbol
EXPECT: (experienced, some_experience, no_experience)
PROMPT: "What is your experience level?"
MULTI: no

NAME: job
TYPE: symbol
EXPECT: (financial, graphics, expert_system, other)
PROMPT: "What are the jobs to be done?"
MULTI: yes

Rules

RULE rec_spreadsheet
IF   job = financial
THEN rec = "Use a spreadsheet."

RULE rec_shell
IF   job = expert_system
AND   495ok = yes
THEN rec = "Use an expert systems shell."

RULE rec_C
IF   job = other
AND   experience = some_experience
THEN rec = "Use the C programming language."

RULE rec_graphics
IF   job = graphics
THEN rec = "Use Graph-a-plot."

RULE rec_assembler
IF   job = other
AND   experience = experienced
THEN rec = "Use Assembler language."

RULE rec_basic
IF   job = other
AND   experience = no_experience
THEN rec = "Use BASIC."

Attributes *rec* and *job* are declared as multivalued. Each of the six rules concludes with the goal *rec*. Because it appears first, *Rule rec_spreadsheet* is considered first.

Rule rec_spreadsheet's premise tests whether *job = financial*. Because the value of *job* is not yet known, it becomes the current goal. Since no rules conclude it, the inference engine checks whether *job* has a PROMPT property. It does, so the inference engine prompts the user, "*What are the jobs to be done?*" The values that may be chosen are *financial, graphics, expert_system,* and *other.*

Because *job* is multivalued, any one *or more* of the values may be chosen by the user. Assume that the user selects two values: *financial* and *other.* Since *job* now has a value, the inference engine evaluates *Rule rec_spreadsheet.* Since one of *job*'s values is *financial,* the premise is true, the rule fires, and *rec* is bound to the string "Use a spreadsheet."

Since *rec* is the goal for the knowledge base, one might conclude that the consultation is now finished because *rec* has been instantiated. But wait! *Rec* is multivalued. Because of this, the inference engine will consider **all rules** that conclude the current goal. Thus the consultation continues and the inference engine seeks other rules that conclude *rec.* This is a key difference of inference engine processing of multivalued attributes. With a singlevalued attribute as the current goal, the inference engine stops searching as soon as a fully certain value is obtained. With multivalued attributes, all rules that conclude it are evaluated.

The next rule is *Rule rec_shell.* It fails because *job* does not equal *expert_ system. Rule rec_C* is considered next. The first premise clause passes because *other* is one of two values that the user assigned to attribute *job.* The inference engine considers the second clause of *Rule rec_C:*

experience = some_experience

Since the value of *experience* is NOTSOUGHT, *experience* becomes the current goal. No rules conclude it, causing the inference engine to check if *experience* has a PROMPT property. It does. The inference engine then prompts the user for the value of *experience, "What is your experience level?"* The attribute is singlevalued and thus the user may choose one of the three possible values defined in its EXPECTS list: "experienced, some_experience, no_experience." Assume the user selects *no_experience.*

Attribute *experience* now has a value and thus *rec* is reinstated as the current goal. Because the actual value does not equal "experience = some_ experience," the premise clause, and subsequently *Rule rec_C fails. Rule rec_ assembler* fails in a similar fashion. Both premise clauses in *Rule rec_basic* are satisfied, causing the premise to evaluate to true. The rule fires, and attribute *rec* is instantiated to "Use BASIC." *Rec* now has two values:

rec = "Use a spreadsheet"
     "Use BASIC"

The last rule, *Rule rec_graphics* fails. Because there are no other knowledge sources that conclude *rec,* the consultation is completed and processing ends. However, if other rules are added, each additional rule concluding the goal will be considered. Defining an attribute as multivalued usually causes the inference engine to consider **all** knowledge sources that conclude the attribute, even when **some** value has already been established. The multivalued property causes the inference engine to undertake an exhaustive search for attributes which have a *multivalued* property.

TESTING MULTIVALUED ATTRIBUTES

The beauty of multivalued attributes is that the inference engine takes on the responsibility of managing those multiple values. The inference engine usually ensures that when a rule premise containing a multivalued attribute is evaluated, each value that attribute contains is tried. For example:

NAME: causes
TYPE: symbol
EXPECT: (low_morale, poor_comp, poor_training, wrong_market, . . .)
MULTI: yes

If the attribute *causes* currently has the values *low_morale* and *poor_training*, then the following rule will fire:

RULE bad_morale
IF   causes = low_morale
THEN solution_part = sales_meeting

It doesn't matter if *low_morale* is the first or last value of *causes*. The inference engine automatically searches the entire list of values that *causes* contains when it tests *causes* in a rule. No matter where in the list *low_morale* appears, its presence causes the rule to fire. Thus the method in which values are stored and maintained in multivalued attributes is not the developer's problem.

MULTIVALUED SINGLE VALUES

Defining an attribute as multivalued changes how the inference engine processes it when that attribute is the current goal. Many shells also treat singlevalued attributes as if they were multivalued when those attributes contain uncertainty.[1]

For example, consider this very similar version of the same knowledge base we looked at before.

GOAL: Rec

Attribute Descriptions

NAME: rec
TYPE: text
MULTI: no

---

[1]The topic of uncertainty—and its close relationship with multivalues—is explored in the next chapter. Suffice for now that attributes may be known with less than complete certainty.

NAME: 495ok
TYPE: boolean
EXPECT: (yes, no)
PROMPT: "Can you spend $495 for the software tool?"
MULTI: no

NAME: experience
TYPE: symbol
EXPECT: (experienced, some_experience, no_experience)
PROMPT: "What is your experience level?"
MULTI: no

NAME: job
TYPE: symbol
EXPECT: (financial, graphics, expert_system, other)
PROMPT: "What is the job to be done?"
MULTI: yes

Rules

RULE rec_graphics
IF   job = graphics
THEN rec = "Use Graph-a-plot" CF 30

RULE rec_shell
IF   job = expert_system
AND   495ok = yes
THEN rec = "Use an expert systems shell." CF 40

RULE rec_C
IF   job = other
AND   experience = some_experience
THEN rec = "Use the C programming language." CF 50

RULE rec_spreadsheet
IF   job = financial
THEN rec = "Use a spreadsheet."

RULE rec_assembler
IF   job = other
AND   experience = experienced
THEN rec = "Use Assembler language." CF 30

RULE rec_basic
IF   job = other
AND   experience = no_experience
THEN rec = "Use BASIC." CF 50

The rules in this knowledge base are identical to the original version with a few exceptions. First, this version of the knowledge base contains rules whose conclusions have *certainty factors* representing some degree of uncertainty. Second, the attribute *rec*, which was before multivalued, is now singlevalued. Finally, the positions of *Rule rec_graphics* and *Rule rec_spreadsheet* have been exchanged. How will the inference engine process this version of the knowledge base?

Since the goal is the same, the inference engine again starts by trying to find rules that conclude *rec*. It first tries *Rule rec_graphics*. It makes *job* the current goal since *job* is NOTSOUGHT. *Job* has a PROMPT property, so the user is asked to respond to the query, *"What is the job to be done?"* This time the user selects one choice: *graphics*. This causes *Rule rec_graphics* to fire and assign *rec = Use Graph-a-plot* with a certainty factor of 30.

Since *rec* is singlevalued and now has a value, we might conclude that the consultation has finished. However, because *rec* is known with uncertainty, many inference engines will continue to consider other knowledge sources for the current goal. This may be desirable because if *rec = Use Graph-a-plot* is true with less than full certainty, we may want the inference engine to continue trying to establish values for the current goal that are more certain or even completely certain. In other words, the inference engine continues trying rules to conclude the *most certain value* for the current goal.[2]

Because *rec*'s value is uncertain, the inference engine continues considering rules. The next rule is: *Rule rec_shell*. Since *job = graphics*, *Rule rec_shell*— and the rest of the rules—fail. The consultation ends with the final value of *rec* equal to *Use Graph-a-plot* CF 30.

Consider one last change to the example. Using the same knowledge base containing uncertainty, assume the user enters both *financial* and *graphics* when prompted for the value of *job*. This is possible because *job* is multivalued. Again, *Rule rec_graphics* fires, instantiating *rec* to *Use Graph-a-plot* with a certainty factor of 30. Consideration continues since the current goal is known with uncertainty. After failing *Rule rec_shell* and *Rule rec_C*, *Rule rec_financial* fires since *job* is also bound to *financial*. It instantiates *rec* to *"Use a spreadsheet."* Because the latter value is completely certain, the final certainty of *rec* becomes 100. *Rec* is now fully certain.

Rec is singlevalued and now fully certain. This causes the inference engine to revert to treating *rec* as it normally treats singlevalued attributes. Other uncertain values (*Use Graph-a-plot*) are purged. The one fully certain value (*Use a spreadsheet*) becomes the sole value of *rec*. Since *rec* is known with

---

[2]A notable exception to this behavior is VP-Expert which stops considering uncertain singlevalued attributes as if they were fully certain. To force the exhaustive search behavior described, an attribute must be declared as multivalued (PLURAL in VP-Expert terminology).

complete confidence, the inference engine stops seeking values for it. The consideration of other rules concluding *rec* is abandoned, the conclusion is presented to the user, and the consultation concluded.

There are some variations in how different shells' inference engines handle multivalued attributes. The basic principle, however, is the same. Aspects of many real-world problems have multiple values. The multivalued attribute property lets you represent these in a nonprocedural way.

COMBINATORIAL EXPLOSION

While using multivalued information can greatly enhance an expert system's power, it also risks making the shell's performance slow. For example, consider the following rule from the shell *M. 1*™ in which multivalued attribute "price" has the value 5, 8, 14, 18, and 25; and multivalued attribute "units" contains values 61, 62, 66, and 80. The rule multiplies these two to obtain (multivalued) attribute "sales."

```
IF     price = P
AND   units = U
AND   P * U = S
THEN sales = S
```

This multiplication produces the following values for the conclusion *sales:*

sales = 496 cf 100
sales = 528 cf 100
sales = 640 cf 100
sales = 854 cf 100
sales = 868 cf 100
sales = 924 cf 100
sales = 1120 cf 100
sales = 1098 cf 100
sales = 1116 cf 100
sales = 305 cf 100
sales = 1188 cf 100
sales = 310 cf 100
sales = 1440 cf 100
sales = 330 cf 100
sales = 1525 cf 100
sales = 400 cf 100
sales = 1550 cf 100
sales = 488 cf 100
sales = 1650 cf 100
sales = 2000 cf 100

Attribute *sales* now has twenty values because each value of *price* was multiplied against each value of *units*. Moreover, if *sales* is now arithmetically combined with another multivalued attribute, hundreds of values could result. It is easy to see how things can quickly get out of hand. Not only is it difficult to test the reliability of such complex results, but the explosion in the number of factors can bog down the shell in maintaining dozens or hundreds of calculations. Too, posting and maintaining so many values eats valuable storage, possibly limiting capacity that could otherwise hold meaningful rules and facts.

USING MULTIVALUED ATTRIBUTES

We have looked at what multivalued attributes are and how they affect inference engine behavior. We now look at several techniques for using this property.

You may want a consultation to provide several recommendations because some key piece of information is missing. For example, the expert system might prompt, "Do you want to vacation in Florida, California, or Indiana?" You may respond "Florida *and* Indiana" to direct the expert system to consider *both* destinations. You can't go to both destinations, but you want recommendations for both states so that you can decide.

In other cases, there may be uncertainty involved. In the example that started this chapter, the president believes his sales force has two problems, with one more likely than the other. This might be represented using a weighting system: *problem = cause_1 CF 80, problem = cause_2 CF 60.*

Tailoring Advice

Expert systems have differing requirements for how final advice should be given. In some, the advice may be a simple "yes" or "no"; for example, "Yes, go ahead with the acquisition." Others, like some diagnostic applications, just need a few words identifying the recommendation: "Replace the battery." Some domains, however, need more tailored Englishlike final advice.

You may want more elaborated advice for a number of reasons. English explanations or justifications may be an integral part of the advice. Users may need step-by-step instructions. Such explanations can be built using a series of English-language text phrases. The advice has various components, each of which is separately concluded.

The effect of tailored advice can be achieved using multivalued attributes. The overall strategy is to declare a goal as multivalued, and allow the inference engine to infer as many conclusions as is appropriate for the particular situation. Each conclusion offers some specific advice. When all conclusions have been inferred, you then provide the accumulated advice. Here are two simple examples:

Example 1

GOAL: investment

Attribute Descriptions

NAME: investment
TYPE: text
MULTI: yes

NAME: risk
TYPE: symbol
EXPECT: (none, some, speculate)
PROMPT: "How much risk are you willing to accept?"
MULTI: yes

RULE 1
IF   risk = none
THEN investment = "Invest in savings bonds.";

RULE 2
IF   risk = some
THEN investment = "Invest in blue chip stocks.";

RULE 3
IF   risk = speculate
THEN investment = "Buy Colorado Penny stocks.";

Example 2

RULE 1
IF   risk = none
THEN   investment = savings_bond
        DISPLAY "Invest in savings bonds.";

RULE 2
IF   risk = some
THEN   investment = blue_chip_stocks
        DISPLAY "Invest in blue chip stocks.";

RULE 3
IF   risk = speculate
THEN   investment = penny_stocks
        DISPLAY "Buy Colorado Penny stocks.";

These examples show two different versions of the same knowledge. The first shows how you accumulate advice in a multivalued goal when the shell allows multivalued attributes to contain text strings. *Risk* can be instantiated with as many values as are named in the EXPECTS list. These values come from the user's responses to the inference engine prompt. In reality, the final system would probably be expanded to include rules that infer *risk* from questions asked about the user's profile. Once *risk*'s values are obtained, all three rules concluding the multivalued goal *investment* can be evaluated. Since *risk* might have any or all of its possible values, the knowledge base's final advice could have up to three components:

Invest in savings bonds.
Invest in blue chip stocks.
Buy Colorado Penny stocks.

The second example represents the same knowledge, but overcomes the fact that some shells do not allow text strings to be instantiated as attribute values. They do, however, enable you to *display* text strings. Therefore, the first part of each advice rule concludes symbols representing an advice segment; the second part contains a DISPLAY statement that prints the related advice.

The same technique can be used to provide recommendations that summarize intermediate conclusions as you go. By summarizing what the knowledge base has concluded at the end of the consultation, you give the user a sense of the rationale for the line of reasoning, and the summary may also be useful as a teaching aid to communicate the vital links in the reasoning process. Although this information may be available in an explanation subsystem, you may want to explicitly display it as part of the consultation.

SUMMARY

We've looked at how multivalued attributes let you represent knowledge that may have more than one value. Understand how your shell's inference engine treats multivalued attributes. Many aspects of multivalued attributes are closely related to certainty factors. Additional uses of multivalued attributes are discussed in the next chapter.

8 | *Handling Uncertainty*

The goal of this chapter is to give you a start at answering the question of *when* and *how* to use uncertainty. Representing uncertainty is one of the more controversial subjects in expert systems. Humans reason in the face of uncertainty. Expert systems differ from conventional software by giving the appearance of humanlike reasoning. Therefore, it seems sensible to expect that expert systems should be able to handle uncertainty.

Beginning expert systems developers often assume that the certainty factor (also called *confidence factor* or *cf*) systems found in rule-based shells work in a globally applicable manner. Experience has shown that this is not the case. Before using cfs, you must clearly understand what they are and how the inference engine calculates them. You must evaluate whether these approaches harmonize with what the expert thinks about uncertainty. Finally, you must evaluate whether the product gives you other cf-related facilities that let you tailor the shell's certainty faculties to domain knowledge. We start by looking at what are certainty factors, common cf blending methods, and some of the testing functions that may be available in your shell.[1] Then we examine some approaches for dealing with the question of when to use cfs to aid you in determining their rightful role in your project.

WHAT ARE CERTAINTY FACTORS?

Certainty factors are attribute and rule properties used to describe the level of certainty or confidence in a particular value. You use cfs to represent the

---

[1] We do not discuss the algorithms used in calculating negative certainty factors, since not all tools offer them and there is little standardization among those that do. Also, vendors use differing terminology to describe the algorithms discussed in what follows. We use the names given these algorithms in the product documentation of the expert systems shell Guru, version 1.1; vendor: Micro Data Base Systems, Lafayette IN 47906; Copyright date 1986.

116

certitude of user input, assertions, and rule conclusions. They are numeric values maintained by the inference engine, usually stored as integer values ranging from zero to 100, or – 100 to 100. Some shells represent them as decimal values from zero to 1.0 or – 1.0 to 1.0. Cf assignments usually occur after a rule's conclusion, preceded by the keyword "CF" or "CNF." For example, "*color = blue CF 80*" means that the attribute *color* is instantiated to value *blue* with a certainty factor of *80*.

The highest possible certainty value (usually 100 or 1.0) means that the attribute/value pair is believed with full certainty. In those shells in which the lowest cf is zero, a certainty factor of zero means that there is "no confidence" or no belief that the assertion is true. In those systems in which the lowest value is negative (usually – 1.0 or – 100), the lowest value indicates negative evidence. The assertion "*color = blue CF – 100*" means that there is complete certainty that *color* is NOT equal to *blue*. Products that support negative cfs make it possible to represent knowledge that contradicts a conclusion.

Certainty factors are linked to each specific attribute/value pair. It doesn't make sense to talk about a cf for *recom* without a corresponding value. Most shells permit attributes to have more than one uncertain value. For example, attribute *recom* may have two values:

recom = take_the_high_road CF 80
recom = take_the_low_road CF 65

Inference engines that use certainty factors have a cf value called the *truth threshold*. The truth threshold indicates the point at which an attribute's value has enough certainty to be considered true. For example:

RULE rain_test
 IF barometer = rising
THEN chance_of_rain = lower

Assume that the truth threshold of the inference engine processing this rule is 30 on a scale of 0 to 100. If the certainty of *barometer = rising* is 40, then *Rule rain_test* fires. However, if *barometer = rising* has a cf of 29 or lower, the rule fails *even though the attribute's value matches the value tested in the premise.* The assertion's certainty has become so low as to make it undesirable to regard the expression as true. This leads to an interesting behavior. The premise may be true from the point of view that the attribute/value binding matches that tested in the premise. Yet the rule does not fire because the premise's cf falls below the truth threshold—it is so low that the conclusion does not warrant being made.

Expert systems shells vary in the value they use for the truth threshold. Some shells allow you to change the default truth threshold. The act of raising the truth threshold can change how a knowledge base is processed. This is because the high truth threshold may cause the inference engine to pass some tests that would otherwise fail if the threshold were lower.

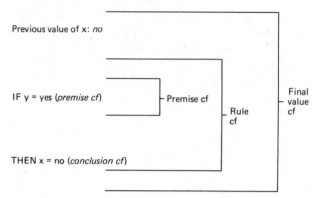

Figure 8.1. The Three "Moments" of cf Calculation: Premise, Rule, and Final Value.

CALCULATING CERTAINTY FACTORS IN RULE-BASED SYSTEMS

Certainty factor "algebras" or "algorithms" are the arithmetic formulas that shells use to "combine" or "blend" cfs. While there are similarities among many shells, there are also differences which make generalization difficult. We provide here an overview of the most common algorithms that rule-based systems use. In addition, we discuss other features that some tools offer for manipulating and testing certainties.

There are three "moments" in which cf blending occurs (Figure 8.1):

1. *Within a premise:* A separate cf is usually calculated for the premise. If all attributes in the premise are fully certain, the premise certainty will be the highest possible value (1.0 or 100). If one or more premise clauses contain uncertainty, their cfs are blended to obtain an overall premise certainty factor.
2. *Within the rule:* The premise's uncertainty must be blended with the certainty of the conclusion. The result is a final certainty factor for that rule. This represents the level of belief this rule contributes to the conclusion.
3. *Final Value:* If the same value has been previously assigned elsewhere, this previous certainty of the conclusion must be blended with the certainty concluded in step two.

Certainty within a Premise

Rules consist of a premise and a conclusion. If the premise is true and fully certain, it follows that this certitude should be passed through to the conclusion. However, if the premise is true with some uncertainty, this uncertainty should likewise affect the conclusion. For example:

RULE veg_cucumber
IF   color = green
AND   shape = cylindrical
THEN vegetable = cucumber

If we are completely sure that the vegetable is green and cylindrical, then we can be fully certain of the conclusion. However, if we are only somewhat confident that the shape is cylindrical, then it follows that the certainty of *vegetable = cucumber* should be reduced. We now look at the algorithms many expert systems shells use to determine how to calculate cfs in premises.

Simple Premises. By definition, simple premises have one clause. To calculate the certainty factor for a simple premise, the inference engine simply takes the cf of the attribute/value pair appearing in the premise. For example:

Truth threshold: 40
Value of *color:* **yellow CF 70**

RULE simple_test
IF   color = yellow → premise certainty: 70
THEN fruit = banana

Because the certainty factor of *color = yellow* is 70, the overall certainty of the premise is also 70. Remember that if the cf of *color = yellow* falls below the truth threshold, the premise is not considered true even though *yellow* is bound to *color.* In this example, if the value of the truth threshold had been above 70, *Rule simple_test* would have failed.

Clauses Connected by AND. When there is more than one clause in a premise and those clauses contain uncertainty, the inference engine usually blends their uncertainty into one value for an overall premise cf.

Expert systems shells treat conjunctions (clauses connected by "AND") as "dependent" clauses. Because every clause in such a premise must be true for the overall premise to be considered true, the thinking is that the overall certainty of the group should never be more than the weakest link in the chain. This is called the "minimum" method of certainty calculation. For example:

Truth threshold: 40
Value of *color:* **red CF 70**
Value of *size:* **large CF 100**

RULE Is_it_an_apple
IF   color = red   → 70 ⌉
                                                               ⌐→ overall premise certainty: 70
AND   size = like_a_rubber_ball → 100 ⌋
THEN fruit = apple

Size = like_a_rubber_ball is true with full certainty. *Color = red,* however, is known only with a confidence of 70. Therefore, the overall certainty of the premise is the minimum of the two values, that is, 70. The premise's certainty is the same as the "weakest link" among those clauses connected by AND.

This characteristic of conjunctions can cause rules to fail in which all a/v pairs except one are known with high confidence:

Truth threshold: 50
Value of *color*: **red CF 70**
Value of *size*: **small CF 100**
Value of *grows_on*: **bush CF 45**
Value of *taste*: **sweet CF 100**

RULE Is_it_strawberry
IF   color = red   → 70 →
AND   size = small   → 100
AND   grows_on = bush → 45   Rule fails.
AND   taste = sweet   → 100 →
THEN fruit = strawberry

Two of the values (*taste = sweet* and *size = small*) are known with complete confidence. However, the confidence of *grows_on = bush* is only 45. Since it falls below the truth threshold, its confidence ranking is not high enough to be regarded as true. It is the weak link in the premise and since every premise must be true in rules whose premise clauses are connected by AND, the overall premise fails. The rule *Is_it_strawberry* fails even though the actual bindings of its attributes all match.

Clauses Connected by OR. Disjunctions (premises whose clauses are connected by OR) are often referred to as "independent" clauses because they don't depend on one another for their truth status. If any one OR clause among many is true, the entire group is considered true. In this sense, each clause is like a small premise in itself.

Since any one true clause among many causes the entire rule to fire, it stands to reason that if more than one clause is true that the overall certainty of the premise should be at least as high—maybe higher—than if only one such clause is true. The presence of additional reinforcing evidence should increase the premise's overall certitude. This "more is better" reasoning means that the certainty of the premise should be at least as high as the highest certainty factor among those true OR clauses. Most shells offer one of two approaches for disjunctions. We look at one now, and the other later in this chapter. The method we examine here is called the "maximum" method.

Truth threshold: 50
Value of *color*: **orange CF 60**
Value of *juice*: **orange_juice CF 100**

RULE Is_it_an_orange
IF color = orange →60
OR juice = orange_juice →100
THEN fruit = orange

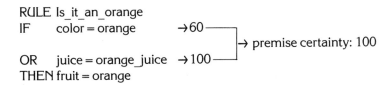

→ premise certainty: 100

Both premise clauses are true. Using the "maximum" method, the overall certainty of the premise is 100 because the highest of the true premise clauses is 100. Therefore, because it is fully certain that *juice = orange_juice,* the premise is fully certain even though one of the attribute/value pairs in the premise contains uncertainty.

Note that when some premise clauses fall below the truth threshold, the overall premise can still remain high. For example:

Truth threshold: 50
Value of *car_type*: **sports_coupe CF 51**
Value of *delivery*: **later CF 90**
Value of *prestige*: **high CF 40**
Value of *price*: **low CF 95**

RULE 4
IF car_type = sports_coupe → 51
OR delivery = now →not true
OR prestige = high →40
OR price = low →95
THEN recommendation = buy

→ premise uncertainty: 95

In this case, only one of four clauses has a high degree of certainty. Clause 1 exceeds the truth threshold only by the narrowest of margins. Clause 2 fails because the actual value of *delivery* is different from what the rule tests. The value for *prestige* matches but its certainty factor falls below the truth threshold, so it too fails. Finally, *price = low* is both true and above the truth threshold. Thus clauses one and four are true, with a cf of 51 and 95 respectively. Using the "maximum method," the inference engine takes the certainty factor of 95. This value becomes the overall certainty of *Rule 4*'s premise.

You can see how the distinction between a conjunction and a disjunction dramatically affects not only its evaluation but how its certainty is calculated. If *Rule Is_it_an_orange* had been a conjunction, the premise certainty would have been 60. As a disjunction, it is 100. *Rule recom_car* would have failed had it had been a conjunction. As a disjunction, it is true with a cf of 95. When using uncertainty, you must think carefully about how rule construction impacts the cf as well as the logical meaning of the rule.

Certainty within a Rule

Premise certainties are only of interest insofar as they are needed to figure the overall certainty of rules. The rule has two parts: the premise and the conclusion. If premises are less than fully certain, the rule's conclusion must reflect this uncertainty. The rule's final certainty must also reflect any uncertainty explicitly named in the conclusion.

The "Product" Method. In *Rule umbrella1*, the premise *rain = yes* is true only with a certainty of 50. It follows that the conclusion *umbrella_needed = yes* should not be more confident than the premise on which it is based.

Truth threshold: 40
Value of *rain*: **yes CF 50**

RULE umbrella1 ─────────────────┐
IF   rain = yes → premise uncertainty: 50 ╫→ rule certainty: 50
THEN umbrella_needed = yes ────────────────┘

Rule umbrella1 has no certainty factor following the conclusion *umbrella_ needed = yes*. In such cases, the conclusion is understood to be 100 or "fully certain." This certainty refers to the confidence we have in this rule's particular knowledge.

The overall rule certainty is calculated by multiplying the certainty of the premise by the certainty of the conclusion and then dividing by 100. This formula is called the *product method.* When applied to *Rule umbrella1*, the overall certainty of the rule is 50.[2]

An expert may sometimes feel uncertain about a rule of thumb regardless of how certain the evidence for the conclusion may be. For example, cloudy weather causes the weatherman to believe there is *some evidence* that it may rain. But he is never fully certain that it will rain based on this guideline alone, regardless of how certain he is that it is cloudy. This could be expressed as:

RULE rain_if_cloudy
IF   cloudy = yes
THEN rain = yes CF 70

The product method works to factor in such uncertainty when it is explicitly represented in the conclusion. For example:

Truth threshold: 20
Value of *color*: **orange CF 60**
Value of *shape*: **round CF 100**

---

[2]Shells representing uncertainty as decimal values up to 1.0 also use the product method. In such cases, you perform the arithmetic without division by 100. Therefore, a premise uncertainty of 0.5 in the premise and 1.0 in the conclusion yields a cf of 0.5 for the rule.

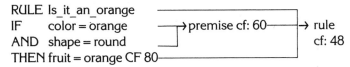

RULE Is_it_an_orange
IF   color = orange   →premise cf: 60   → rule
AND   shape = round   cf: 48
THEN fruit = orange CF 80

Because it is a conjunction, the cf of *Rule Is_it_an_orange*'s premise is 60 (the minimum of the two clauses). The certainty factor of the rule's conclusion is 80 (because the cf is stated as such in the conclusion). By applying the product formula to this rule, we get an overall certainty factor of 48 (60 * 80 / 100).

The "Probability Sum" Method. Earlier, we noted that most shells use one of two methods for handling certainty factors in disjunctions. We looked at one called the "maximum method." We now look at the other method which is called the "probability sum" method.

The probability sum method is different from other certainty approaches in that it does not separately compute a cf for the premise. Instead, it immediately applies each true premise clause against the rule's conclusion using the product method. Each resulting value is then applied against a new formula.

Truth threshold: 20
Value of *price*: **low CF 60**
Value of *appearance*: **good CF 80**

RULE should_I_buy_it
IF   price = low
OR   appearance = good
THEN buy_it = yes CF 90

Both premise clauses are true. Using the "maximum method," the inference engine would take the higher of the premise certainties, giving an overall premise cf of 80. This would be blended with the conclusion cf using the product method to give an overall rule certainty of 72 (80 * 90 / 100).

The probability sum method works as follows: It evaluates the first premise clause. After determining that it is true (*price = low*), the inference engine immediately applies that premise clause's certainty against the conclusion's certainty using the product method (60 * 90 / 100 = 54). It then temporarily stores this intermediate value of 54. Next, it evaluates the second premise clause. Since *appearance = good* is also true, it repeats the product method evaluation against the conclusion (80 * 90 / 100 = 72). The two intermediate values are then used in the probability sum formula: A + B − (A * B / 100). (See Figure 8.2.) This leads to the following calculation:

54 + 72 − (54 * 72 / 100) =
126 − (38.88)   =
                        = 87.12

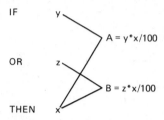

IF

OR

THEN

$A = y*x/100$

$B = z*x/100$

Figure 8.2. Method for Calculating cfs Using "Probability Sum" Formula:
$A + B - (A*B/100)$

The result then is either rounded to the nearest integer or truncated. The resulting cf of *Rule should_I_buy_it* is therefore 87. Note that the rule's overall certainty is significantly higher than it would be using the maximum method (72). The idea behind the probability sum method is that the whole is more certain than the individual parts. If there is more than one OR clause supporting the conclusion, the conclusion's overall certainty should be greater than any one clause's certainty factor. In fact, the probability sum is an *optimistic* cf algebra—it moves quickly towards maximum certainty.

Truth threshold: 30
Value of *car_type*: **sports_coupe CF 50**
Value of *delivery*: **later CF 60**
Value of *prestige*: **high CF 35**
Value of *price*: **low CF 65**

RULE   recom_car
IF   car_type = sports_coupe
OR   delivery = now
OR   prestige = high
OR   price = low
THEN recommendation = buy

Using probability sum, the first clause is true, therefore the first intermediate certainty factor is 50 (the implied certainty of the conclusion is 100):

$A = (50 * 100 / 100)$
$A = 50$

The second premise clause fails because its value does not match the premise clause. The third premise clause is true with a certainty value of 35:

$B = (35 * 100 / 100)$
$B = 35$

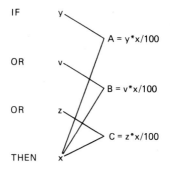

IF

OR

OR

THEN

A = y*x/100

B = v*x/100

C = z*x/100

A + B - (A * B/100) = D
D + C - (D * C/100) = cf

Figure 8.3. Method for Calculating "Probability Sum" with Multiple Attributes.

Finally the clause *price = low* is also true with a cf of 65:

C = (65 * 100 / 100)
C = 65

These are then applied against the probability sum formula. Since there are more than two factors, the first two are applied against the formula, and the result of that computation is applied against the next factor. This continues until all have been factored. (See Figure 8.3.)

50 + 35 – (50 * 35 / 100)   =
85 – 17.5   = 67.5

And then that result is factored against the third true clause.

67.5 + 65 – (67.5 * 65 / 100)   =
132.5 – 43.875   = **88.625**

Even though one of the four clauses is false, another barely passes above the truth threshold, and the other two have certainty factors less than 65, the resulting certainty factor is 88. Use of the "probability sum" method implies that the whole is more certain than any part and always produces certainties higher than the highest individual clause certainty.

Using the probability sum method, when any one premise clause has a certainty factor of 100 together with a fully certain conclusion, the rule's overall certainty will always be 100. For example:

Truth threshold: 50
Value of *color:* **orange CF 60**
Value of *juice:* **orange_juice CF 100**

RULE Is_it_an_orange
IF   color = orange
OR   juice = orange_juice
THEN fruit = orange

A = (60 * 100 / 100)   = 60
B = (100 * 100 / 100)   = 100
60 + 100 − (60 * 100 / 100) = 100

The result makes sense: 100 represents full certainty, so a certainty factor higher than 100 would have no meaning. Thus if any premise clause *and* the conclusion are fully certain, the rule will be fully certain regardless of the certainty of other premise clauses.[3]

Calculating Final Values

When a rule fires, it instantiates an attribute to some value. If the attribute had no prior value, it takes on the final certainty value concluded for the rule that instantiated it. For example, if *Rule recom_car* above is the first rule to conclude that *recommendation = buy*, then the resulting cf for *recommendation = buy* is *88*—the same as the certainty of the rule. Once an attribute has an initial value, other rules may reconfirm that conclusion. Thus the cfs of these several instantiations must be blended into a final value.

When the same attribute/value is concluded in more than one rule, the additional instantiations bring confirmative weight in favor of the conclusion. In other words, since more than one rule concludes the same value, additional evidence is being brought to bear. For example:

Truth threshold: 50
Value of *raindrops* = **yes CF 100**
Value of *looks_like_rain* = (no value yet established; current goal)
Value of *temperature* = **falling_fast CF 100**
Value of *cloudy* = **yes CF 100**

RULE 1
IF   raindrops = yes
THEN looks_like_rain = yes cf 95

RULE 2
IF   temperature = falling_fast
AND   cloudy = yes
THEN looks_like_rain = yes cf 60

---

[3]This assumes that only positive cf values are used.

The certainty of *looks_like_rain* = *yes* becomes 95 after *Rule 1* fires. When *Rule 2* also fires, it would be difficult to imagine why the certainty of *looks_like _rain* = *yes* should be less than 95. After all, here is *another* rule that confirms that *looks_like_rain* = *yes*. Most shells use the probability sum method to guarantee that the final certainty will reflect this added confidence.

Looks_like_rain is instantiated to 95 in the first rule. Because it has no previous value, it takes on the certainty of the rule that concludes it.

Premise certainty: *raindrops* = *yes*   → CF 100
Conclusion certainty: → CF 95
Overall rule certainty (using product method)   → CF 95
Certainty value assigned to *looks_like_rain* = *yes*   → CF 95

After *Rule 2* is evaluated and fired:

Premise certainty (using minimum method):   → CF 100
Conclusion certainty: → CF 60
Overall rule certainty (using product method)   → CF 60

Apply the probability sum operation to the previous value of *looks_like_rain* and *Rule 2*:

Previous cf = A, this rule's cf = B
A + B − (A * B / 100)   =
95 + 60 − (95 * 60 / 100)   =
155 − 57   = 98

Therefore the adjusted certainty of *looks_like_rain* = *yes* is 98.

Because this blending occurs with the probability sum formula, if either of the two factors is 100, the final certainty becomes 100. Certainty factors greater than 100 have no meaning since 100 already means "full certainty."

OTHER CERTAINTY FACTOR FEATURES

We have looked at some of the most common cf blending algorithms that many rule-based expert systems shells use. The Appendix shows how some popular shells handle cfs. If the shell you use is not among them, check your product documentation, or create some sample knowledge bases that calculate certainty and checks its result against the algorithms described in this chapter.

You may find that the way in which your shell's built-in algebras calculate uncertainty doesn't match the manner in which the human expert handles it. The method may be completely different. It may approximate the automatic algorithms, with important exceptions. The expert may explicitly reason about uncertainty, thus requiring some way of testing the uncertainty itself. Perhaps a much simpler approach to representing uncertainty is used.

To help you tailor how certainty is handled in your expert system, some shells provide additional features for testing and manipulating uncertainty. Many of these features are product-specific and cannot be generalized among shells. This is not an exhaustive analysis. We briefly discuss some classes of these features to give you a broad sense of what these capabilities are and why they are useful.

Testing Uncertainty

Regardless of how uncertainty is assigned, you may find that your human expert reasons and makes inferences based on how certain some knowledge is. This kind of knowledge is called *metaknowledge*, that is, knowledge about knowledge. Metaknowledge capabilities enable you to create rules that help the expert system "reason" about its own knowledge. As it applies to this discussion, we are interested in aspects of expert systems shells you can use to "reason" about the uncertainty contained within the knowledge base.

One of the most common uncertainty metaknowledge features enables rules to test for specific certainty values in a premise. For example:

RULE convict_only_if_sure
IF   alibi = none CF 100
AND   motive = established CF 100
AND   witnesses = yes
THEN verdict = guilty

In rules we looked at before, each premise clause was evaluated on two criteria:

1. Does the value tested in the premise match the actual binding of the attribute?
2. If so, does its certainty exceed the truth threshold?

However, when a certainty factor value appears in the premise, this second question is replaced by a new criterion:

2. If so, does the certainty factor named in the premise match the actual certainty factor of the a/v pair?

This is a much more rigorous test. *Rule convict_only_if_sure* only fires if *alibi = none* and *motive = established* are fully certain. While a rule without a certainty factor test in the premise would fire if *alibi = none* had *any* certainty factor over the truth threshold, any cf value other than 100 causes this rule to fail. In this way you actually test two facts in one expression: the correct a/v binding, and a specific uncertainty value or range.

This method can also be used to test for less than completely certain cf values an a/v pair might have. Some shells also provide Englishlike expressions for testing ranges of confidence. For example, consider this Texas Instrument's Personal Consultant Plus™ rule.

RULE 001
IF   APPLICANT IS MIGHTBE QUALIFIED
THEN recom = ask_for_2nd_interview

This rule tests whether *applicant = qualified* as well as whether its certainty falls within a range called *MIGHTBE*. (This range happens to be a certainty factor value greater than − 20 and less than 100. It is intended to help check for just enough certainty in an expression that it "might be" true.)

Finally, some shells allow you to test the confidence of an attribute *independent of its value*. For example, consider this rule in the syntax of Information Builder's LEVEL5™ expert systems shell:

RULE   recom_hire_if_quite_sure
IF   CONF (honesty) > 90
AND   CONF (past_success) > 90
THEN recom IS hire

The two premise clauses of this rule test *only* the certainty of the attributes *honesty* and *past_success*. The translation of this rule would read something like this: "If there is substantial evidence that (he/she) is honest and has been successful, then the recommendation is to hire the candidate." Note that such a rule implies that attributes *honesty* and *past_success* have quite well-defined values. For example, if *honest = no* were possible in this knowledge base, then it might be considered faulty since the rule could fire if *honest = no* had a certainty factor higher than 90.

Multivalued Attributes and Uncertainty

Sometimes, your interest in a particular multivalued attribute may depend on its relative certainty. For example, you may want to process only the most likely among a set of uncertain values, or a value with some particular uncertainty rating. Several shells provide functions that give you more control over this aspect of knowledge base processing. Consider the following rule:

Value of *color* = blue CF 60
            = yellow CF 55
            = red CF 90

```
RULE  recom_red_likely
IF        color = red
THEN recom = color_red_most_likely
```

Attribute *color* has multiple values. You want the rule to succeed only if *color* is the most likely value among those *red* contains. The question is how to ensure that only the *most likely* value is considered. Some shells enable you to sort the values from highest to lowest cf. Others provide functions that return the highest certainty factor. These can help you write rules that test *only* the most likely value of the attribute. Consider this Guru construction:

```
RULE  test_only_best_chance
IF        HIVAL(color) = red
THEN recom = color_is_red
```

This rule fires only if *color = red* AND *red* is the value of *color* with the highest certainty. This type of rule is useful when you want to test a condition **only** when it is the most likely. In effect, it allows you to design rules that reflect lines of reasoning dependent on the most probable value of an a/v pair.

Another capability found in some shells is the ability to reorder a group of uncertain attribute values from most to least likely. When rules test the various values an uncertain attribute has, the most likely values are tested first. This can reduce the number of unsuccessful premise considerations as the inference engine tries the highest likelihood values first. Consider this example:

```
Value of color = blue CF 70
                = yellow CF 55
                = red CF 90

RULE  recom_red
IF        color = red
THEN recom = color_is_red
```

The values of attribute *color* have accumulated in the order of the rule firings that concluded them. Thus *red,* the most likely, was concluded first, then the least likely *yellow,* and then the somewhat likely *blue.* When trying *Rule recom_red,* the most recently concluded value *blue* is tried first. Next *yellow* is tried, and finally *red.* The inference engine manages these premise considerations automatically because *color* is multivalued. However, the inference engine must nevertheless consider and fail the first two values as the engine tries the values *blue* and *yellow* against the rule. Finally, when *red* is tried, the rule fires.

However, if the values of *color* are reordered from highest to lowest certainty, the order of *color's* values becomes

Value of *color* = red CF 90
            = blue CF 70
            = yellow CF 55

After this operation takes place, *red* now gets tested first, and the rule fires immediately. The others will *still* be tried. But in cases where the attribute may have many values, this may help you improve performance.

Absolute Assignment of Uncertainty

You may occasionally want to assign uncertainty to attributes without subjecting them to the automatic blending algorithms we've looked at. We call this capability "absolute assignment."

Absolute assignment enables you to override built-in certainty factor systems. For those cases in which the normal blending algorithms would otherwise produce inappropriate certainty factors, absolute assignment enables the developer to correct the situation by forcing a "hard-coded" cf into the rule's conclusion.

Some of the shells supporting absolute assignment enable developers to assign uncertainty with constants and attributes. Thus some rules might reason and assign a numeric attribute value representing some confidence level. Then this attribute's value could itself be used as a certainty factor somewhere else.

KINDS OF UNCERTAINTY

So far in this chapter, we've examined the various concepts and some of the certainty factor features offered in rule-based expert systems shells. But the important question remains: *when* and *how* should you use these uncertainty resources in your knowledge base? Unfortunately, there are no easy answers. To understand why this question is perhaps more difficult than it may at first appear, we need to look at some of the various concepts that "uncertainty" can represent.

Probability

One common way we think of uncertainty is in terms of *probability*. Probability is usually expressed as the chance of some particular state occurring as a percentage of the population of all possible states. For example, when you flip a coin there is a 50 percent chance that "heads" will occur face-up. We know this because there are two possible outcomes in a coin flip, and there is an equal chance for either result to happen. Probability is useful when we have a model of how a system works. For example, we know the coin is weighted proportionally, has equal area on both sides, and thus either side has an equal chance of appearing. This concept is sometimes referred to as mathematical probability. The probability flows from the mathematical or physical essence of the phenomenon. As a result, the probability can be deduced from a model of the object.

Statistical Uncertainty

Statistical methods of determining uncertainty are similar to those determining mathematical probability, except that they rely on empirical evidence. If you have a data base of examples, you may be able to statistically determine the certainty of various results by examining past behavior. One such method is called the "Bayesian" approach to uncertainty. Statistical uncertainty systems do not predict based on a model of the system under consideration. Instead, they look at actual frequencies in the real world. This is both their strength and weakness. Their strength is that they are grounded in real-world observation. Their weakness is that in order to use statistical uncertainty you must have an accurate, up-to-date data base of observations. Because expert behavior is often not well documented, this is exactly what may be missing. For problems in which a human expert is the sole problem-solving source, statistical data may simply not exist.

Limitations of Probability and Statistical Systems

These two prior certainty systems have an important advantage. Because they are built on models and real-world behavior, they portray a verifiable view of the probability in question. However, two important problems limit their usefulness and make them difficult to employ in many rule-based expert systems.

Mathematical and statistical models assume neat, quantifiable relationships. This is rarely the case in expert systems. Expert systems domains are by their very nature difficult to nail down. This quality is one of the reasons we use expert systems: they enable us to represent rules of thumb and other reasoning processes that work "much of the time." If the problem was well defined and well understood, it could probably be automated using conventional programming algorithms. It is almost by definition that such problems are difficult to apply against mathematical and statistical analyses.

"Heuristic" Certainty Factors

We have seen expert systems shells allow you to capture heuristics—rules of thumb that help solve a problem by inference. They are useful for solving problems when algorithms alone are not enough. So far in this chapter, we've seen that the method shells use to calculate uncertainty *is* algorithmic. At once, we have a tool that acknowledges that human expert problem-solving is nonalgorithmic, and yet the system for representing that knowledge's uncertainty is algorithmic! Isn't it possible that the way in which humans use uncertainty is more like the rules of thumb which represent the expert's reasoning? This is a question that must be asked for each domain you investigate. The answer has a deep impact on how you represent uncertainty in your expert system.

There is little doubt that human experts use uncertainty in inexact ways at least some of the time. The expert may relate the likelihood of one occurrence in relation to another based on a gut feeling: "It's more likely that the battery is dead than that the coil is damaged." The expert may classify possibilities in likelihood categories: "It is *very likely* that the battery is dead (because the temperature was −20°F last night)"; or "Chances are *low* that the coil is damaged." The expert may see certainty accumulate in an exponential manner: "If the suspect has some nervous mannerisms, there is a low chance that he is smuggling. If the suspect holds himself in an erect manner, there is a low chance that he is smuggling. However, if he has nervous mannerisms *and* holds himself erect, there is a high chance that he is smuggling." The expert may believe that either behavior is normal if observed independently. When combined, those behaviors indicate a strong confirmative evidence—but only when they appear together.[4]

In many cases experts use uncertainty in a heuristic or rule-of-thumb manner. Translating the expert's handling of uncertainty into rigorous arithmetic models may defeat the very reason an expert systems tool was selected—the knowledge or method is not algorithmic. This is an important point. Uncertainty can mean many things. It can be grounded in a mathematical model or based in a statistical examination of empirical evidence. It can also have nothing to do with algorithms, based instead on a human expert's intuitive approaches which may or may not coincide with the facilities provided in the expert systems shell.

Moreover, as we've already seen, uncertainty usage can cause subtle changes in inference engine behavior. These changes need to be factored into

---

[4]Note here that this last example is a conjunction that would use the "minimum" method for figuring certainty. The expert concludes just the opposite.

the certainty factor decision in order to judge whether this impact is appropriate to the domain.

DESIGNING CERTAINTY FACTOR SYSTEMS

We've briefly outlined how the term "uncertainty" actually stands for a diverse group of concepts including rigorous mathematical models, examinations of empirical evidence, and heuristic approaches. Certainty factor algebras may be unable to capture this latter category. For beginning developers, we now provide some guidelines for evaluating the role of uncertainty in their applications. While there are no hard and fast rules for deciding how to proceed, the following section provides some questions developers should ask before proceeding.

When in Doubt, Don't Use Certainty Factors

If you are unclear about how the human expert uses uncertainty, do not use certainty factors. Without a clear and specific understanding, any implementation you choose will be at best a guess and, therefore, the results generated by the certainty system may be misleading.

It is our experience that certainty factors' importance is often overrated. New developers may feel compelled to use a certainty factor system simply because the facility is present. Unless you have identified some specific benefit, and understood how the human expert uses uncertainty, the best decision is to omit certainty factors.

When interviewing the expert, avoid asking specifically about uncertainty. Concentrate instead on understanding how the expert reasons about the domain in general. If the expert identifies uncertainty as a meaningful part of that decision making, this is a signal that you should probably go further in thinking through the uncertainty question. If uncertainty is not raised as an issue, don't feel compelled to raise it yourself. There is no rule that says you must use cfs solely because there is a software facility for representing them.

Understand How the Expert Uses Uncertainty

Once you determine that uncertainty does play some role in the expertise, nail down as precisely as possible what that role is. This is not always easy to do. Experts tend not to isolate uncertainty as a separate category of thought. They may use words or phrases like "likely," "if it looks like . . . ," "doubtful." These words are signs that you should further explore exactly how much these concepts can be quantified. Quantification can mean many things. Here are some important questions you should try to answer.

Is There a Data Base of Examples? Is the expert's use of uncertainty based on empirical evidence? If so, this makes your task easier. Examine this evidence to understand how various factors combine and blend to achieve a certainty recommendation. Is uncertainty statistical? If there is a data base of examples, consider using a shell that supports the representation of statistical uncertainty. This often means that the shell offers a Bayesian model of uncertainty.

Is There a Model of the Uncertainty? Is there an underlying model that can generate correct uncertainty results? Does the expert use some arithmetical formula for computing certainty? If so, does it match the cf algebras provided in your shell? If it does not match, consider choosing a shell in which you can add your own certainty factor algorithms or integrate to an external program in which you can maintain your own certainty factors. If the shell's facility and the expert's method are similar but not exactly the same, can you use testing and other supplementary functions? Does the ability to test confidence levels in rules let you represent the expert's reasoning? If none of these options appears suitable, don't use that shell's cf facility.

Does the Expert Think About Uncertainty in Numeric Terms? Once uncertainty is established as a decision-making factor, have the expert describe prior cases in which uncertainty played a role. Does the expert use an arithmetic process to calculate likelihood? Or does she or he use imprecise language to describe certain decision points? Again, if the expert uses words and phrases like "probably," "likely," "doubtful," and "possible," you are being tipped off that the expert may be using heuristic methods of handling uncertainty. Numeric certainty factor systems may be of little use.

Is Uncertainty Used as a Weighting Mechanism? Sometimes the expert uses uncertainty to prioritize various options or conclusions. The expert may reason using many bits of knowledge, none of which is individually strong enough to prove a hypothesis or imply a decision. Thus the expert considers many factors. When many of these "evidence chunks" accumulate in support of one conclusion, the expert lets the overall weight of the evidence prevail. This "accumulated evidence" technique or *scoring system* is relatively easy to implement.

Scoring systems use certainty factors to weigh solution candidates versus competitive peers. At the end of the consultation, the solution with the highest value "wins." Scoring systems can be useful even when conclusions are not uncertain. They can be used to measure how often evidence for a conclusion

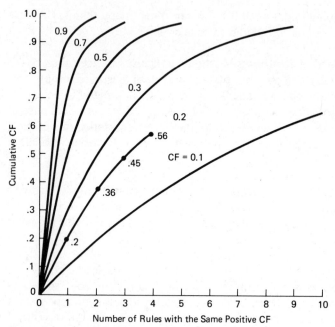

Figure 8.4. "Scores" Resulting from Blending Rules with Same cf Using "Probability Sum."

was found, how attractive a certain approach might be, or how many times a rule (a piece of evidence) has fired in favor of a particular conclusion. Figure 8.4 illustrates this kind of situation.

The x-axis represents the number of rules concluding a particular attributes/ value pair with an identical certainty factor. The y-axis represents the cf value used for the conclusion (for shells representing uncertainty on an integer scale, multiply the y-axis value times 100). The graph shows that, for example, five rules concluding an a/v pair with a cf of 0.3 (or 30) gives a final certainty of 0.83 (or 83). Consider this example:

Truth Threshold: 10

GOAL: animal_class

RULE mammal_hair
IF   body_cover = hair
THEN class = mammal CF 20

RULE mammal_warmblood
IF   cold_warmblood = warm
THEN class = mammal CF 20

RULE mammal_livebirth
IF   birth = live
THEN class = mammal CF 20

RULE bird_warmblood
IF   cold_warmblood = warm
THEN class = bird CF 20

RULE bird_eggbirth
IF   birth = egg
THEN class = bird CF 20

RULE fish_coldblood
IF   cold_warmblood = cold
THEN class = fish CF 20

This example uses uncertainty to cause the inference engine to treat attributes as multivalued. Each time a rule fires in favor of a given class, certainty factor blending causes the overall certainty of that conclusion to increase. Using probability sum, if all three *mammal* rules fired, the overall certainty of *class = mammal* is 48. If the two *bird* rules fire, *class = bird*'s cf is 36. Of course, if the one *class = fish* rule fires, its certainty factor is the same as the rule: 20. As more rules concluding a value are added, the potential certainty of that conclusion increases. By writing rules that incrementally add certainty to a multivalued goal, the developer lets the inference engine hold a competition whose winner is the conclusion with the most fired rules.

Scoring systems are most useful when conclusions contribute about the same amount of evidence to a recommendation. If some are slightly more important than others, you can experiment by giving a bit more value to those rules' conclusions. Also, determining which cf value to use in the conclusion can be a bit tricky. If you use too high a certainty factor, the conclusions bunch up quickly, close to full certainty. If the value you choose is too low, they move up too slowly. You can use Figure 8.4 to determine what cf to try. Estimate the maximum number of rules that can fire in favor of a conclusion. Find that number on the x-axis. Then choose a value that gives a cf of about 0.90 to 0.95, assuming all fire. Run some consultations and fine-tune results from there.

Does the Expert Reason Negatively? Does the expert consistently reason using negative evidence? For example, does he or she start with a handful of likely conclusions and concentrate on *disproving* them? Under what conditions does evidence against a conclusion become so great that a line of reasoning is abandoned? Such an approach may lend itself to using shells that let you represent negative cfs.

Testing Uncertainty. Experts rarely think of uncertainty apart from the domain itself. Instead, they are likely to associate it with a particular decision or issue. For example, the expert may say,

> First, you check the battery cable. It *must be* attached correctly or else you tighten it and try again. If the cable *is* tight and *it appears that* the cable is not damaged, then you go on and look at the coil. . . . (Later, after determining that the coil is not the problem), . . . and if that's not the problem, then you do a *detailed check* of the cable to *make sure* it isn't damaged.

The quotation illustrates that the expert accepts some uncertainty in the early stages of problem-solving. Later, he or she returns to remove that uncertainty if the problem is still not solved. You recognize the presence of uncertainty by the use of key words like *"must be," "appears that," "probably," "perhaps,"* and *"sometimes."* The above knowledge might be represented by the following knowledge base fragment:

GOAL: *recom*

NAME: cable_ok
TYPE: symbol
EXPECT: (yes, no)
PROMPT: "Does a casual scan of the cable show it to be all right?"
MULTI: no

RULE cable_tight
IF   cable_tight = no
OR   CONF (cable_tight = yes) < 100
THEN recom = tighten_cable_and_try_again

RULE cable_quick_check_replace
IF   CONF (cable_tight = yes) = 100
AND   cable_damaged = yes
THEN recom = replace_cable

RULE cable_complete_check
IF   CONF (cable_tight = yes) = 100
AND   cable_damaged = no
AND   coil = ok
AND   CONF (cable_damaged) < 100
THEN recom = do_complete_check_of_cable

RULE prelim_no_cable_damage
IF   cable_ok = yes
THEN cable_damaged = no CF 80

RULE prelim_cable_damage
IF   cable_ok = no
THEN cable_damaged = yes

Rule cable_tight verifies that the cable is tight with complete confidence (the second premise clause tests that the CONFidence of *cable_tight = yes* is less than 100). If this rule fails, the first premise clause of *Rule cable_quick_check_ replace* causes backward chaining to *Rule prelim_no_cable_damage*. Backward chaining on *cable_ok* in turn generates a prompt asking for a quick estimate of whether the cable seems ok. The response *yes* fires *Rule prelim_no_cable_ damage* with a certainty of 80. A response of *no* causes the expert system to recommend that the cable be replaced. If the first two rules fail, rule *cable_ complete_check* then causes chaining to check that *coil = ok*. If the first three clauses pass, the rule tests whether the certainty factor in *cable_damaged* is less than 100 (fully certain). Since *cable_damaged = no* with less than full certainty, the rule fires and recommends that the user "do complete check of cable."

The example shows how the expert uses uncertainty in making decisions. In order to simulate this in an expert system, you must be able to test certainty. Note here that you may need only two values to represent the uncertainty in the problem: "certain" and "uncertain." If this is the case, the uncertainty might possibly be represented using an attribute with two pre-enumerated values. If the expert uses uncertainty as a decision-making criterion, it is important that the shell offer some uncertainty metaknowledge facilities that give you access to the certainty of the symbols with which you reason.

Is Uncertainty Based on Heuristics? If so, your best path may be to explicitly represent uncertainty as an attribute. Instead of forcing the expert's representation of uncertainty into algorithmic form, express it symbolically in a manner that corresponds to the expert's descriptions and reasoning process. For example, look at this form of the previous example:

GOAL: recom

NAME: cable_ok
TYPE: symbol
EXPECT: (yes, no)
PROMPT: "Does a quick scan of the cable show it to be all right?"
MULTI: no

RULE cable_tight
IF   cable_tight = no
OR   cable_tight = yes_not_sure
THEN recom = tighten_cable_and_try_again

RULE cable_quick_check_replace
IF   cable_tight = yes_sure
AND   cable_damaged_prelim = yes
THEN recom = replace_cable

RULE cable_complete_check
IF   cable_tight = yes_sure
AND   cable_damaged_prelim = no
AND   coil = ok
AND   cable_damaged_final = yes
THEN recom = do_complete_check_of_cable

RULE prelim_no_cable_damage
IF   cable_ok = yes
THEN cable_damaged_prelim = no

RULE prelim_cable_damage
IF   cable_ok = no
THEN cable_damaged_prelim = yes

Here knowledge items like *cable_damage* and *cable_tight* are split into finer parts to reflect the various uncertainties that make up the knowledge in this domain. Attribute *cable_tight* now has three values: *no, yes_not_sure*, and *yes_ sure*. The second represents a fact reflecting some belief that the cable is tight; the last reflects complete certainty in the same belief. Rules in the knowledge base can now reason about the two states as separate ideas with important meaning in the context of this domain. Attribute *cable_damaged* has been split into two: *cable_damaged_prelim* and *cable_damaged_final*. This enables reasoning to represent the first preliminary inspection of the cable and subsequently support later reasoning based on the *final* or thorough inspection after other reasoning lines fail.

When the manner in which the expert uses uncertainty is inherently symbolic, this approach to representing uncertainty is often best. It also offers the benefits of specifically expressing uncertainty within the knowledge base as an integral component of the expert's knowledge.

Are the Particular Areas of Uncertainty Limited to Narrow, Well-understood Reasoning Paths? If the uncertainty is limited to the interaction of a few specific attributes, you may be able to fashion a system that uses certainty factors based on your precise understanding of the interaction of those knowledge items and the particular algorithms your shell offers. The key here is that uncertainty is contained within a box that you and the expert understand. Therefore, you can predict, test, and confirm certainty factor outcomes.

Does the Domain Coincide Exactly with the Shell's Certainty Factor Algebras? Among all the possible ways certainty can be represented, the specific combination of certainty factor algorithms your shell offers produces certainty results exactly the way the domain expert does. For some applications, this may be as likely as winning the lottery. For others, there may be important correspondences between the underlying rationales chosen for a certainty factor system and the domain itself. Where these exist, take advantage of them.

Is a Scoring System Used? Does the expert let potential solutions "compete" for evidence? This is the approach used by the landmark expert system MYCIN. The diagnostic method used by physicians—after whom MYCIN was modeled—tended to give weight to those possible diseases in which many rules brought confirmative evidence, as opposed to those which only a few rules supported. A certainty factor scoring system propagated certainty for those hypotheses that many rules confirmed. The consultation ends with a relative ranking of those hypotheses that exceed the truth threshold ranked from highest to lowest cf.

SUMMARY

We've seen how certainty factor algebras are automatically applied to premises, rules, and instantiated attributes. Some certainty algorithms are pessimistic, that is, they tend to lower the overall certainty of a conclusion. Others are optimistic: they raise certainty. The algorithm is chosen by the inference engine depending on a number of factors. In premises, certainty is determined by whether clauses are connected by AND or OR. Premise and conclusion cfs are then combined. For determining new cfs for attributes already containing certainty, old and new values are combined in an optimistic fashion using the probability sum formula. The algebras are not arbitrarily chosen, but neither is there any guarantee that they are relevant to a particular domain.

It is easy to exaggerate the importance of certainty factors. Don't feel compelled to use them or bring them up in your discussions with the expert. When you hear the expert using key "uncertainty" words, then you should begin looking at the issue in more depth. If uncertainty plays a significant role, grasp exactly how the expert uses it in order to determine whether it has a mathematical, statistical or heuristic basis. If uncertainty is heuristic, you may be able to simulate the expert's use of it using testing functions, localized use of certainty factors, scoring systems, and symbolic representation of uncertainty.

Whatever decisions you make, remember that "uncertainty" is a broad umbrella term. How you represent uncertainty in a particular domain may be unique to that domain. The implementation may well be unique to your shell. Therefore, document clearly the assumptions and dynamics of how the expert uses uncertainty to make the knowledge base as clear, maintainable, and portable as possible.

9 | *Integration*

A computer information center struggles to staff its "help desk" with competent people.[1] The help desk provides debugging and information services to users of the company's diverse computer resources. A dozen people rotate throughout the week, one "helper" on duty per shift. The expertise level of the helpers varies, turnover is high, and training is a constant challenge.

To address these problems, the department decides to implement a help desk expert system. The top performer is chosen as expert. An information center specialist with no previous experience in expert systems is chosen as knowledge engineer. A leading expert systems development shell is chosen, and the new knowledge engineer attends a one-week training course offered by the vendor.

The domain is properly analyzed and limited to communications problems, the most difficult and highest payback area identified. The helpers test the system, and provide corrections and ideas for new rules. The 70-rule application is finished and fielded.

Several months later, the project is evaluated. It is declared a theoretical success and a practical failure. As a reservoir of knowledge, the project has been successful, capable of aiding helpers diagnose problems in many instances. The system has also been successfully deployed as a learning tool.

As a *practical* aid, however, the project is a failure at this stage. The system's inferencing process imposes a questioning order that sometimes doesn't match the natural flow of a human consultation. Helpers become impatient with the seemingly random question pattern generated by backward chaining. Sometimes they have useful data at hand that are not requested until late in the consultation. This information could quickly narrow the range of likely solutions if asked early. This makes some consultations frustrating.

---

[1]Portions of this chapter are based on an article taken with permission from Ken Pedersen, "Connecting Expert Systems and Conventional Environments," *AI Expert* 3, no. 5 (May 1988): 26.

Details about the caller's computing environment are often needed to reach a conclusion. This somewhat static information could be accessed through a data file interface using an indexed key. In the current expert system, however, helpers must manually enter these data as requested by the expert system, adding to the amount of extra keyboard work necessary.

While the system's expertise is adequate, helpers must document each call to a paper log. The log is retained for administrative reasons, and the procedure forces helpers to manually copy many consultation attributes into the log—a frustrating and time-consuming duplication.

The expert system is itself unable to produce the log for several reasons. The shell does not support a print function; therefore it cannot print the necessary reports. The expert system, because it is driven by a backward chaining inference engine, gathers the minimum amount of information required to solve the problem. However, the paper system requires entry of certain "nonessential" data, like name and student ID number.

This example describes a situation that can best be described as follows: "The project has met its knowledge-based expectations, but we underestimated our need for integrated facilities."

WHY IS INTEGRATION IMPORTANT?

The information center example shows several common needs that drive the incorporation of integration techniques into expert systems. The inevitable result of these problems is that in many cases the "finished" expert system is not regularly used by those for whom the software was originally intended. Some of the major tasks to which integration techniques can be applied include the following:

The Need to Refine the Query Process. Backward chaining can produce questioning orders that don't match the sequence expected by human users. Many shells don't supplement the shell with facilities for letting developers refine the questioning order. Integration techniques can overcome this problem.

Enhancing the Shell's Primitive or Stylized Interfaces. Some shells provide only the most primitive of user interfaces. Others hardwire their display screens, interfaces, and screen layouts in ways not acceptable to the developer or user. Accessing outside programs or languages may be the only way to improve the situation.

Accessing Common, Repetitive Data. Entering one data item often implies a set of associated information that could be imported from a data file using an index. For example, the discovery that a call comes from "mainframe site 5," might imply a set of data about the site's data communications hardware configurations. These data can be stored in an outside data file and automatically extracted by the expert system when "mainframe site 5" is selected. In the information center example, help desk workers must manually enter these data items as requested by the inference process.

Archiving Consultation Results. It may be useful to archive consultation results for later analysis. Some shells lack a print or data file *write* function; again, integration may be necessary.

Fitting into an Existing Administrative System. If the expert system supplements or replaces some existing administrative system, it may be critical for acceptance of the project that the expert system use and propagate the original system's information flow. Data base and worksheet access, telecommunications, and external programs may all play a part in meeting this need.

Installing a Security System. Shells offer varying degrees of knowledge protection. Where the shell's knowledge is accessible, integration techniques can deny or limit access. Where explanation facilities are inadequate, integration can enhance or add to these facilities.

Creating an Application Head and Tail. Many applications require an initialization and completion sequence not dependent on inferencing. For example, some attributes may need specific starting values. Perhaps data files or other outside information may be required. It may be desirable to show an introductory screen or graph.

After completing a consultation, the application may call for a report, or need to update a file or worksheet. Since these tasks require procedural control, and because many tools do not offer good procedural tools, integration to an outside program or language may be the only option for accomplishing the job.

INTEGRATION NEEDS UNDERESTIMATED

These are some of the reasons that integration techniques are desirable in expert systems projects. Some of these points address major requirements of any software project and represent vital concerns for ensuring the project's success—and the user's perception of its success.

However, it is common that beginning developers do not think through their integration needs because of their concern with other higher profile concerns like knowledge acquisition and representation. They possibly become overly focused on using unique expert systems facilities such as uncertainty and explanation systems. Often they simply put off dealing with integration until after getting a better handle on the expert-system-specific portions of their project. While this decision seems logical on the surface, it can be a critical mistake in terms of making the right design decisions.

Perhaps the worst result of premature or uninformed choices made in this manner is that the impact of the decision may not always become readily apparent until it is too late. The situation can be compared to children who build their playhouse with a five-foot roof. The playhouse provides adequate headroom today, but in several months or years when the kids bump their heads on the ceiling, they will wish they had taken future needs into account and given themselves more room to grow. Based on their perspective at the time, five feet seemed like a cathedral. As they mature, they realize it was never even close to leaving room for growth. Their recourse is to tear down the playhouse and build something new, having only the experience to show for their effort.

This is a perspective gained with experience, and eluded only by proper and complete needs analysis. Without probing and understanding how the system fits into the organization's administrative flow and interacts with "how people do it now," no amount of programming excellence will compel people to use the expert system in their daily routine.

PROGRAMMING LANGUAGE HOOKS

Integration can be defined as any software facility that provides links to computing resources outside the expert system itself. These links vary widely. We examine here some of the most important links and some of the uses you can put them to.

In the past, one of the earliest and most common methods of meeting the demand for accessing outside resources was built-in programming language interfaces. Using a language interface, you empower the expert system to call executable code written in a conventional programming language. The hook allows you to supplement the capabilities of the expert system. The most common language that expert systems shells hook to is the C language.

For example, consider an expert system that monitors an analogue readout from a manufacturing device. In order to process input from the device, the expert system requires a short program to accept the device's input, convert its analogue signal to digital form, and feed those data to the expert system at a moderate speed. Some expert systems shells may not have a facility for accepting input from a source other than keyboard. But if they do offer a programming language interface, this code can be written in the program- ming language and linked into the expert system. One of the advantages of this code is that it may execute considerably faster than it could if the function were driven by inferencing from within the knowledge base.

This is by no means the only circumstance under which a conventional programming link might be beneficial. Here are some other general circumstances in which programming language links may prove useful.

Procedural Need

If the shell does not offer facilities that make it easy for the developer to execute step-by-step sequenced tasks, a programming interface may provide this facility. Report writing, for example, is a task which requires many small tasks to be executed in a precise order. After the expert system comes to a conclusion, it could call a program through its language interface in order to write the report.

Supplemental Facilities

The shell may lack certain capabilities you desire in the expert systems application you choose. You may be able to program these in a conventional language and call that program when it is needed. In this manner, a programming language interface helps you add new capabilities to the shell as you need them.

Access Outside Data Sources

If vital data sources exist in a form that the shell cannot access with built-in features, you may be able to get those data using code written in a programming language. We consider why you would do this, below. Note that not all shells may offer built-in data file access in a form you can use. For example, at the time of this writing, many shells do not offer links to many minicomputer and mainframe data bases. Also, few provide the ability to download through a telecommunications link. A programming language may be the answer to add this capability.

Drawbacks

While language interfaces provide much flexibility and potential power, they can also have drawbacks. They add another level of technical complexity. You must master the technical aspects of handshaking between the shell and the programming language. These often require programmers with specific experience in the language. If you are an "expert" working with a shell for the first time, the burden of learning the shell plus another programming language may be more than is practical.

Language interfaces require knowledge of the target language. For example, Pascal programmers are out of luck for tools using C language interfaces. Thus developers, too, face learning foreign languages in addition to becoming competent with the shell.

The compiler issue adds to the complexity. "Compilers" are computer programs that turn your programming language statements into a form the computer can use. Most shells support one or two compilers. If you are already using a compiler that is not supported by the shell, you may have to switch to a new one to take advantage of the language interface. This process can be painful and implies a big learning curve.

There are also financial costs. If you don't own the compiler, you will have to buy it. This increases the cost and development time involved in the project. While the price of purchasing such software may be modest, you must include learning and training time, as well as maintenance, in the overall project equation in order to accurately gauge the real cost of such involvement.

Some language interfaces are so designed that language functions get access only to those *arguments* that are explicitly passed to them through subroutine or function calls. This may be acceptable if the task the language component is to perform can be isolated from other parts of the knowledge base. However, it may not be acceptable if you require that the new code have access to the knowledge concluded to that point in the consultation. You may have to limit the use of the language interface to coding short procedures, interfacing with external devices or files. The interface becomes a subroutine handler; useful, but not capable of accessing the overall knowledge base.

Finally, it may become more difficult to test the knowledge base. Knowledge base values may be concluded from outside the inference engine. Errors in the conventional programming may cause unpredictable problems during knowledge base processing. Depending on the specifics of what you do with the programming language hooks, you may end up with a knowledge base that contains problems that the debugging facilities designed to test the knowledge base cannot handle.

We cover some of the problems that proceduralizing the knowledge base may cause for testing in Chapter 14. Suffice it to say now that when considering custom programming links, you should investigate what facilities the shell offers to test knowledge bases which use external interfaces.

EXECUTING EXISTING PROGRAMS

In some cases, you may have existing software that performs exactly the task you want to integrate into the expert system. In this case, you don't need to write a custom program. Many shells allow you to execute existing software directly from the expert system.

The benefits and drawbacks of this approach are generally similar to those you encounter if you use a custom program interface. However, this integration method is often technically much easier to implement than the custom software method. In those shells that support the execution of outside programs, invoking the outside program is usually easy. There are, however, technical questions you must answer.

Memory and Performance Requirements

If you are running in a PC-based environment, you may run into memory requirements that limit the size of the program and/or knowledge base you may create. When you call the outside program, usually some portion of the expert systems shell remains memory resident. This memory overhead, when combined with the program you call, can cause the called program to fail, or give unacceptable performance. Also, if the program you want to invoke runs under a graphic interface environment like Microsoft Windows or Presentation Manager™, be sure to verify that the shell will operate properly in this environment. Make sure you research what the performance and memory constraints are for the shell you use.

Parameter Passing

You may need to communicate with external programs or processes the expert system invokes. Evaluate how this can be accomplished. There are two basic flavors for such communication. The fastest—and most technical and machine specific—is the ability to pass parameters through memory. Implementing memory parameter passing sometimes requires technical competence and requires the partner software to leave pointers or other values in specific memory locations. This latter point means that many "off-the-shelf" programs don't support memory parameter passing, but custom software written specifically for the concerned tool could.

If you are using the OS/2™ operating system or other multitasking environments, check to see if the shell supports interprocess communications. This could provide a powerful, painless, and efficient method for communication between the expert system and the task with which you want to communicate.

Given the technical demands of communication through memory, you may need an alternative method for trading information. Most shells offer the ability to pass information through disk files. This function is designed for communication among knowledge bases or with outside programs. Such communication files often reside in ASCII form, a standardized form of representing information that many products can produce. Disk data passing can be slow. For applications in which performance is critical, explore setting up a cache for the purpose of trading data.

DATA FILE INTEGRATION

Data file integration refers to the reading and writing of information from outside sources. When properly implemented, it can substantially increase the perception of intelligence, user satisfaction, and flexibility of expert systems. It can also foster poor design techniques and the use of expert systems shells for applications which contain little or no expertise.

When Should You Use Outside Data Sources?

When should you consider using outside data files as part of the expert system? Here are some questions to help you evaluate those needs.

Do Important Consultation Values Already Reside in Electronic Form? Many good domains deal with information that may already exist on a computer. Whether it exists in data base, spreadsheet, hypertext, or other form, you can usually improve the speed, user satisfaction, and accuracy of the system by accessing that information from its electronic source instead of asking the users who consult the system.

Does One Data Item Imply a Set of Related Data? Most data bases are organized around a data structure called a "record." Records are groups of logically related data items grouped together for convenient handling. For example, an employee personnel record might include name, address, phone number, social security number, date of hire, and salary earned. Each item is relevant because it relates to information about an employee.

Some expert systems may similarly require groups of related data to undertake a consultation. For example, in the information center example, when the helper discovers that the user is calling from "mainframe site 5," she needs a set of related information detailing the various data communications configurations that the site has. This information remains relatively unchanged.

Applications that require groups of related information based on a key can benefit from the use of data file integration. The technique saves users from having to manually enter the associated data or code the entire data base into the knowledge base, which saves development time, improves accuracy, and ensures better user satisfaction. As the data base evolves, only the data file requires change. This can lower the maintenance burden on the knowledge base itself.

Is Questioning OK? Some domains may need facts that cannot or should not be asked of users. For example, an expert system examining financial results may need some intermediate accounting data that the chief financial officer (CFO) previously provided, since this person played the role of the expert. These intermediate values may not have been stored on a computer system. The solution could be to have the accounting system post these values to a data file. The latter scenario may be desirable for reasons ranging from performance (the shell may not perform math calculations sufficiently fast) to security (the shell's explanation system would reveal the CFO's analysis to users).

Other expert systems may require sensitive data (e.g., personnel records) to complete consultations. Management may deem that, because of its sensitive nature, such information should not be available to users. By enabling the expert system to access the data through a data file interface, the consultation can take place without requiring the sensitive information from the user.

What Are the Technical Issues? Sometimes there are technical issues that constrain or prevent the ability of your expert system to access data files. Are the files secured from outside access? Is there password protection? If the environment is a multiuser or network configuration, can the expert system honor record-locking or other protection protocols? You may need to consult the data base administrator or other technical personnel.

Roles of Data File Integration

Once you've established a need for data file integration, what are some common approaches for implementing it?

Selection Menus. Most shells enable you to ease user entry by displaying "menus," lists of selection items from which users choose. Menus can be used for giving simple yes/no selections or choosing from much larger lists. If those items change regularly, it may be desirable to put the choices in a data file and build the menus from data file links.

Selection can be "qualified." Based on the state of a particular consultation, the expert system may infer that only some subset of the possible choices included in the file are applicable to the situation. Based on this information, the expert system searches the file for those records that match some specific condition. Values for building the menu are taken only from records that satisfy the search. This gives you added flexibility in tailoring the consultation.

For example, this VP-Expert statement creates a user selection menu based on a search of the dBASE® data base *staff*, choosing those records in which the field *salary* has a value greater than the value found in the VP-Expert variable *min_salary*, and creating a menu whose values come from the field *name* from each record which satisfies that search. When the user selects from that menu, the value or values are placed in the field *candidate*.

MENU candidate, salary > (min_salary), staff, name

Question and Answer Shortcut. An easy way to use outside data files is as a shortcut for avoiding excessive user questioning. In this situation, the answers to questions already reside somewhere. The expert system interrogates this source instead of forcing users to manually enter the information. A common approach is to have the user enter one key piece of information (e.g., *mainframe site 5*), and have the expert system use this key to perform a data base search that succeeds when the key and the key field contents match. The complete record is then brought into the expert system and its contents become known as assertions as if the user had entered them or the inference engine had concluded them.

Not all such systems depend on an index. For example, financial spreadsheets, like Lotus 1-2-3, can be accessed to provide starting figures for a consultation. Too, most shells can read ASCII (or on mainframes, EBCDIC) files. A common approach then is to have some program create a data file that feeds the expert system starting values.

Hypothetical Reasoning. Some applications may require that certain possible lines of reasoning be processed by the inference engine before their relevance can be determined. This can be thought of as "hypothetical reasoning," referring to the strategy in which certain portions of the expert system's values are stored in an external data source and loaded for the purpose of exploring that model's relevance. If the results of such an exploration seem to match the user's case, the consultation proceeds. If not, the model's values are retracted and another is tried, or the consultation is abandoned.

For example, consider a diagnostic expert system in which only partial evidence is available. Based on the few facts that are available, the expert system determines that there is enough evidence to suggest problem "x." Contained in an external source are values containing all the values implied by problem "x." These are loaded into the knowledge base and the appropriate attributes are instantiated with values from that external source. The expert system now processes the model, and can proceed in several ways:

• It could generate a list of additional symptoms, problem characteristics, or problem implications and ask the user if these match the current scenario in an attempt to further confirm the hypothesis.

- The expert system might use these values to suggest certain remedies and ask the user if these repairs improve the problem.
- The software might look for contradictions between other user observations and those implied in the hypothetical model.

Based on this processing, confidence in the hypothetical model is raised—or the model is rejected. The expert system may load other models or determine that the problem is outside the scope of its knowledge.

Audit and Reason. This approach to using outside data files is an extended version of the shortcut method. Instead of using data files to supplement information obtained from users, the data base is the primary source of information. This approach can be used to create intelligent analysis expert systems that run in batch mode at the end of transaction processing systems, providing interpretations or "smart" summaries of data.

The level of integration for these kinds of systems is usually high. Audit and Reason applications may be technically challenging if the job of the expert system is to interpret trends or changes in the data source. For example, if the expert system looks at the record-by-record changes in several data base fields, it must be able to represent changes as if they occurred over time. Such interpretation or prediction type applications may require forward chaining and sophisticated representation facilities. Such applications are usually not suitable for novice developers, and may not be suitable for strictly rule-based approaches.

A simpler form of this kind of integration approach is based on reasoning about summarized versions of the data source. The expert system accumulates and examines factors like averages, totals, or statistical deviations of the entire data source. Because the record-by-record stream is now summarized by one or several values, it is handled more easily.

Data Base Front-End. This type of expert system performs inferencing in order to develop a profile of requirements. It then examines all or parts of a data file to find records that match these user requirements. For example, a student financial aid advisor uses a rule-based approach for getting values, from which it infers eligibility characteristics. It then performs a qualified data base search looking for records that contain data about different financial aid vehicles for which the user may qualify.

Other applications may require extensive text elaboration of the recommendation. Instead of storing the recommendation internally, the developer might conclude the recommendation as a record number or other key. When the conclusion is noted, the expert system performs a data base search and displays or prints the recommendation stored in an associated record or file.

Using expert systems to front-end data bases in this way may seem attractive. However, there are reasons to closely examine whether or not an expert system is really the right tool to implement such applications. Is there really meaningful inferencing taking place in the expert system? For example, if the financial aid advisor simply accepts family income and student work status information and subsequently accesses records that match those two values, you really have a simple data base application that can be implemented with almost any data base program owning a query facility. On the other hand, if student financial aid eligibility is based on a reasoning process that includes many rules of thumb that manipulate basic information like family income and student work status, and perhaps factors like academic performance, equal opportunity law, and special case scholarships, then the expert system may serve appropriately as an *intelligent* front-end.

When you integrate outside data into the expert system, you break down the perceived dichotomy between expert systems and other software like data bases, fourth generation languages, and conventional programming languages. If you use a shell to implement simple query-and-match qualified data base search applications, you may end up with an expert system that contains no real expertise and is difficult to control. On the other hand, if the project requires expertise *and* data base lookup, taking advantage of the integration facilities of the shell gives you the tools to provide a complete solution that can give the impression of a high degree of intelligence with easy access to information that already exists.

Integration Supplements Inferencing. Some shells allow you to access outside data sources as an alternate knowledge source. This lets you go to outside files on an "if needed" basis as part of the search performed by the inference engine.

For example, when backward chaining occurs on an attribute, it becomes the current goal. If the value is NOTSOUGHT, most inference engines first seek values for this attribute by looking for rules that conclude the attribute. If none exists, the user is queried for its value. In those shells that support it, you may add other search steps. After the inference engine determines that no rules conclude the value, it may allow you to check to see if an external search is defined. If so, the inference engine seeks a value for the current goal by accessing the defined outside data source. This could be a data base search, worksheet interrogation, or execution of some outside program. If the search is successful, the current goal is satisfied and the next goal from the goal backlog becomes the current goal. If the search is unsuccessful, then the inference engine looks for the next knowledge source, which is often a user prompt.

This method is valuable because the external search, like a user prompt, only takes place if the attribute/value is NOTSOUGHT and cannot be obtained from within its own rule base. The process is transparent to users. You only incur the cost of the external access on an as-needed basis.

Embedding Expert Systems

In some applications, inferencing or other expert-system-specific components may play an important, but secondary, role. You may wish to add an expert system component to existing "conventional" software. In others, procedural processing may be the most natural way to address much of the problem. For those parts in which inferencing make sense, you'd like to provide access to an inference engine.

Several shells allow "the tail to wag the dog," or let external application programs drive their inference engine as a subroutine. This can be especially useful for those wanting to add intelligent behavior characteristics to existing software. It may also be an appropriate approach for writing monitoring or process control programs, where processing speed is especially critical.

Several approaches are used. Many programming languages enable their developers to call external programs from within the language itself. This is exactly the same capability that those shells offer that enables developers to execute outside programs from within the shell. Using this method, the shell is executed from the inside of the external program. When shell processing is completed, control returns to the calling program. Some vendors offer the inference engine as a programming language library, usually for C. Here the shell is unbundled into its functional components. C language developers call inferencing components when needed.

Another approach that is becoming increasingly popular is the generation of C language code from a finished knowledge base. Developers create standalone knowledge bases. Then they run the knowledge base through a conversion program that translates it into C language source code. Developers then link this code into their source program.

BACK TO THE EXAMPLE

Let's take a brief look at how the help desk application we examined earlier is being improved to incorporate some of these integration aspects. What might the information center developer do in order to improve the system through the use of integration techniques?

All current computing environments throughout the company could be entered and archived in a data base file. Helpers would then be able to access these environments by choosing a name from a single menu, pulling in all relevant site information with a single keystroke. Helpers would interact with a single input form, making the consultation run more consistently each time and enabling random, immediate entry of known information without wading through inference-driven prompts.

After input is entered on the form, the expert system processes the data and typically suggests several remedies based on this input (the expert system plays the peer role). The expert system pushes the questioning process to a single recommendation only when explicitly told to do so by the helper. This enables helpers to choose the lines of reasoning they consider promising and keeps them at the fore of the consultation instead of playing the passive role of data entry operator. The expert system contributes by pointing key directions, naming top candidate suggestions, with the potential for autonomously completing many consultations if the helper so desires.

The developer could design the expert system to replace the manual administrative log by generating it in data file and hard copy form. The data file would include the administrative information the old system required, plus system recommendations and success ratings in resolving the problem. A later development phase would add code examining the log to evaluate and improve application behavior.

SUMMARY

The following are suggestions we recommend you use in the design phase of your expert system as part of your standard evaluation activities. These will better prepare you to evaluate and plan for your integration needs.

Apply Standard Systems Analysis Techniques. The modern expert system is more and more often a hybrid of knowledge-based and data processing techniques. Apply standard systems analysis techniques to the data processing aspects of the application as you would any conventional business program. If possible, work the application into your current information flow. Seek user feedback early in the prototyping phase to understand their concerns and how they might use the application. Keep in mind that ergonomic and ease of use concerns are at least as critical in expert systems as in other software.

See the Application in the Data Processing Continuum. Expert systems programming techniques are just one group of tricks in the software development bag. While you need to be cognizant of their unique issues, don't forget the pragmatic, problem-solving techniques you already know from conventional programming.

Evaluate Your Future, as Well as Current, Integration Needs Now. Try to look down the road on what you want to do in the future, in terms of interacting with outside resources. While you may not implement all of these concerns now, the analysis process will enable you to choose a tool with which you can grow.

PART THREE

Designing the Knowledge Base

10 | *Knowledge Acquisition*

This chapter gives a method for structuring your first knowledge acquisition efforts. We start by offering guidelines for managing unfavorable, but common, biases toward expert systems that participants may bring to the project. We then propose ideas for aiding the knowledge acquisition process in general. These ideas are based on the notion that the expert's job of describing knowledge is not an easy one. We propose a simple three-stage model for understanding how experts articulate their knowledge. Then we suggest communication techniques you can use in all knowledge engineering sessions. The topic here is *how* you communicate with the expert. Finally, we look at the *what* of the first interviews: the goals you set and the topics you cover during those early sessions. We propose goals for early knowledge acquisition that are particularly relevant for diagnostic, classification, and selection problems. These are the most common types of problems pursued with rule-based tools. The underlying assumption of this material is that the domain is suited for backward chaining rule-based systems. These assumptions are examined in Chapter 11.

WHY EXPERTS SHOULDN'T BE THREATENED BY EXPERT SYSTEMS

Let's first deal with the "threaten the expert" issue. The expert and others may fear that the expert system may replace them. These fears are usually based on the misunderstanding that *the software is potentially smarter than they are.* You must be prepared to deal with this anxiety to ensure the expert's cooperation and support.

Experts Are Smarter than Expert Systems

Given the hype and selling of expert systems technology, many believe that expert systems are some fundamentally new and improved way of writing computer software. We've seen that expert systems excel at different aspects of computing than conventional software. However, like any other computer software, the end result is only as good as the development job done. Specifically, commercial expert systems do not improve themselves spontaneously, cannot "learn," and can easily contain bugs and provide wrong recommendations even if the expert does not. Because the expert system has the limitations of any other software, it can't be trusted to play the prominent and authoritative role that the expert does. It must necessarily be judged, evaluated, and perhaps even maintained by the expert. Therefore, it remains subordinate to the expert.

The Expert System: Always a Subset of Subsets

The expert system can be vastly useful, but even in the best of circumstances will always be a subset of subsets. Here's what this means. Consider the whole of a human expert's knowledge. The expert system can only represent what the expert articulates. This verbalization is limited by time, the expert's facility for articulating his or her knowledge, and the nature of the domain. It is always a subset of what the expert knows. This in turn is limited by what the knowledge engineer captures. The knowledge engineer may miss pieces of knowledge, not grasp the relevance of various points, and so on. (See Figure 10.1.)

The developer can only encode that captured knowledge which is suitable for the shell he or she chooses. In the case of rule-based shells, suitable knowledge is constrained in many ways. For example, it should not be based on common sense or sense data. Representable knowledge is more or less limited to knowledge about the common behaviors *about* the domain as opposed to *modeling* or *simulating* the domain. While you choose areas that conform to the guidelines recommended in Chapter 2 in order to ensure that the shell and domain knowledge coincide as much as possible, inevitably these constraints trim some of the knowledge the engineer can encode.

Once you have determined what parts of the articulated knowledge can be represented, the scope of the expert system will possibly be further narrowed by performance and capacity limitations of the hardware or software environment. Finally, given what now remains from the starting point of the expert's knowledge, the final product is then dependent on the talents of the developer. If he or she does a *perfect* job, the final result is a subset of a subset of a subset

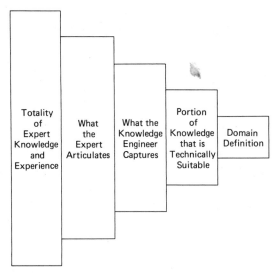

Figure 10.1. An expert system contains only a subset of the expert's knowledge and experience.

of a subset of a subset. If the developer does a less than perfect job, the result is something less than that.

This fact is not a criticism or downgrading of the significance of that final result. The remaining well-chosen kernel can still be vastly useful and important. The expert system offers its own advantages, like the ability to deliver that kernel to various parts of the organization when needed, not limited by the expert's availability. Clearly though, the delivered product is about as far from a human expert as Pluto is from the sun. The expert represents many orders of magnitude more knowledge—and therefore value—to the organization. This needs to be stressed to the expert.

The Expert System Will Be a Trainee

Even for the limited scope of the expert system, the software will be a trainee in its subdomain just as an inexperienced new hire would be. The system's performance must be tested before giving it substantial responsibility. When it makes mistakes, it needs to be corrected. When the knowledge in the domain evolves, the expert system needs to be updated. Who is qualified to recognize when mistakes are made and judge when knowledge has changed? The expert probably plays a prominent role here. Loss of the expert could damage or destroy the ability to evaluate and maintain the system over its lifetime.

The Expert System May Improve Quality of Work Life

The expert system may improve the expert's quality of work life. Since the problems the expert understands best are among the easier problems, the expert system holds the potential to off-load many of the mundane, easy problems with which he or she deals. Because the expert's problem-solving method becomes the standard for the organization, much of the "putting out fires" part of the job may be reduced. The reduction of defensive problem-solving can relieve stress, open up opportunities for the expert to become more proactive, and possibly allow her or him to address other areas which hold strategic interest and value.

All organizations have a shortage of qualified talent. No expert system can get close to replicating a human's ability to deal with new situations creatively. The expert system can free the expert for more interesting and challenging work, while freeing him or her from many of the familiar, mundane tasks.

SET EXPECTATIONS

After covering the above points, help the expert understand the acquisition and engineering process in which she or he will engage. This includes describing the interviewing process and the role of taping. Describe the prototyping method as it is laid out in the next chapter. Stress the active, guiding role you hope to have the expert play, and give a rough description of the time commitment that will be necessary. If you sense there's a problem here, make a note of it because the issue will have to be dealt with explicitly by you, management, and the expert. Let the expert feel comfortable with the prominent role in the development process he or she must play. Make clear that experts control much of what the expert system contains since its knowledge depends much on what they can tell you about the domain.

How much of this material is relevant to your expert varies. However, one point is clear. Expert systems today do not replace experts. Instead, they enhance experts' value, and make more of what they know available more often. The state of the technology is such that management, users, and expert alike must understand that the expert system plays a well-defined, limited, yet still vastly useful role in the organization, a role which is subordinate to the uniquely flexible approach to problem-solving that characterizes human experts.

GETTING READY

Review Background Sources

An obvious first step to take before interviewing the expert is to learn as much as you can about the domain. Read whatever written sources you can get that provide a high-level perspective on the domain. As you read, note key terms, definitions, and ambiguities in meaning. You want to clarify these in the form of a keyword glossary as you pursue the project. Therefore, strive to understand key jargon of the domain as specifically as possible. Early on in the interviewing process you will compare your definitions to those used by the expert. Your glossary should then be updated and maintained as the project continues.

Write down questions about areas you don't understand. Try to get several views on each topic. Read introductory materials, then some intermediate discussions of specific topics. Reading different technical levels, writing styles, and perspectives will serve to broaden your view of the domain.

Use Tape

Everything we describe in this chapter assumes that you tape discussions with the expert. Good knowledge engineering technique dictates that when the expert begins providing meaningful output, you do not interrupt. The only way to reliably capture the expert's output is to commit it to some medium that you can review and analyze.

Video tape offers the advantage of observing the expert while he or she speaks. This also helps you capture any diagrams, visual output, and nonverbal cues the expert may provide. Its main disadvantage is that the equipment must be set up and may not be portable enough for some situations. Audio tape is also useful. Tape recorders can be toted wherever they are needed, including off-site locations if this is a necessary part of the acquisition process. The choice of which medium to use is ultimately up to you.

Some people feel uncomfortable being taped. Let the expert know in advance that this is an essential part of the knowledge engineering process. If the expert is anxious about the uses to which the tapes will be put, note the confidential and limited purpose of the tapes: to support the knowledge engineering process and make best use of the expert's time. Most people lose their anxiety after a session or two.

After a taping session, the tape must be transcribed. Transcription involves listening or viewing the recording and putting its content into prose descriptions or diagrams that summarize what the expert said. The transcription process is useful as it gives you a second hearing. Inevitably, you clarify or pick up new information from these hearings. The transcription is then sent to the expert, who comments on any misunderstandings. The transcription can also be used as a starting point for future acquisition sessions.

Use audio or video tape recordings of the sessions. By listening and watching the dialog a second or third time, you usually get information that would otherwise be lost. Because you participate in the interviewing process, it may be difficult to objectively grasp everything that is happening in the heat of the interview. Taping helps you detect gaps in understanding, and recapture important details.

Take Notes

While we urge that you tape interview sessions, we also suggest that you take notes during the interview. The goal of the notetaking is to keep track of the agenda of the interview, to capture essential ideas, and to diagram relationships. Ideally, your notes present an outline review of structure of the session, as well as the key findings.

This provides many benefits. First, it gives you a mechanism for organizing your own goals for the interview session and evaluating its progress as the session unfolds. Second, it gives you a written record of the interview before you transcribe the taping session. It also provides a backup in the case of technical failure of the taping process. Notetaking can serve as a useful stimulant to the expert. By graphically depicting relationships and requesting feedback from the expert as you try to understand them, you can help the expert correct and refine outputs. We strongly encourage the use of such graphical summaries of what is being said at the end of each acquisition session.

WHAT IS KNOWLEDGE ACQUISITION?

The knowledge acquisition process has three stages, depicted in Figure 10.2.

1. explanation
2. capture
3. organization

The acquisition format in which we are interested in this chapter is the interview. Knowledge may be acquired from other sources—for example, from written sources. We stress the interview format here for three reasons. First, it remains the most commonly used way to gather knowledge. Second, it is the most difficult due to considerations we will examine shortly. Third, it is the

Figure 10.2. Three Steps in the Knowledge Acquisition Process.

form that most typically lacks an organizational format to guide the activity. Knowledge that exists in written form has already undergone the explanation stage and exists in an articulated form. Thus, most other knowledge sources can be seen as a subset of the knowledge acquisition process based on the interview format.

The "capture" stage refers to the process of documenting the objects, relations, and actions that make up the knowledge. The "organization" stage refers to the process of ordering that knowledge in such a form that it is ready for mapping to rules. The organizational stage is discussed in the next chapter. It is easy to become enamored with the technical challenges of encoding knowledge. However, encoding logically comes second to extracting the material. Since the second and third points of the acquisition process become irrelevant if no knowledge can be drawn from the expert, it is vital to understand the dynamics and challenges inherent in the interview format.

A KNOWLEDGE EXPLANATION MODEL

Most experts have difficulty in clearly explaining their problem-solving methodology in a step-by-step fashion. We offer here a three-step model for recognizing different stages of the explication process. This is not a proposal for describing how experts really think. Instead, the author has found that the model fits how most acquisition interviews seem to work. By applying this model to your interaction with the expert, you will better understand where in the acquisition process you stand, and help guide the interview accordingly.

The model has three parts, depicted in Figure 10.3.

1. Generate explanation hypothesis.
2. Test hypothesis.
3. Revise and refine hypothesis.

Generate Explanation Hypothesis

The process begins with the invitation to the expert to explain some aspect of her or his problem-solving behavior. This request asks the expert to translate some experientially acquired knowledge into language. While the request

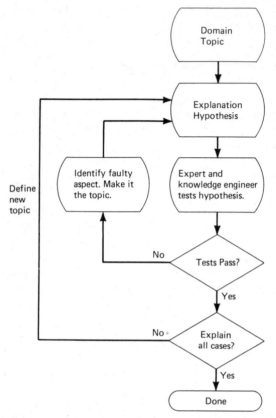

Figure 10.3. Model for Understanding Explanation Behavior.

sounds natural, it may pose daunting problems, of which we name two. First, the expert may have little experience using words to describe a decision-making or reasoning process of which at least some aspects have been made at a nonlanguage level. This fact forces the expert to *create* this descriptive language. The expert may exert substantial creative effort at uncovering a good way to explain and narrate the problem-solving strategy and each decision-making step. For this reason, early explanations tend to contain areas of inaccuracy as the expert "feels" his or her way to an interpretation of the reasoning process.

Second, it is impossible for most humans to consider all the cases that may impact how a problem is actually solved. Experts will typically believe that their reasoning process is rather simple. When they try to explain it, they usually begin by offering a route that may describe a default approach in the face of no particular significant circumstances. It may contain certain general

Knowledge chunks

Explanation I	Revision II	Revision III	Revision IV	*Actual Reasoning*
X	X	X	X	X
	–	–	–	–
–	O	O	O	O
		O	O	O
			–	–
	O	O	–	O
O	O	X	O	–
		–	X	X

Figure 10.4. Explanations evolve toward their final form.

principles that the expert applies. Until you can test specific cases against these early outputs, the explanation will almost certainly be incomplete. These two points combine to make early explanations a starting point for further work. Figure 10.4 depicts this evolution from early to final explanation, using symbols to represent a reasoning process.

In the acquisition process, early explanations play the role of "hypotheses." As the acquisition process unfolds, the expert mentally self-tests these proposed theories by checking them against a battery of common cases that come to mind. You fuel this process by asking for more information and pursuing particular lines of reasoning.

Putting into language a nonverbal thinking process is more than simply "telling how it's done." The final account of the problem-solving method to which you and the expert agree may have little resemblance to the initial attempts at putting that nonlanguage decision process into words. Therefore, treat the hypothesis as a preliminary explanation. While the expert works at verbalizing how he or she performs a certain task, his or her outputs should not be regarded as knowledge, but as working theories that must still stand up to the tests that you and the expert put to them.

Test Hypothesis

As soon as a hypothesis has been proposed for some particular knowledge item, the expert immediately begins to test it. This is not so much a conscious decision to improve the theory as a first chance for the analytic side of the expert's mind to evaluate what the creative side has just produced. This process can be compared to the way a painter puts a few strokes of paint on the canvas, stands back, and says, "Hmm . . . ." The analytic side is "seeing" the theory in language form for the first time and now gets to decide if it agrees. For example, you will find the "analytic" side of the expert may interrupt the "creative" side when the analytic side finds a hole in the theory being proposed—even while the creative part articulates the theory for the first time.

Some experts are adept at producing plausible explanations that seem to fit their behavior. Such experts are called articulate. Another aspect of the expert's personality that will show itself is how aggressively the expert critiques his or her own initial explanations. Some will believe what they say is true and accurate simply because they said it. They critique only the most obviously contradictory of their own statements. Others' analytic side will immediately jump into action and find problems with the theory, generating new hypotheses that solve the flaw without prompting from you.

At some point, the expert accepts his or her explanation—either in its initial or revised form. How do you know if you should accept it? After all, you are not an expert in the domain. The answer is that you do not judge the hypothesis but involve the expert in further testing it. You do this by getting the creative side of the expert involved in generating new theories for the expert's analytic side to evaluate. This is done by asking for more information. By focusing attention on some ambiguous aspect of the expert's explanation and asking for more output, you engage the expert's creative side to produce additional explanations. After the expert complies, those outputs become fodder for the analytic side. This gets the expert back into the critiquing mode. As you dig deeper into the domain and gather more information, any problems that exist begin to emerge. Usually the expert discovers these as his or her words create inconsistencies. If the expert does not acknowledge them, you point out these inconsistencies and ask for clarification.

A productive questioning technique for engaging the expert's creative side is to ask for case descriptions. For example, "What do you do when the (factor a) is (factor's proposed value)?" This is the type of question that lets the expert add depth to the hypothesis and causes that person to evaluate whether solving this proposed new case supports the hypothesis or forces its revision.

As the project proceeds, the major testing vehicle you provide is the software prototype. By showing the expert a working prototype, you give a vividly concrete version of the expert's explanation hypotheses for testing. For this reason, working side-by-side from a prototype can be extremely productive. The expert can now pose cases to an expert-in-development and test its performance removed from his or her own background knowledge and assumptions. In this sense, the software prototype is probably the best hypothesis testing vehicle you have for engaging the expert's analytic side.

The testing process is a recursive process that can operate at many levels of abstraction. Large generalizations the expert makes will trigger analysis of the detail implications of those statements on test cases. When explaining test cases, new information may arise that requires the expert to reevaluate her or his explanation of the overall problem-solving framework. The more active this analysis activity is in the expert, the better the expert will be at refining explanations to conform with his or her actual performance.

Revise and Refine Hypothesis

At some stage the expert may reject the entire explanation. This happens because the analytic side thinks up test cases that fail the hypothesis. In such a case, she or he must replace the prior hypothesis with a new one. When this occurs, the generate/test/revise cycle begins anew. More commonly, the expert refines an explanation. Refinement includes such activities as detecting and filling in missing steps in the original explanation, adding steps to explain new cases, and unpacking steps previously thought of as a single entity into several parts.

The "revise and refine" step, then, is the step in which the need for a new hypothesis is discovered. Both the act of correcting and expanding knowledge restart the explanation cycle and generate new hypotheses that must be tested and refined. Thus, it is important to realize that any new information, even the detailed filling out of cases within a framework which you and the expert currently accept, is not knowledge, but a hypothesis. The acquisition process starts by having an expert propose some explanation of a bit of knowledge, test that meaning, refine the explanation to better match the actual thinking, and then provide more information to deal with new cases. You then both mutually continue with this acquisition cycle while holding open the possibility that previous knowledge may yet be refined further.

One of the core assumptions underlying the knowledge acquisition and expert systems prototyping method is that knowledge cannot be gotten all at once. Knowledge is often unsystematic, nonverbal, and therefore difficult to acquire and nail down. Rules are good at representing the knowledge items because of their self-standing, independent nature. Therefore, incompleteness of knowledge is a fact of life you accept and plan for during the development cycle. You do not immediately try to learn everything about the domain. Instead, you harness the generate/test/refine explanation model to get the information you need in the order you need it. You do this by structuring interviews with the expert in such a way that the expert is encouraged to focus attention on areas you are ready to accept. We now look at interviewing techniques that give you this control. We first examine general interviewing rules of thumb you can use in all interviewing situations. We then propose an interview structure for the first interview session. In the chapter that follows this, we expand that structure to include subsequent interviewing sessions.

GENERAL INTERVIEWING GUIDELINES

In order to be effective with the expert, you need to practice good listening skills. These support your goals of encouraging the creative side of the expert to provide initial hypotheses, and getting the expert's analytic side involved in testing and refining those hypotheses. The better you support this activity, the fewer false starts and "dry" interviewing sessions you will have. Here are some simple, but important, interviewing guidelines you can use in all your knowledge acquisition efforts.

Don't Interrupt

During the interview, the expert may make statements you don't understand. The expert may make statements that superficially touch on areas about which you will need more information. The expert may make statements that appear to contradict previous statements, contain ambiguities, or bring up new subjects.

Your knee-jerk reaction may be to focus attention on these points by asking questions immediately. Resist this urge. Instead, write keywords in your notes that will remind you of your questions. Let the expert finish his or her thought. This allows the expert to complete a line of thought without your imposing a left or right turn that may stop the flow of a productive hypothesis.

The number one goal of early acquisition interviews is getting the expert to produce hypotheses. For this reason, you should value everything the expert says. Your urge to prioritize his or her thoughts at this stage is a mistake. If you constrain the process around your ability to immediately absorb everything that is being said, you may get insufficient output. The knowledge engineering session becomes "choppy" and blocked, without flow. When you interrupt a statement with a question, you may sway the expert's attention so far that the person simply does not remember what was being said. The information may be lost for that session, perhaps for the entire knowledge engineering process.

Sometimes when the expert makes a statement it will "trigger" another thought. Make sure you do not interrupt him or her at this time. You can recognize "triggers" as moments of insight the analytic side of the expert has. The expert may say things like, "Oh yes, this reminds me," or "and another thing. . . ." These may continue for many minutes. When a knowledge engineering session becomes a monologue of meaningful information connected by these triggers, this is a clue that you are working at a productive level. Ten minutes of such trigger-driven output can provide days and weeks of knowledge engineer fodder. Gather it now, absorb and organize it later. For this reason, you tape the acquisition sessions.

Stay Out of the Way

You are the knowledge engineer. Like a psychiatrist, you try to help that which is already present to come forth. Like a translator, you work at rendering one form of communication into another while retaining its essential value. This is an interesting and challenging task.

To facilitate this process, do not impose yourself on the acquisition process. It can be tempting to try to improve the expert's performance, or comment on perceived efficiencies or other aspects of what the expert does. This can be especially tempting as you experience the excitement of learning the domain and how the expert attacks it. Yet it is essential that you not comment on the expert's methods or results. Expert behavior is not required to be "reasonable" or conform to our idea of "correctness." If it did, it might be logically deducible and not worth a knowledge engineering effort. Unless you also have expertise in the expert's area, you should dedicate yourself to encoding how the expert does what he does, not trying to improve it.

When you engage in the knowledge acquisition process, you participate in a human relationship. It is easy to fall into the behavior of volunteering your personal opinions. Your comment may get the interview off track so that it loses its focus. It may serve as a distraction or excuse for talking about something other than the reason you are taking the expert's valuable time. Limit your opinions to areas in which your opinion carries weight: acquiring and encoding knowledge. Realize that when you impose your own personal thoughts on the interview that you throw unfamiliar ingredients into the recipe. If you sensitize yourself to recognizing this conduct, you will become better able to control it.

Ask One Question at a Time

Make it easy on the expert. Use a logical questioning sequence, don't badger or give the "third degree." You are trying to get information. Ask one question at a time. Then be quiet and listen.

Ask Questions in the Subjunctive

To learn more about alternative paths or results, propose hypothetical scenarios that assume different circumstances. For example,

> Assuming for the moment that it is not a hardware problem, how would you proceed?

This gets you further inside the expert's reasoning process, and gives you a broader context in which to grasp what the expert is doing. Use words like "might," "should," "could," "would," and "assuming" in your questions. These words are keys for getting information about scenarios the expert may not be addressing.

Rephrase, Summarize, Gain Agreement

Another way to test assumptions and ensure that you precisely understand what is being said is to rephrase a statement or group of statements. After the expert finishes, say, "So if I understand you correctly . . ." and repeat back the facts. The expert then agrees, clarifies, or corrects you.

This rephrasing approach for checking your grasp of what experts say is also a useful transition technique. When you gain agreement to your summary, you also get the ball thrown in your court. It allows you to ask the next question. First, the expert gives you some information. You then restate what was said and ask for agreement to your summary's accuracy. You get the feedback. Now it is your turn to speak. You ask the next question, state your reading of the implications of the statement, or make whatever move best fits the situation. By asking for agreement, you get to make the next move after the expert agrees. Asking for agreement caps the past conversation, and gives you the initiative to establish the next direction. This is a subtle, yet effective, method for getting your information right while keeping control of the interview.

When an interview session is over, summarize where you stand. Summarize new knowledge. If you are working with a software prototype, note changes the expert suggested and errors that were detected. Go over this information as specifically as necessary to ensure your grasp of the material. Gain agreement to this summary. Then write it up as a memo, and send a copy to the expert. The process of writing is a good discovery and organizational experience. If the information is wrong, you have a better chance of catching it immediately. Away from the heat of the moment, the memo may jog additional thoughts from the expert. The paper trail serves as a useful documentation of the progress of the project and puts the ball in the expert's park to discover any errors you've made.

After summarizing, restating, or saying anything else of importance, make a point of gaining agreement. Gaining agreement is vital for involving the expert and checking your information. When you draw a conclusion, you've reached a milestone. *Cause the expert to agree with your summary.* If you simply make a statement and move on, you don't know if you've said something with which the expert disagrees. You may think you are making progress when you are actually standing still or going backwards.

Gaining agreement involves the other party. Getting agreement provides you valuable information about whether or not you are on the right track. If she or he won't agree, you have may not have understood the point correctly. Therefore, when you ask for agreement and *do not* get it, you are gaining valuable information you must act on.

Aggressive listening, summarizing, and gaining agreement communicate that you are absorbing the information. By repeating back in a manner that shows this grasp, you check your understanding and guide the next step. By gaining agreement, you ensure clear communication. All the while, the expert senses a clear intelligence and interest through your simple act of feeding back what he or she tells you.

Three Don'ts and a Do

Here are some important points that can particularly affect how well you involve the expert in the production and analysis of explanation hypotheses.

Don't Critique Too Soon. Quell your analytic urge in the early stages of the knowledge acquisition process. As the expert verbalizes, that person may seem to struggle to express his or her reasoning. Therefore, early information only may be approximately correct or applicable. Your role is to let the expert describe that reasoning. Only after it appears in language and has been given time to mature should it be regarded as a target for direct critique.

Turning intuition into language is a creative activity. Regardless of how silly, contradictory, or wrong the expert's verbalizations seem to be, don't seem too anxious to start working through those conflicts. Conversely, early output may make sense, but also can be wrong. Be neutral to the content of what the expert says, regardless of how right or wrong it seems. Neutrality is important in order to give the expert a chance to refine the thinking or even to change her or his mind.

Don't Jump to Conclusions. You can't see the puzzle's picture until enough pieces are connected. It is hard to put the pieces together until you know what the picture is. Our human nature constantly tries to see a picture, even before we have enough pieces. Good knowledge engineers let the pieces *present* the picture when enough of these pieces have been put together. In the early stages, then, your goal is to help the expert produce enough hypotheses about the domain so that a picture can present itself.

Don't Put Words in the Expert's Mouth. Too much direction from you can taint what the expert says. See yourself as a producer, not a director. It is the expert's job to decide when descriptions match the "actual" reasoning. You facilitate the process by documenting, asking questions, but not suggesting solutions or filling in the blanks for her.

You may also catch yourself answering your own questions. For example:

"How is that done? Do you . . . ?"

You then spout forth your understanding of how " . . . " is done. In the process, you limit the expert's response to yes or no. This often happens when you get insecure about asking for information that the expert may regard as obvious or trivial. Even though you ask the question, you want to appear knowledgeable. So you try to answer the question for the person. This is a poor interviewing technique. Don't answer your own questions. The expert has the know-how. Your goal is to bring forth the expert's answers and explanations. You cannot do this if you answer for the expert. Even if the answer seems obvious, hearing the expert use language may supply you with important insight. Ask the question. Then be silent and listen to the answer.

Do Be a Knowledge Midwife. The creative process of explaining the reasoning process may be frustrating, embarrassing, and difficult for the expert. Be supportive. Display lots of quiet behavior, as well as tempering the analysis of what the expert says with thoughtful compassion. This can be especially effective with individuals who, because of their expert stature, are used to controlling the situation.

Stress how difficulty in explaining the reasoning process is normal and common. Perhaps outline the explanation model used in this chapter. Be empathetic and, if appropriate, agree to make the nature of the interpersonal process you use confidential. It is important to gain the expert's trust and establish a comfortable working relationship.

Do not add an aura or mystery about what you are doing. This is important because the success of the project depends first of all on the expert's cooperation. You should provide encouragement and recognition to the expert. Propose ideas and alternatives in a consultative, subjunctive manner. While your underlying confidence and competence must come through, help the expert feel in control.

These points address *how* you interact with the expert. They refer to presenting your behaviors to the expert in a manner that encourages open communication and builds trust. If followed, you will create a relationship in which you relieve the expert of the responsibility of presenting you with a finished package called *"How I think."* Instead, you become partners. This nurtures the knowledge acquisition process and draws the expert into active partnership as his or her reasoning prowess begins to take shape in the form of an expert system.

THE FIRST MEETING

The first interview session has special importance. It is here that you set expectations, establish rapport, and start to gain the expert's support and trust. These are all important for ensuring the success of the project. Moreover, it is technically the most difficult session. Much of your role is helping along the testing, refinement, and expansion of hypotheses about how the expert's reasoning happens. However, in the first session there may be no existing hypotheses for you to work on. In this session, you must help the expert create such hypotheses. To this end, we here suggest an agenda whose questions can produce this starting fodder. This saves you the embarrassment and possible damage to the project of starting out with a "dry session" that appears unstructured and pointless. It puts you in control of the interviewing process and gets the acquisition process into a systematic routine in which you and the expert's expectations coincide. It helps make the acquisition process less art and more craft.

You start the acquisition process with whatever knowledge you've gained from reviewing written background sources. While this may be substantial, it may also be nonexistent. Moreover, whatever sources have been reviewed may not necessarily include the particulars of the expert's expertise. Thus the primary acquisition goal you have in the first interviews is to understand the big picture. You want to learn the expert's view of what the domain includes. You'd like to know what typical cases she or he encounters and solves. You want to determine what a problem and a solution look like. This helps you begin to address the question of domain definition and gives you information about certain technical decisions you must make. The answers to these questions become the material from which you start digging deeper. Finally, the results of these early acquisition sessions will give the basic essentials needed to produce a simple software prototype that you can demonstrate to the expert and use as a catalyst for further work.

Get High-Level Descriptions

Start the first session by asking the expert for an overview of how she or he goes about addressing the problem. This starts the person at a somewhat superficial level that should be easier to articulate than other areas. If the expert asks for more specific information about what you mean, you might try any of these questions:

- "Describe the overall strategy you use in solving the problem."
- "Are there a few basic categories of information you use to arrive at a conclusion?"
- "What *things* do you reason about when you solve this problem?"

These questions also give you basic information about the domain. What are the objects of reasoning in the domain? Does the expert have a default approach for solving problems? Are there conceptual categories of investigation? Encourage the expert to describe the task in whatever way is comfortable. If the expert has difficulty getting started, ask the person to use a very simple case and walk you through the process of solving it.

You may find that the expert rambles somewhat in these early stages. This is acceptable. It provides you a broad smattering of the expert's thinking. Note key concepts so you can come back to them later. Don't interrupt. If this stage does not seem to generate useful output, go on to the next step. When you've worked through the remaining points, you will come back to this one at the end of the session.

Determine Constant Information

What information is always needed to solve the problem? Get the expert to talk about the data he or she *always* gathers for any consultation. This can be helpful for determining which data are critically important for solving the problem. It also aids in designing the user interface, since you may want to allow the user to enter this information before starting inferencing.

Determine Knowledge Sources

Does all input come interactively from users who consult the expert? Or does the expert use reference and other written sources? Is more than one expert necessary to solve the problem? Are there subspecialties that each expert performs? You need to know this information in order to make domain suitability decisions. If there are sources other than the expert, can they be accessed from the expert system? Must a human find the answers and manually enter them? Is this action acceptable?

Gather Symptoms

If the domain type includes facets in which debugging, repair, or diagnosis plays a role, ask the expert to describe the *symptoms* that are encountered in the problem-solving process. By "symptoms," we mean the traits that superficially signal a problem. For example, if the problem involves fixing a malfunctioning device, symptoms are the abnormal behaviors presented by the device. If there are clients who consult the expert, symptoms may be the user's surface level complaint. Have the expert name the symptoms in a manner that coincides with how a typical client might describe them. Any of the following could qualify as symptoms:

- The software displays the message "Out of disk space."
- The terminal won't respond and there is a capital "K" under the blue line.
- The car whines when I try to start it.
- My nose is running and I feel run down.

The job here is to get into brainstorming mode in order to name and list as many abnormal symptoms as the expert encounters in the course of his or her work. Remember that this is appropriate only in those domains in which the expert is remedying a suboptimal state. Encourage this process to go on for as long as it produces results.

Naming and listing symptoms has three benefits. First, it gives you a good general picture of the various abnormal conditions in the domain. Second, each item that is named represents a trigger for getting the expert to describe a problem-solving line of reasoning. You don't want to investigate that line yet, but by naming and documenting the symptom, you get the trigger for investigating it later. At this stage, you still want to explore the big picture. On the other hand, by capturing this information you now have a key to get back to this subject by asking, "How do you handle cases in which symptom x appears?"

Finally, the discussion may give valuable clues as to how the user interface should be structured. If the symptoms you gather serve as the expert's starting point for problem-solving, selecting a symptom or symptom group may be the best way for users to start a consultation. You can start to evaluate this after you've gathered symptom information.

Gather Conclusions

Now do the same thing with the recommendations or conclusions that the expert makes. Ask the expert to list as many conclusions or types of final advice that she may give. This serves two important purposes.

First, you get a feel for the type of advice the expert gives. Is the advice selected from a shelf of prepackaged possible answers? Selection and classification expert systems share this trait with diagnostic domains. If the domain's solutions are preenumerated, you begin to build a list of the potential values that the final advice can have. The better you nail these values down, the better you begin to get a feel for the scope of the domain. Since you cannot know at this point if you have them all, don't jump to the conclusion that the domain is manageable. On the other hand, if you identify dozens, it may be a warning sign if the number exceeds your expectations.

Note conclusions so that later you can begin work by asking, "Earlier you noted that you sometimes conclude x. What kind of situations produce a conclusion of x?" From there, you can nail down the specifics of that case.

Note that not all conclusions can be listed in this manner. Another possibility is that there are too many solutions to practically name. This may be because solutions are built or tailored depending on many combinations of factors. For example, if the problem is configuring a computer, it may not make sense to name every configuration possibility because there are too many. The expert may combine many component parts in varied ways. For example, if the configuration includes "amount of memory" (512K, 1M, 2M), "graphics type" (none, medium resolution, high resolution), and "disk storage" (floppies, 20 megabyte, 40 megabyte), we already have 27 different combinations of these three simple factors. Since an actual system would probably take into account other factors, there could plausibly be hundreds of possibilities.

This information is in itself valuable. It clues you that the expert systems project is possibly more complex than the selection and diagnostic types just discussed. There may be dependencies among factors that must be understood. Possibly it may not be appropriate for development using a solely rule-based shell. For cases in which there are too many final conclusions, have the expert name the component pieces that go into making a final conclusion. In the configuration example, determine which items go into making up a configuration. Try to exhaustively list as many of these considerations as possible.

Group and Order

The above activities start to give you a feel for the domain. This part of the process may take less than an hour, or could take many hours over several sessions. Once you've gotten to the point where you have this information, you have started to grasp the building blocks that the expert uses in solving the domain problem. The next step is to let the expert help you prioritize this raw material. Order the symptoms and conclusions list by frequency and importance.

Ask the expert to order symptoms from most to least commonly encountered. This gives you a sense as to what problems occur frequently. Have the expert identify the "80/20" group, if one exists. The "80/20" group is that 20 percent of the symptoms which cause 80 percent of the cases. If such a phenomenon exists, it can help you define the scope of the project in such a way as to maximize the coverage the expert system provides.

Create a similar list that orders symptoms by importance. Importance may mean those symptoms that have the worst consequences, those that ordinary performers are least competent at solving, or those which cause the longest delays. The criteria will vary, and the expert will probably have a point of view. Getting this information helps you understand from where the real value of the expert system may come. By contrasting this list with the list ordered by frequency, you get a view which covers the common and important cases in the domain.

Repeat this exercise for preenumerated conclusions. Expect both sets of lists to evolve and change. For purposes of early prototyping, these ordered lists give you an agenda of those cases which should be addressed first.

What Problems Are Easy to Solve?

Get a sense of which problems—if any—are "easy" to solve. You do this so you can analyze if problems with many potential solutions can be easily narrowed, and so you can encode these easy cases early in the prototyping stage. It also clues you as to the overall problem-solving strategy the expert may use. There are several ways to get at this information.

Ask the expert if there are ever cases in which one or two questions immediately lead to a conclusion. In diagnostic-type domains, this is common. Problems often take on an 80/20 character, and the expert is usually skilled at recognizing the signs that indicate those common situations. If a conclusion is gotten quickly with just one or two questions, you want to try to capture and understand this reasoning now.

Another angle to pursue is to find out if there are inferences the expert makes that eliminate large chunks of the problem space. These are common because one of the essential qualities of expertise is first addressing those considerations that get to the solution quickest and focusing attention on the most meaningful aspects of the problem. The expert may have one or two key questions she asks right off that get rid of many possibilities. These may also give her vital insight into what kind of a problem it is. Try to capture these now.

Table 10.1. Goals for Early Knowledge-Acquisition Sessions.

Get high-level descriptions
Determine constant information
Determine knowledge sources
Gather symptoms
Gather conclusions
Group and order
What problems are easy to solve?
Again: is there an overall problem-solving strategy?

Again: Is There an Overall Problem-Solving Strategy?

Finally, return to the first issue of problem-solving approach you discussed. In the earlier question, you asked about this from a speculative point of view. Having now gathered much more information, can generalizations be drawn with respect to the overall approach? Does the expert have an agenda which drives the investigation? For example, does she ask a group of questions designed to eliminate common problems first, followed by questions designed to assign responsibility in some functional area?

Try to determine if this agenda exists in your expert's approach. It may legitimately not exist; therefore, don't feel forced to find one. On the other hand, if it does exist, this knowledge is useful for organizing the architecture of the expert system.

SUMMARY

We've look at the basics of knowledge acquisition in this chapter. Knowledge acquisition has three stages: explanation, capture, organization. The interview is the most common and most challenging acquisition format—challenging, because the expert must bring into language a reasoning or decision process which may be essentially nonverbal. We showed a three-step approach for understanding the process of knowledge explanation. First, experts try out some way of expressing their thinking. They then test it against real-world instances, and finally revise and expand it—which starts the cycle over again. Your job as knowledge engineer is to facilitate the process and capture its results. We urge the use of some recorded media to permanently capture the interview so that you may focus on helping the process of bringing that knowledge forth. Early knowledge acquisition sessions are most difficult because you have nothing to work from. We presented a set of questions you should pursue that allow you to move into later acquisition stages.

Once gathered, this information must be evaluated and organized. If the domain is suitable for a rule-based expert system, you go on to produce a prototype. Otherwise the domain definition must be revised, or the project abandoned. We address these issues in the next chapter.

11 | *Prototyping*

Knowledge engineering translates knowledge into the symbols, rules, algorithms, and other representation structures that enable computer software to mimic humanlike interactions. Having completed the initial interviews described in the last chapter, you now move to this stage. The method by which you carry out knowledge engineering is called prototyping. We discuss a method for carrying out knowledge engineering through the development of a prototype in this chapter.

THE NEED FOR PROTOTYPING

Two factors dictate the method you use to develop rule-based expert systems. The first factor is the nature of what you are encoding: knowledge. This can most easily be seen by contrasting how you come about knowing expert knowledge as opposed to what you code in conventional programming. Conventional programs are created by painstakingly specifying each step the computer performs. These steps are usually planned and designed before coding begins. From a design point of view, systems designers plan the inputs and outputs of the system. On a smaller scale, the programmer/analyst plans each code module based on a program specification. This is possible because conventional programming usually handles well-understood processes.

While this works for conventional languages, it is less applicable to expert systems development. Since much of the challenge in creating expert systems lies in extracting knowledge, you spend considerable time gathering and refining the expert's explanations. Given the difficulty of this task, it is usually unrealistic to fully design the knowledge-based portions of the expert system before you start to code. The "design before you begin" approach that conventional software encourages is impractical when what is being designed is a representation of someone's knowledge, which itself may not be fully understood at the beginning. Knowledge-based problems are usually understood in small pieces or "chunks."

The second factor that influences development method is the relatively independent nature of rules. Each rule is more or less a standalone unit that expresses some kernel of knowledge not reliant on other rules. This means that you can add and remove rules without altering the "correctness" of the remaining knowledge. Contrast this to conventional software in which one small change can dramatically impact the logical flow—and correctness—of the program. The independent nature of rules lends itself to expressing knowledge in chunks.

For these reasons, it is desirable to code the knowledge base in small groups of chunks that can be tested before risking too much on an extensive detailed design process. By showing the in-progress prototype to the expert and getting feedback early, you quickly refine your understanding of the knowledge before investing too much. Moreover, you give the expert a chance to test his or her explanations for accuracy and completeness. By feeding back the expert's explanations in the form of a prototype, you give those explanations an objective, concrete form which greatly aids testing and refinement. This process of building and refining the system a little bit at a time is called "rapid prototyping."

RAPID PROTOTYPING

Rapid prototyping is a method made up of several steps repeated until the application is finished. These steps are depicted in Figure 11.1. First a topic is proposed. Based on available facts, you make a preliminary judgment as to its suitability and value. If the project seems promising, you research it. This research may include knowledge acquisition sessions with an expert, reading written sources, or observing an expert in action. You then organize this information and evaluate it. If the results remain promising, you develop a requirements statement for the expert system. You then either return to the knowledge acquisition process to obtain more knowledge and repeat those steps or encode what you have learned in a prototype. When you proceed to the "encode" step, you make decisions about knowledge representation. For rule-based systems, these decisions include defining attributes that represent the things about which the expert reasons, summarizing rules of thumb, and choosing a primary inferencing paradigm (forward or backward chaining). The first time through this loop, you create a simple prototype expert system that represents the essential structure of how the expert represents and solves the problem. The prototype is then demonstrated and tested. You get feedback from the expert in additional acquisition sessions, giving you information on changes, errors, and new cases. You then organize this input. As the prototype

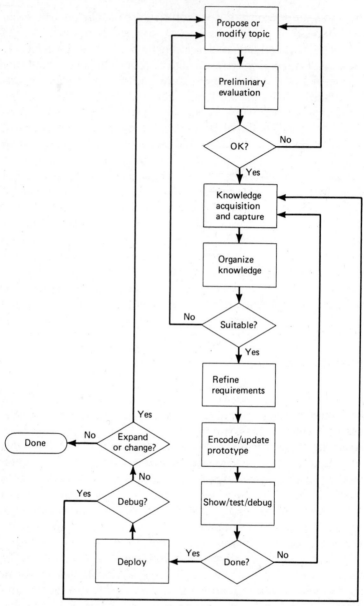

Figure 11.1. Flow Diagram of Rapid Prototyping Method.

matures, the expert's evaluation is supplemented by testing against test cases. The cycle is repeated until the expert system meets the requirements set out for it.

Incremental Evaluation

Two important points arise from using the rapid prototyping approach. First, you continually evaluate the suitability of the system as it progresses. This means that you evaluate the suitability of new knowledge as you acquire it, as well as the suitability of existing knowledge which you refine as work progresses. You treat the expert's explanations as hypotheses. You can't be sure of your grasp of those hypotheses or their validity until the system is tested. Thus you continually reexamine the suitability of the knowledge as your understanding of it evolves.

Also, you continue to reevaluate and refine the expert system's requirements. While you may start the project with a firm notion of what you would like the expert system to do, you probably do not start with a solid understanding of how the expert's underlying reasoning works. Accordingly, you hold a less than fully certain view of how reasonable that initial expectation is. As you learn more, you get a more accurate view. Thus you may find that you can expand the expert system past your original expectation, or conversely, that the original requirement was too ambitious.

The key issue here is that it is difficult, once and for all, completely to evaluate the factors which go into the reasoning process. The concreteness with which you can nail down the suitability and requirements of the expert system is bottlenecked by how much knowledge you elicit and organize. Thus you should remain open to reexamining the project's suitability and to refining its requirements throughout. You accomplish this by taking an incremental approach not only to the development of the expert system, but also to refining its goals and evaluating its suitability.

The First Prototype

When you've gathered enough knowledge, you develop a prototype. You strive to make this first prototype reflect the expert's high-level knowledge representation and problem-solving strategy. Depending on the scope of this work, you perhaps also get it to the point where it solves one or two common problems, often with only one or two simple reasoning levels. You then seek the expert's feedback. You note what portions of the system meet with approval and document corrections and omissions for those aspects which do not. The prototype also serves as a catalyst for defining new cases and deepening the existing knowledge. This new knowledge is then organized and the process repeated.

The prototype thus plays two important roles in the knowledge acquisition process. First, it is a vehicle *for improving your understanding of the problem.* The prototype helps the expert tell you where mistakes have been made. This feedback lets you find out early in the cycle what areas require revision, as well as what parts seem to reflect well the expert's reasoning. Second, the prototype *helps the expert correct and expand his or her own descriptions.* Because it concretizes the expert's verbal descriptions, the expert system is something tangible which helps the expert's analytic side more easily find wrong descriptions. It also triggers more detailed descriptions and accounts of new cases. Thus the prototype serves as a brainstorming vehicle.

ORGANIZING KNOWLEDGE

After completing background research and the first acquisition interviews described in the last chapter, you have obtained a set of data that needs to be organized. You begin this organizational process by answering several questions:

- What concepts or events *directly* impact the conclusion? (*Understand the highest level concepts the expert uses.*)
- Is there an overall problem-solving strategy? If so, what is it?
- What are the concepts, factors, and objects with which the expert reasons? (*Determine the "things" that need to be represented.*)
- How does the expert express the *values* of these concepts, factors, and objects? (*Are their values numeric, yes/no, or symbolic? If the latter, what are those values?*)
- What questions does the expert ask that eliminate possible lines of reasoning? (*Understand how the expert avoids considering every combination of factors.*)
- What are the conclusions the expert makes? (*Are they selected from a small group of possibilities? If there are constructed conclusions, how does the expert build them?*)

Once you have some knowledge toward these questions, you have enough to produce the first prototype. Let's illustrate how you might address these questions by organizing the higher-level information in Chapter 2 to produce an expert system which evaluates expert system topic candidates.

What Concepts, Factors, and Objects Directly Impact the Conclusion?

The expert uses three concept categories for evaluating a domain: the expert system's *economic return,* the *need for the expertise,* and the *suitability* of the domain. While there are other factors, these are the "big picture" considerations for which the expert seeks to establish evidence.

Is There an Overall Problem-Solving Strategy?

The next step is to work out your understanding of the problem-solving strategy used by the expert. In others words, determine the order-dependent categories of inquiry the expert says are used to drive the reasoning process. The best way to document this understanding is in the form of a flow chart, pseudocode, or prose description. Usually a graphic form such as a flow chart works best at triggering the expert's feedback.

The expert first examines whether the domain provides sufficient economic return to warrant further consideration. The expert reasons that if the organization cannot benefit economically from the project, it will not get the necessary support to succeed. Therefore, if economic return cannot be established, the topic is dropped from consideration. Next, the expert examines the issue of expert need. If there is no perceived shortage of expertise, no expert available, or no significant difference in performers, then it does not pass this test and the expert rejects the project. Finally, having established economic payback and a shortage of know-how, the expert examines whether the project meets various suitability criteria.

The above paragraph summarizes the problem-solving approach. A flow diagram representing this description appears in Figure 11.2. The description implies a certain order of inquiry and also establishes the necessary conditions for pursuing those topics that occur later in the order. Such information—if it exists—is essential to developing a control structure for the consultation that reflects the expert's approach to the problem.

In the early stages, you may have only the most general understanding of the problem-solving strategy. A strategy may not even be apparent at this stage. One legitimately may not exist. If you cannot determine this aspect of the expert's knowledge, skip ahead to the next step. Otherwise, work through this topic as thoroughly as possible. When you present to the expert a prototype missing a procedural structure, one of the more immediate responses you will often get is the expert's feedback on the order of questioning. This is a trigger for you to more specifically refine and learn about the questioning and processing order the expert believes is necessary to best solve the problem.

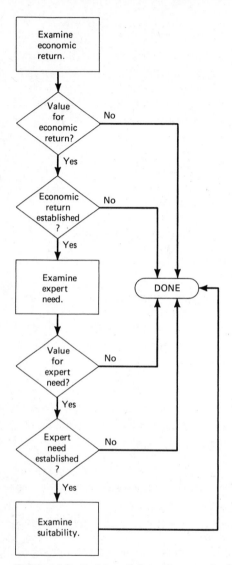

Figure 11.2. Problem-Solving Strategy for Sample Problem.

Thus you may come back to address this question later in the development process.

Make sure you differentiate between questions that are grouped together and those in which the particular order is critical. In the former case, it is not important to nail down the exact order since that order is not critical to the correctness of the knowledge. The issue of determining problem-solving strategy is one in which the exact order of questioning is an essential part of the expert's knowledge. Thus in the example, the order among economic return, expert need, and suitability is essential to properly representing the knowledge. Questions that conclude economic return, thus, are grouped and asked together. However, the order among those economic return questions is not a critical component of the expert's knowledge, and may even differ from consultation to consultation.

With What Concepts, Factors and Objects Does the Expert Reason?

We just named three key factors: economic return, expert need, and suitability. In addition, there are many other factors the expert considers. Here are some of them:

technical suitability	topic suitability
organizational suitability	multiple objects in domain
large difference in performers	costly mistakes made
problem well defined	domain stable
depend on common sense	dependent on sense data
solutions preenumerated	granular time descriptions required
three levels of object description	more than object in domain

What Are the Values of Those Factors?

Having itemized the concepts, factors, and objects we know about so far, we identify those for which we have values. For example, the expert expresses economic need as *justified* or *not justified.* These are determined by asking questions about financial return. The expert seems to use three terms to express expertise shortage or need: *no need, clearly needed,* and a variety of terms that could best be described as *ambiguous.*

The expert has stated that it is desirable that *suitability* be rated *high.* However, we don't know what other values he or she uses for this factor. As seen above, we have noted factors that the expert uses in thinking about suitability including three secondary factors named *topic suitability, technical_ suitability,* and *organizational_suitability.* However, we are not sure exactly how the expert uses the values of those factors to conclude suitability. Early in the process, there may be many factors like "suitability" about which your information is incomplete. Make a note of these areas at this time.

How Does the Expert Eliminate Possible Solutions?

How does the expert avoid investigating every possible combination of factors? Usually experts accomplish this by quickly narrowing the problem space. As an expert chess player quickly removes from consideration those lines of play that offer poor chances, most experts get rid of the low-potential options in order to focus their attention on those that offer better possibilities. Certain "knock-out" questions immediately end a consultation when a fatal answer is encountered. In our example, if the expert cannot establish a justified *economic return*, the expert immediately dismisses the domain. If there is not a justified *economic return* and acceptable *expert need*, the expert dismisses the domain without pursuing the *suitability* category of consideration. Thus the expert—and so the expert system—doesn't need to pay attention to combinations of factors that include unacceptably low values for economic return and expert need.

Similarly, certain conclusions can direct or deflect the expert's gaze toward or from particular lines of reasoning. For example, in a car diagnostic system, if the car won't start, the electric system becomes a primary target of inquiry. If the car *does* start, we know the problem is not the battery.

What Conclusions Does the Expert Make?

The next step is to determine as specifically as possible the kinds of conclusions the expert makes, and their values. In the example, the expert essentially does one of the following:

- recommends the domain *not* be pursued and explains why.
- ends a consultation having identified certain essential missing information. The user must get this information before a recommendation can be made.
- recommends the domain be pursued, perhaps qualified by certain improvements as a prerequisite to that approval.
- unconditionally recommends it be pursued.

The conclusions are not simple selections from a list of preenumerated answers, or if they are, we have not yet identified all the list members. Rather, the expert seems to contrast findings on the topic of economic return, expert need, and various facets of suitability to arrive at a conclusion.

Diagram the Relationships

The next step is to graph the implied relationships among the concepts and questions the expert asks in an "attribute hierarchy" or "attribute dependency" chart. This helps clarify how the "lower" concepts and questions make up the reasoning grist used by the expert to infer higher concepts. In other words, the chart shows which factors are used to conclude the major categories the expert says are used to drive the decision process (Figure 11.3). You use this chart to translate this knowledge into rules.

To create such a chart, you start by placing the goal at the highest level since the goal is the most dependent factor. In this case, the goal is *"advice,"* which can only be dispensed when one or more of the key factors below it have been inferred. Directly below the goal, you place the *primary factors*. Primary factors are the "big picture" concepts that the expert directly uses to conclude the goal. The attributes you use to represent these primary factors we call *primary attributes.* Below each primary factor, place those secondary factors that make up the primary factors—and so on.

As you fill in the attribute hierarchy, you will find that the facts that the expert asks the client fall at the bottom of the hierarchy. The request for facts gives the expert the building blocks with which to reason. The expert infers the higher-level concepts from these user responses to form intermediate con-

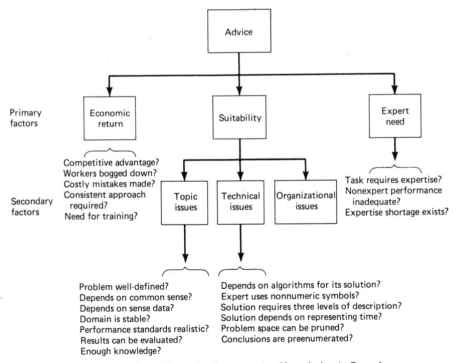

Figure 11.3. Partial Attribute Hierarchy Representing Knowledge in Sample Problem.

cepts. These are in turn formulated into primary "top-level" concepts which impact the conclusion directly. Thus you have four possible levels in the attribute hierarchy:

1. GOAL
2. PRIMARY CONCEPTS
3. INTERMEDIATE CONCEPTS (level two through n)
4. QUESTIONS (level n + 1)

Not all domains will display this four-level structure. For example, domains which can be represented by a truth table may have only two levels in which user responses to questions directly conclude the goal. Such expert systems work by asking questions and matching the answers to those questions directly to a conclusion. Figure 11.4 shows the structure of just such a small knowledge base. It recommends a software development language.

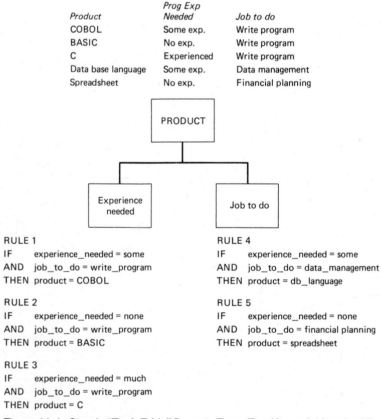

Product	Prog Exp Needed	Job to do
COBOL	Some exp.	Write program
BASIC	No exp.	Write program
C	Experienced	Write program
Data base language	Some exp.	Data management
Spreadsheet	No exp.	Financial planning

RULE 1
IF   experience_needed = some
AND   job_to_do = write_program
THEN product = COBOL

RULE 2
IF   experience_needed = none
AND   job_to_do = write_program
THEN product = BASIC

RULE 3
IF   experience_needed = much
AND   job_to_do = write_program
THEN product = C

RULE 4
IF   experience_needed = some
AND   job_to_do = data_management
THEN product = db_language

RULE 5
IF   experience_needed = none
AND   job_to_do = financial planning
THEN product = spreadsheet

Figure 11.4. Simple "Truth Table" Domain Type: Two Hierarchy Levels; All Rules Conclude the Goal.

The factors you use to represent the problem-solving strategy may be the same as the conceptual categories the expert uses to reason about the problem. In the example, the strategy is to first establish economic return, then expert need, and finally, suitability. The order of these items is important, according to the expert. They also happen to be important concepts the expert uses to develop a recommendation. This synonymous character is not always present. For example, a diagnostician may first ask a wide range of questions covering different topics before evaluating particular answers. Only then does he or she pursue detailed questioning sequences designed to pinpoint a cause. While this first step of the expert's problem-solving strategy could be described as "ask general questions to evaluate possible causes," the expert does not reason using a concept called "get general information." Therefore, make sure you independently distinguish the problem-solving approach from the ideas that the expert uses to reason about the domain.

The beneficial outcome of this diagramming exercise is that you gain a more concrete understanding of how the various reasoning components relate to each other. This helps you prioritize your work, determine where you stand so far, and eventually allows you to gather feedback from the expert in a focused way.

IS THE DOMAIN SUITABLE?

Having organized the preliminary findings of the early knowledge acquisition sessions, you now closely reexamine this information for compliance with the guidelines in Chapter 2 before continuing. You try to choose projects that offer good chances to provide economic return, supplement a shortage of expertise, and meet various suitability criteria.

How would the information we have just organized stand up against the suitability questions? At this point, we believe that the project would pass. The domain at this point seems well-defined, since the expert has been able to articulate a problem-solving approach that at this point seems to handle all cases in a manageable manner. By manageable, we mean that the expert has been clear at naming the factors he or she uses to evaluate the domain.

We believe that there is enough knowledge for the expert system to be useful. The expert examines one case at a time, and therefore there does not seem to be a need for three levels of description. The expert does not use a formula for evaluating the domain and thus the problem-solving method is not algorithmic. Time plays little or no role in the evaluation. The expert seems to be able to prune the problem space by eliminating possibilities quickly—for example, the consultation ends immediately if economic return cannot be established.

Yet there are some areas of uneasiness that we must pursue before completely declaring this domain as finally suitable. The expert claims the factors named so far represent the entire consideration process. This is a claim we do not accept at this point. We realize that when we show the prototype to the expert it is likely to trigger him or her to find other considerations that have not yet been articulated. We also realize at this point that we do not understand all of the concepts—for example, our understanding of how suitability is processed is incomplete. This is a warning sign that we must especially pursue clarification in the area of suitability in forthcoming acquisition sessions. Another area of concern we must focus on is that the recommendations do not seem to be preenumerated. There are many different recommendations the expert gives depending on a number of circumstances. We must better understand how these recommendations are developed.

Given this analysis, we believe that the goal of being able to evaluate candidate expert systems topics remains reasonable. We do not revise its scope given what we now know. We realize that, at this stage, it is normal and acceptable to have areas of uncertainty. At this stage, it is common that you have gaps and mistakes in your understanding. You have probably omitted essential elements. There may be technical aspects of the domain you simply have not yet grasped. This is normal and to be expected. It *should not* discourage you from trying to document what you do know in a prototype. The task of documenting your knowledge is a learning process that clarifies what you do and do not know. The outputs you produce then serve as a discussion topic for you and the expert.

CREATING THE FIRST PROTOTYPE

We've seen that knowledge explanations are hypotheses that require testing. The goal of the first prototype is to create a vehicle for testing your grasp of the expert's descriptions of the *most important* domain factors. It is not your goal, at this early stage, to encode everything you learned. What is most urgent is to test that your formulation of problem-solving strategy and "primary" concepts is as the expert describes it, and that these descriptions are capable of providing the desired results. Thus the primary focus of the first prototype is to capture and represent these two areas.

Create Control Rules

Control rules are those rules that represent the problem-solving strategy of the expert and control the rule consideration pattern of the inference engine. The order in which the expert considers various aspects of the problem may be an essential part of his or her expertise. Therefore, the skillful representation of this procedural knowledge in rules can be as important as representing the declarative knowledge that represents the expert's experience. Because many rule-based shells do not provide explicit procedural control, you often must use rules in order to achieve the control over consultation behavior you desire. By creating control rules as presented here, you can achieve control in a manner that makes these rules easy to read and maintain.

Control Rules in the Example. Let's look at how we might encode the control structure developed in the evaluation example. In backward chaining systems, you start by defining a goal. For this example, we will call the goal *processing_complete*. *Processing_complete* will be assigned a value when the consultation is finished—we'll use the value *done*. Because attribute *processing_complete*'s function is to control the order in which the consultation runs, the value it eventually gets is not important. This is one way to recognize attributes whose primary role is that of representing the problem-solving strategy within the knowledge base: they receive a "dummy" value. The attribute is used to force backward chaining in a certain direction. By using the value *"done"* we signify this.

One rule will conclude *processing_complete*:

RULE 1
IF consideration_order = done
AND advice = KNOWN
THEN processing_complete = done

Because *Rule 1* will be the only rule that concludes the goal *processing_complete*, it is guaranteed to be the first rule considered in the knowledge base. The attribute *consideration_order* will be assigned the value *done* when the problem-solving strategy represented in the diagram has been carried out. Afterwards, the control rule *Rule 1* will force backward chaining on the attribute *advice*. The inference engine then considers those rules that conclude advice, producing a recommendation. When that advice becomes known, the knowledge base's processing is complete. Thus there will be two kinds of knowledge in the knowledge base: rules concluding the attribute *consideration_order* representing the expert's problem-solving strategy, and rules representing the inferential knowledge that conclude the attribute *advice*.

The next step is to encode the rules that represent the expert's problem-solving strategy as shown in Figure 11.2. The high-level control structure of the example is straightforward. The expert pursues economic return, expert need, and suitability in sequence. Pursuit of the latter primary factors depends on successfully establishing values for the earlier ones. This can be represented by the following rules:

RULE 2
IF economic_return = not_justified
OR economic_return NOT = KNOWN
THEN consideration_order = done

RULE 3
IF   economic_return = justified
AND expert_need = no_need
OR   expert_need NOT = KNOWN
THEN consideration_order = done

RULE 4
IF   economic_return = justified
AND expert_need = clearly_needed
OR   expert_need = ambiguous
AND suitability_script = done
THEN consideration_order = done

RULE 5
IF   suit_immediate_rejection = KNOWN
THEN suitability_script = done

RULE 6
IF   suit_immediate_rejection NOT = KNOWN
AND topic_suitability = done
AND technical_suitability = done
AND organizational_suitability = done
THEN suitability_script = done

Because the knowledge base's goal is *processing_done,* the inference engine first considers *Rule 1. Rule 1* in turn forces backward chaining on attribute *consideration_order. Rule 2* is processed forcing consideration of as yet unwritten rules that conclude *economic_return.* This exactly reflects the expert's strategy: first pursue the question of *economic_return. Rule 2* tests that *economic_return's* value becomes known and is instantiated to *justified.* This reflects the expert's belief that *economic_return* must be positively established for the consultation to continue. If these conditions are not confirmed, then the information seeking portion of the consultation is done. Control returns to *Rule 1* which then must conclude advice based on this situation.

Rule 3 and *Rule 4* work on similar principles. Note that each rule begins by testing that *economic_return = justified.* Since finding *economic_return* is a precondition for proceeding to the next categories, the first premise clause of each rule is a key part of the knowledge. The first premise clause screens the applicability of the rule's remaining knowledge, that is, it guarantees that economic return has been sought before considering subsequent clauses.[1] If the first clause passes, a value for the next primary concept is pursued. *Rule 3* establishes that *expert_need* is known and not contraindicated, or else process-

---

[1]This idea is essential to good rule construction and is pursued in Chapter 12.

ing is completed. *Rule 4* forces backward chaining on rules concluding *suit-ability_script,* assuming that its necessary prior conditions are verified in its first three premise clauses.

When the rules concluding *consideration_order* have been processed, the inference engine will have driven the consultation according to the expert's problem-solving strategy. No advice is yet given, but *Rule 1* will now cause the advice-producing stage of the consultation to occur.

What If There Is No Problem-Solving Strategy? If there is no problem-solving strategy, or that strategy turns out to resemble the two-level hierarchy discussed earlier, you simply move on to the next step. For example, if the expert in the example had explained that the primary concepts *economic_return, expert_need,* and *suitability* were all pursued in no particular order, there would be no problem-solving strategy to encode. Similarly, if the domain resembles the language advisor example in which there are no intermediate levels of inference, there would be no need for control rules.

Create Rules Using Primary Concepts That Give Advice

Once you've expressed in rules whatever problem-solving strategy seems to exist, you write those rules that conclude final advice. Don't worry about the form of the advice, that is, "prettying up" how the consultation works. Instead, focus your efforts on representing as many rule combinations that provide the *final recommendation* as you understand the expert to have described them. Thus the rules you write at this stage should conclude *advice* and contain attributes representing primary concepts or other factors directly impacting that advice (Figure 11.5).

The expert may have described somewhat detailed lines of reasoning that conclude primary concepts. Don't encode this knowledge yet. To get values for the primary concepts, create prompts that ask the user to enter values for these factors. For example, even though the primary concept *economic_return* is inferred by secondary concepts, for now, create a user prompt that asks, "What is the economic need?"

Create Rules for Which You Don't Have Information

Depending on how many primary attributes you define, and how many values those primary attributes can have, you may have as few as two and as many as fifty or more rules resulting from your work on the section above. The knowl-

RULE 7
IF   economic_return NOT = KNOWN
THEN   advise = get_answers

RULE 8
IF   economic_return = not_justified
THEN   advise = don't_do_project

RULE 9
IF   economic_return = justified
AND   expert_need NOT = KNOWN
THEN   advise = get_answers

RULE 10
IF   economic_return = justified
AND   expert_need = no_need
THEN   advise = dont_do_project

RULE 11
IF   economic_return = justified
AND   expert_need = clearly_needed
AND   suitability = high
THEN   advise = definitely_do_the_project

RULE 12
IF   economic_return = justified
AND   expert_need = clearly_needed
AND   suitability = low
THEN   advise = don't_do_project

RULE 13
IF   suitability_immediate_rejection = yes
THEN   suitability = low

Figure 11.5. High-Level Rules Based on Initial Understanding of the Domain.

edge contained in those rules may not cover every possible combination of primary attributes' values. In other words, there are probably combinations of factors for which you don't yet know the final advice. These are gaps in your knowledge. Create rules that describe these gaps. Make them conclude some place-holding symbol you design to mean "conclusion not yet provided." When you demonstrate the prototype to the expert, you will want to bring up these cases so you can fill in the gaps. Creating these rules helps you define exactly what these missing areas are. If there are broad ranges of unknown conclusions, use disjunctions to summarize the options included in the range.

For example:

RULE 14
IF   economic_need = justified
AND   expert_need = ambiguous
OR   expert_need = clearly_needed
AND   suitability NOT = KNOWN
OR   suitability = ambiguous
THEN advise = not_yet_known

In this form, the rule covers four conjunction cases—each containing the first premise clause, one of the two values for *expert_need,* and one of the two values for *suitability.*

Many of the scenarios these rules encode may be unlikely or impossible outcomes. Let the expert tell you this. For instance, in the above example rule, the expert may say that there is no such thing as UNKNOWN suitability. If the user does not respond to questions, then you simply ask the question again, or ask the user to find out the answer. This input gives you valuable insight on how to treat input to the secondary concepts later, when you encode these lower aspects of the expert system.

Some of these gaps may represent situations which are real and plausible. In this case, the expert will provide you the correct recommendation. You can then jointly explore how such a line of reasoning might occur, engaging you in a knowledge acquisition session for the case. Rule-encoding the high-level cases you don't know gives you examples to show the expert. They provide a vehicle for getting information about new cases that expand your knowledge and, hopefully, give you a deeper insight into the domain.

If you omit this step, the expert system will usually give a final recommendation of UNKNOWN when the inference engine infers a combination of factors that no rule covers. You try to anticipate these combinations and encode them as above so that the inference engine's UNKNOWN response uncovers gaps in response combinations you failed to anticipate. This makes the UNKNOWN response of the inference engine more meaningful.

Code Knock-Outs

Regardless of where they appear in the hierarchy, some individual factors may force immediate rejection of a case. These are called "knock-outs." For example, if the answer to the suitability category *domain_well_defined* is *"no,"* the topic is rejected regardless of its other merits. A poorly defined domain makes an unacceptable topic, and causes immediate rejection of the topic in that form. Because of its dire and direct impact on the recommendation, you code this rule now.

Most domains have knock-out factors. Knock-outs are important because they narrow the space that the rest of the expert system must address and help you gauge the breadth of the remaining space. This narrowing by rule of thumb is a classic expert behavior. You acquire these knock-outs from the responses to your question, "Are there ever cases in which one or two questions lead immediately to a conclusion?"

RULE 15
IF   domain_well_defined = no
OR   results_can_be_evaluated = no
THEN suit_immediate_rejection = yes

Code Full Cases?

When you have completed the above steps, the prototype may still be rather small. This is completely acceptable. For example, some diagnostic applications may have only a few primary decision factors with a limited number of values and an equally small number of preenumerated conclusions. Such a system may yet have many detailed and in-depth inferential levels in order to reach the right conclusion which the prototype does not yet include. The small size of the prototype is acceptable because of the importance of the knowledge it contains. You are ready to get feedback from the expert.

If you have more time to work on a small prototype that has just a few conclusions and primary concepts, you may code one or several "typical" cases if you've acquired the knowledge to do so. This will allow you also to get feedback from the expert that you indeed understand the "character" of the typical consultation as well as to gain insight into the correctness of the case or cases you encode (Figure 11.6).

When encoding these test cases, do not necessarily try to encode every possible value one branch could contain. One branch may require several questions, which lead to various inferences, each of which has several possible values. You do not need to create rules that encompass all possible combinations. Instead, create one or several rules that produce a consultation effect that reflects your current understanding of how a consultation proceeds. When you create these additional rules, you will most likely add rules that use secondary and tertiary level attributes. Some of these will prompt for values. Accept the fact that since you are now working depth-wise down the hierarchy, the expert system will require very specific answers in order to get the line of reasoning to work for that particular case. The idea here is to test the consultation character, questioning order, and concept hierarchy by getting expert feedback as to how you believe it works.

Remember, don't feel obligated to add full cases at this stage. This is especially true if you have many rules that use primary concepts. Getting

RULE 16
IF   competitive_advantage = yes
OR   workers_bogged_down = yes
OR   costly_mistakes_made = yes
OR   consistent_approach_made = yes
OR   need_for_training = yes
THEN   economic_return = justified

RULE 17
IF   task_requires_expertise = yes
AND   nonexpert_performance_inadequate = yes
AND   expertise_shortage = high
THEN   expert_need = clearly_needed

RULE 18
IF   few_experts_in_short_supply = yes
AND   expert_travels_often = yes
AND   difficult_to_see = yes
THEN   expertise_shortage = yes

Figure 11.6. Detail Rules Filling Out Several Full Cases.

feedback on your grasp of that top level is the most important goal of the first prototype. If time permits and the problem is relatively simple at the top, then go ahead and work down the hierarchy by coding several representative cases.

SHOWING THE PROTOTYPE

When you have completed the first prototype, you are ready to meet with the expert. This meeting has the following two major goals, as will all future meetings:

to test the knowledge you acquired from prior meetings.
to get new knowledge so you can expand the knowledge base.

This continues until the expert system is finished.

Set an Agenda

Because time with your expert may be scarce, you need to make the best use of the time you have together. Before each acquisition session, set focused goals and a clear agenda. In these sessions, you use the prototype as a starting point. Usually you will first allocate time for the expert to "play" with the prototype. Once he or she feels comfortable using a computer and the software, you may be able to have the expert review it before the meeting. However, it can be instructive to watch the expert work with a new version for the first time. This is especially true early in the development process. A good format is to review what you did at the last meeting, outline the progress you think the prototype represents, and identify key questions that remain. Then let the expert work independently with the software for a while. Allow him or her to provide unstructured feedback on what is being seen (make sure the video or audio tape is running). When opportunities arise, ask questions about points of special interest to you.

The second agenda point should be to deal with points raised by the prototype review. This includes getting corrections as well as new information. For the first meetings, focus on high-level, big-picture feedback. Here you may direct the expert's attention to particular areas of the prototype.

You have several particular topics for the first meeting in which you show a prototype. You want to test your formulation of the problem-solving strategy and attribute hierarchy. You want to make sure you properly represent primary concepts. You also need to make sure that the values you use for those primary concepts are correct and complete. Moreover, you want to verify that your understanding of the final advice the expert gives is correct. Get feedback on any knock-outs you encoded.

For each area in which you encounter omissions, misunderstandings, or errors, you move back into the knowledge acquisition phase.

Continuing Knowledge Acquisition: A Three-Step Approach

When you identify areas requiring more work, you return to knowledge acquisition mode. Insofar as the acquisition categories examined in the last chapter require refining, you return to addressing those questions. However, as you firm up the expert system's conceptual framework, your acquisition work will begin to evolve more to the analysis of particular detailed cases. This is the stage at which you probably spend the most development time. For this activity, we recommend the straightforward, three-step approach put forth by Walters and Nielsen in *Crafting Knowledge-Based Systems*.[2]

Determine Next Step. Using the list of symptoms and conclusions you've developed, select one. Ask the expert to step you through how she or he solves that problem with a query like "What do you ask or do next?" The expert describes the problem-solving activity as a series of actions or steps. You

---

[2]John R. Walters and Norman R. Nielsen, *Crafting Knowledge-Based Systems: Expert Systems Made Realistic* (New York: Wiley Interscience, 1988), 37.

determine how each step works. For each step that is named, get two other pieces of information.

What Does It Mean? The expert may name the step using some domain-specific jargon. The meaning may not be clear. Dwell on the step until you clearly follow the description. The question "What does it mean?" gets the expert to focus enough attention on the topic to flush out the assumptions that may underlie the step. For example, the conversation may disclose that this "one step" is actually a number of discrete steps. In such a case, you would separate them and deal with them one at a time.

"Why Do You Do That?" This helps you grasp the rationale used by the expert for taking the step. When you ask, "What are you looking for when you ask this?" or "Why do you do that?", you're asking what *conclusions* the expert draws from that step. Once you understand this, you've understood the implications of the question or step.

Example

Knowledge Engineer (KE): What do you do next?
Expert: Next I determine whether or not the domain is well defined.
KE: What does that mean?
Expert: It means that the project definition must have borders. There must be a definition of what it will and will not do.
KE: How do you determine that? *(asking for more "what does that mean?" information)*
Expert: I ask some questions. *(Aha! This step is actually a number of steps. Let's get the "why do you do that?" information and then investigate the component steps further.)*
KE: Why do you need to know whether the domain is well defined?
Expert: It is important in order to establish a finishing line for the project as well as to evaluate whether the problem space is a reasonable size. My experience is that these are both important for the project to eventually succeed.
KE: You mentioned that you "ask some questions" to determine whether the domain is well defined. Do you ask them in any particular order? *(Again, asking "what do you do next," giving insight into the problem-solving strategy.)*
Expert: Yes. First, I ask what cases of the problem they anticipate solving. Then, I ask what cases the expert system will *not* solve. Often, the client has not thought about this. Finally, I find out if there are knock-outs. That is, I determine if there are ways in which the expert rapidly narrows the problem space.

KE: (after capturing each question) Can you tell me more about how you get the information about which cases they anticipate solving? *(More on "what do they do next," leading to "what does it mean"?)*

Apply this three-question approach repeatedly as you unpack the steps taken by the expert in solving the problem. Your success at getting at the meaning and rationale for each step dictates how fast you can proceed. Sometimes, the process is smooth and clean. At other times, the expert may continually refine the description inserting step after step into what was first described as a "simple" two- or three-step process. Remind yourself to remain flexible as you gather this information. While you want to understand what is being said, do not get frustrated as the process evolves and certain steps are replaced or supplemented by others.

The three-question approach is also useful early in the knowledge engineering process. This is especially true when the expert has a hard time initially describing his or her reasoning in the abstract. In such cases, turn your efforts to having the expert describe how he or she solves a few actual or hypothetical cases. You use the three-question technique to help along these descriptions. When these descriptions are captured, investigate whether those steps represent problem-solving strategies or representation schemes that can be generalized to other cases.

Other Prototyping Issues

As we observed at the start of this chapter, prototyping is an iterative process in which you build the expert system little by little. Each interview presents to the expert what you learned in prior meetings in the software form of a prototype. Then you discuss areas in which you are uncertain, knowledge is incomplete, and you cover new cases. In the early stages, the proper representation of the problem-solving strategy and attribute hierarchy is the most important issue. As you progress, you fill in each line of reasoning using the three-phase interviewing technique. As the prototype matures, a number of issues will become more important. We itemize some of these questions here.

What is the Role of UNKNOWN? What if the user doesn't know the answer to a question? Most shells let users answer UNKNOWN. If you decide to accept this, the knowledge base must contain knowledge for handling this response. There are three typical strategies:

Don't Allow It: If the user answers UNKNOWN, end the consultation. Inform the user that the information is mandatory for the expert system to give meaningful advice.

Reason with It: Most shells allow rules to test for UNKNOWN. Therefore, you can create rules that reason about the known or unknown status of an attribute. Such rules are usually created for primary concepts and other information that is essential for carrying out the consultation. For example, *Rule 14* on page 199 shows a rule that tests to see if attribute *suitability* is unknown. If the expert reasons about known/unknown status of information, you can create rules that make decisions based on the fact that values for important conceptual categories cannot be inferred.

Ignore It: The user's UNKNOWN response eliminates the path being currently considered. In this case, the UNKNOWN entry simply causes those rules depending on a specific value to fail. This is analogous to the expert's ignoring paths in which data are missing; he or she simply goes on to consider others. In such cases, let the inference engine fail those rules that depend on a value other than UNKNOWN by ignoring any particular processing of the status of the attribute. If none of the normal lines of reasoning succeeds, the higher-level concept depending on that answer may also become unknown.

For more on reasoning about the unknown, see Chapter 6.

Ask for Facts, Not Judgments. A common error in formulating user prompts is asking users to draw conclusions and inferences they are not qualified to make. For example, the question *"Is the problem one that relies on sense data?"* could be regarded as one that asks the casual user to draw a conclusion he or she is not qualified to make. The issue here is whether or not users will interpret "sense data" in precisely the same way that the expert does. Since the concept of "sense data" could plausibly be regarded as ambiguous, the question should be reformulated as one or more questions that ask for facts instead of judgments. The expert system should then reason about these facts to make its own judgments that represent the expert's view. For example:

```
RULE sense_data_test
IF     color = yes
OR     shapes = yes
OR     sounds = yes
OR     textures = yes
THEN sense_data = yes
```

Each attribute in the rule's premise has an associated prompt which asks for data based on simple observations. For attribute *sounds,* for example, the prompt might read *"Does the expert use the sense of hearing to solve the problem?"* Based on these more objective responses then, the rule "decides" whether the problem relies on sense data or not.

DETECTING LEVELS OF ABSTRACTION

One of the more conceptually difficult and important steps in mapping the expert's descriptions to rules as you continue work is detecting "levels of abstraction." Finding an "abstraction level" here means determining that several consideration steps used at different points of the reasoning process can be represented by one concept. This is important because detecting and representing implicit abstraction levels can generalize the knowledge in the expert system, separate procedural knowledge representing the problem-solving strategy from declarative knowledge, reduce the knowledge base's size, and improve its clarity.

For example, consider an expert system that diagnoses problems in printers and display terminals. The expert describes one aspect of the strategy for solving terminal problems as "checking for simple problems." This can be represented as follows:

RULE 1
IF   terminal_turned_on = no
OR   terminal_not_plugged_into_wall = yes
OR   plug_not_connected_to_terminal = yes
THEN terminal_problem = found

The rule concludes a dummy value which signals that *terminal_problem* is an attribute representing procedural knowledge. Later, you find that the expert uses a similar reasoning line for printer problems.

RULE 2
IF   printer_turned_on = no
OR   printer_not_plugged_into_wall = yes
OR   plug_not_connected_to_printer = yes
THEN printer_problem = found

Upon closer examination, you can see that what we really have is a common problem-solving approach that could be called *easy_general_causes;* that is, the expert screens the problem for easy causes. This would allow you to simplify these rules so that the pursuit of one attribute would drive all questioning associated with determining a value for *easy_general_causes*. This gives us:

RULE 1
IF   easy_general_causes = yes
THEN terminal_problem = found

RULE 2
IF   easy_general_causes = yes
THEN printer_problem = found

RULE 3
IF   device_turned_on = no
OR   device_not_plugged_into_wall = yes
OR   device_not_connected_to_printer = yes
THEN easy_general_causes = yes[3]

Note how you started with two different rules that concluded basically the same thing. Once this realization was made, you were able to generalize that knowledge and make it apply to more than one situation.

Also notice how the details get pushed out of *Rule 1* and *Rule 2* as you abstract them to a higher level. As you learn of other high-level strategies the expert uses for attacking the problem, you may be able to detect other abstraction levels for those investigations too. Thus *Rule 2* may evolve to look like this:

RULE 2
IF   easy_general_causes = yes
OR   easy_printer_problem = yes
OR   spooler_problem = yes
OR   . . .
THEN printer_problem = found

RULE 4
IF   printer_not_online = yes
OR   printer_out_of_paper = yes
OR   . . .
THEN easy_printer_problem = yes

The detail questions are pushed down into rules that conclude attributes standing in for those detail questions. Therefore, the high-level rules express the problem-solving strategy, and the lower rules actually drive the questioning for detail data. The conceptual rules summarize the overall approach and drive the pursuit of those attributes that are needed to conclude the higher-level concept.

Not only does this approach make explicit the implicit strategy of the expert, it makes the questioning process easier to control and refine. This happens because one attribute (*easy_general_causes*) represents an entire group of attributes on whose values it depends. Therefore, whenever you refer to that attribute in a rule premise, you cause the inference engine to seek values for those needed attributes. For example, suppose the expert decides later that the reasoning actually involves considering printer-specific problems

---

[3]The example assumes that terminal problems and printer problems are mutually exclusive, which for the example from which it was taken, they were.

first. In this case, you simply exchange the places of *easy_general_causes* and *easy_printer_problem* in *Rule 2:*

RULE 2
IF   easy_printer_problem = yes
OR   easy_general_causes = yes
OR   spooler_problem = yes
OR   . . .
THEN printer_problem = found

The inference engine now seeks those rules that conclude *easy_printer_problem* first, causing questioning and inferencing on that group of topics.

How do you detect levels of abstraction? First, you develop them explicitly in the attribute hierarchy. Those concepts that appear directly below one factor directly contribute to concluding its value. Thus your rule-building approach should reflect this. Second, listen for hints the expert gives you during the knowledge acquisition process. This often happens in the form of labeling groups of questions. For example, when the expert says "Then I check for operational problems," or "First I check to make sure that it's not something dumb like . . . ." In the first case, the use of the plural clues you that there is more than one question in the category called *operational problems.* In the latter, there may be a category called *dumb causes* of which one example is (. . .).

SUMMARY

Prototyping serves two critical purposes: it helps you test your understanding of acquired knowledge, and it helps the expert refine his or her descriptions. Because of its tangibility, the software prototype offers the best possible vehicle for both activities.

In this chapter, we offered a method for prototyping. It helps you turn your initial acquisition efforts into software in a way that quickly gets you maximum feedback in the most critical areas: understanding the expert's problem-solving strategy, the advice he or she gives. You refine this understanding before traveling too far down a wrong path. Because the acquisition process is one in which you learn a little at a time, you continue to examine the project's suitability and requirements as you learn about the domain. Once you firm up your understanding and confirm the project's merit and feasibility, you deepen the knowledge base's reasoning and add cases as necessary.

12 | *Guidelines for Knowledge Base Development*

The goal of good knowledge base design is to realize the advantages which expert systems promise over conventional programs. These include transparency, ease of maintenance, and the separation of knowledge from the processing of that knowledge. An expert system's architecture differs from that of conventional programs. Creating that structure can confound first-time expert systems developers. Therefore this chapter is especially important if you are relatively new to developing rule-based expert systems.

If you are the expert or are new to software development, you may have only the mostly vaguely defined notion of software development methodologies and knowledge base organization. If this description fits you, you may suffer from a lack of direction in organizing your work.

If you are experienced in conventional software development, you may have the opposite problem. Thoroughly versed in the rules of "structured programming" and other methodologies, you bring a rigid, formalized point of view to your work. While this is useful in conventional programming, it may cause you to try to "over-control" and proceduralize the knowledge bases you write. Structured programming approaches, now taken for granted by many, often lead down fruitless paths in expert systems development. Trying to use these approaches in expert systems development may lead to poorly organized, bug-ridden, opaque knowledge bases that are difficult to read and maintain. You are using a method which is not applicable to rule-based expert systems.

This chapter discusses knowledge base organization. We cover here those principles you should keep in mind when developing rule-based expert systems regardless of the domain. By applying these principles, you can avoid testing and debugging problems that many developers needlessly encounter. These guidelines remain constant regardless of the shell you choose.[1]

---

[1] The exception is the "state-based" tool, such as Radian's RuleMaster™ and AION's ADS™. While the guidelines for organizing rules within states may apply, their big picture architecture is usually different enough that the general approach does not.

GOALS OF KNOWLEDGE BASE ARCHITECTURE

Effective use of organization techniques provides three major benefits for your development effort. First, it enables you to minimize the procedural content of rules. By keeping knowledge separate from the inference engine that processes that knowledge, the knowledge base becomes easier to maintain. Second, following these guidelines makes the knowledge base easier to read. Third, the knowledge base will be better organized, making it easier to find your way around the knowledge base during development and debugging.

Organizing Rules

Rules can appear throughout the knowledge base with much less concern for order than in conventional programs. In conventional software, the statement order *is* the program. When you change the order, you change the operation, functionality, and character of the program. Such changes modify what the program does and thus statement order is a crucial element of the code's "correctness."

The backward chaining inference engine selects those rules that can conclude the current goal. The forward chaining inference engine processes all rules based on the facts that have accumulated, usually in a sequential manner. Therefore, a rule's relative position does not determine whether or not it will be considered. This makes the position of rules much less significant.

How you organize rules within the knowledge base can affect when the rule is processed, however. This may be significant in influencing user satisfaction and the performance of the system. Moreover, rule organization can also influence how easy the knowledge base is to read, maintain, and debug. Because one of the goals of the expert system is to document domain knowledge, readability is an important goal in itself. Just as structured programming eases maintenance and debugging of conventional programs, good rule organization can increase productivity and ease the upkeep of the expert system.

Three guidelines for organizing rules follow.

Organize Like Rules Together

Group rules that conclude the same thing together. This provides a framework for expansion, providing areas for future developers, maintenance engineers, or experts to add new rules. It also makes it easier to read and debug.

A common bug you will encounter is that an attribute seems to bind to incorrect values. This usually happens because a rule is misstated or its knowledge is improperly formulated. It may be difficult to determine which particular rule fired and instantiated the incorrect value. Any one of many different rules might apply.[2]

By grouping rules together by conclusion, you make it easier to locate the incorrect rule. You will also have an easier time comparing like rules and, therefore, detecting syntax errors among attributes you meant to be the same. Moreover, if the development shell offers a "trace" capability, this technique makes it easier to identify ranges of rules while the inference engine considers the knowledge base.

Place Most Likely Rules First

Within each group of rules that conclude the same attribute, order the rules from most to least likely. This serves several purposes. Virtually all backward chaining inference engines select the first rule they find that concludes the current goal. By placing the most likely rule first, you reduce the number of rules the inference engine must consider. This can improve performance.

You may also reduce the number of questions the inference engine asks. The more rules the inference engine considers, the more likely it is to encounter other unknown attributes which cause it to backward chain and ultimately seek additional information. By placing the more likely rules first, you avoid having these less likely lines of reasoning explored when the most likely scenario is true.

Finally, the order you establish for the rules within the knowledge base serves as documentation of rule importance to the reader of your work. Place a comment at the top of your knowledge bases stating that rules concluding the same attribute are grouped together and ordered from most to least likely. Have the expert help you order rules along these lines. By following this convention, you add knowledge content to the knowledge base.

There are times you may want to break this rule. The "most likely" line of reasoning may require an involved reasoning or query process. If this is the case, you may have a less likely rule that nonetheless requires no user prompts or a very short line of reasoning. You may want to consider this less likely route first, because of its low cost, for those times when it does happen to apply. Be sure to add comments to the knowledge base that document this choice of route.

---

[2]This trait of rule-based systems is called "poor behavior visibility."

Organize Rules Hierarchically

Once you have grouped rules together by what they conclude, which groups should appear first? Place first those groups that conclude the highest-level attributes. This means that you should place rules that conclude the knowledge base goal first. Place next, those rule groups that are directly necessary to conclude the goal. These are the attributes that appear in the premises of concluding the knowledge base goal. Follow those rule groups by sets that conclude the attributes necessary to conclude the second group. The guideline can be summarized as

> Place rule groups concluding an attribute below those in which the attribute appears in the premise.

Figure 12.1 shows the attribute dependency relationships for a knowledge base that screens prospective bank tellers. Figure 12.2 shows an abbreviated version of that knowledge base to illustrate how this translates to the organizational approach just discussed.

This approach offers the potential for increasing performance in some expert systems shells. Because this method ensures that the rules concluding the goal always appear first, the inference engine's search is often more

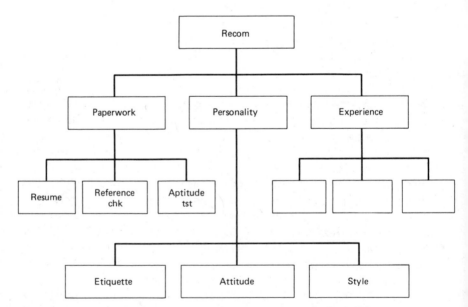

Figure 12.1. Dependency Relationships among Attributes for Bank Teller Hiring Knowledge Base.

```
!        Bank Teller Hiring Knowledge Base                                      *
!        The exclamation point to the left means this line is a comment         *
!        The goal is a recommendation we want to offer

Goal: RECOM

!******************************************************************************  *
!******************************************************************************  *
!******* Level One. The first rules conclude the recommendation                 *
!******* because this is the top level goal.                                    *
!******************************************************************************  *
!******************************************************************************  *


RULE Paperwork_knockout
IF      paperwork = fails
THEN recom = don't_hire

RULE Best_case
IF      paperwork = passes
AND   personality = very_good
AND   experience = very_good
THEN recom = make_top_offer;

!******* Here appear the rest of the rules concluding "recom"


. . .


!******************************************************************************  *
!******************************************************************************  *
!****** This starts Level Two: those rules that conclude the                    *
!****** attributes used in the rules that conclude "recom."                     *
!****** The following rules determine "paperwork": the first of three           *
!****** attributes ultimately needed to conclude the recommendation.            *
!****** "Paperwork" is yes/no: it either fails or passes the candidate          *
!******************************************************************************  *
!******************************************************************************  *


RULE Is_paperwork_ok
IF      reference_chk = fails
OR     aptitude_tst = fails
OR     resume = misrepresented
THEN paperwork = fails

!****** Note we write out the following rule instead of using ELSE above.

RULE Pass_paperwork
IF      reference_chk = passes
AND   aptitude_tst = passes
AND   resume = passes
THEN paperwork = passes;
```

Figure 12.2. Bank Teller Hiring Knowledge Base.

```
!**********************************************************************    *
!******* The following rules determine if the candidate's personality is   *
!****** conducive to working as a bank teller. This is the second of the    *
!******second-level attributes that conclude "recom."                       *
!**********************************************************************    *


RULE personality_knockouts
IF     etiquette = fails
OR     attitude = fails
OR     style = fails
THEN personality = fails

RULE perfect_personality
IF     etiquette = very_good
AND   attitude = very_good
AND   style = very_good
THEN personality = very_good

!******* The rest of the personality rules appear here.

. . .


!**********************************************************************    *
!******* The following rules determine if the candidate's experience is    *
!******* acceptable. This is the last of the three attributes that          *
!******* conclude the recommendation.                                       *
!**********************************************************************    *

!******* Rules concluding "Experience" appear here.

. . .


!**********************************************************************    *
!**********************************************************************    *
!****** Here starts Level Three. Below here would appear the rules          *
!****** necessary for concluding those attributes used in the premises      *
!****** of the second level rules concluding "paperwork," "personality,"    *
!****** and "experience" above.                                             *
!**********************************************************************    *
!**********************************************************************    *


!**********************************************************************    *
!****** "Paperwork" rules: they conclude "reference_chk," "aptitude_tst,"   *
!****** and "resume."                                                       *
!**********************************************************************    *


. . .


!**********************************************************************    *
!****** "Personality" rules: they conclude "etiquette," "attitude,"         *
!****** and "style."                                                        *
!**********************************************************************    *
```

Figure 12.2. *Continued.*

. . .

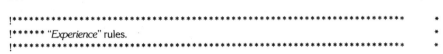

```
!*********************************************************************    *
!****** "Experience" rules.                                              *
!*********************************************************************    *
```

Figure 12.2. *Continued.*

efficient. More importantly, this approach makes the knowledge base more readable because it shows the most important rules first. These rules reflect the high-level reasoning of the domain expert and thereby give readers a sense of the general approach the expert uses. Readers can subsequently pursue those parts of that reasoning in which they are interested. Those rules appear immediately following the rules that conclude the goal.

If your expert system allows the user to choose the consultation goal, there may be more than one knowledge base goal. In this case, it's your choice which goal should appear first. If you have a default goal or one that users choose most often, put it first. Whatever choice you make, always try to organize the knowledge base from the highest conceptual level downwards. First, rules that conclude goals. Next, the rules concluding attributes needed to conclude the goal. Next, those rules that conclude the previous group of attributes. And so on.

One final problem you may encounter is that some expert systems shells don't give you direct control over rule order. They provide an integrated editing environment with which you cannot directly control where the rule resides. If this is the case for you, you will usually find that some mechanism exists for controlling rule order indirectly. Some shells enable you to create "rule groups" in which you can place logically related sets of rules. Others provide a PRIORITY feature for expressing the relative importance of a rule in relation to other rules concluding the same attribute (we examine this more in-depth in Chapter 13).

REFRAIN FROM "PROCEDURALIZING" THE KNOWLEDGE BASE

One of the most common obstacles encountered by veteran conventional programmers building their first expert system is the urge to control *exactly* how the knowledge base is processed by the inference engine. This feeling is natural: conventional programs follow step-by-step instructions. Programmers write those instructions. This is usually counterproductive in rule-based expert systems programming.

The job of the expert systems developer using rule-based shells is to acquire and declare domain knowledge in the form of rules. Stated another way, their job is to tell the computer *what to know,* not *what to do.* The "what to do" aspect is already done in the inference engine. The inference engine is specifically designed to process the knowledge base. Thus developers must undergo a shift in thinking that can, at first, be frustrating. In effect, you must give up control.

The benefits of properly adopting the nonprocedural approach are twofold. First, because the knowledge is not intertwined with how the knowledge is processed, you can more freely change the knowledge base without concern for adversely affecting other parts of the knowledge base. Because each rule is a *declaration* instead of a procedure, each is a relatively independent unit. Second, because you keep procedural coding out of rules, you improve their readability. Again, you gain the benefit of easier maintenance and better transparency.

We saw in the previous section that organizing rules is useful for documentation and maintenance. Do not confuse this, however, with the urge to predict and control how every rule gets processed. The former makes it easy to find a specific rule. The latter tries to force the inference engine to process rules in a lockstep manner. If your application really requires extensive step-by-step control, you have probably chosen a task that is better suited for conventional programming languages. The following guidelines are intended to give you a start in overcoming the urge to overcontrol the expert systems environment.

The "Nested IF" Problem

Perhaps the classic first-time mistake new developers run into is what we call the "nested if" problem. It arises from the observation that conventional programmers are experienced working with IF/THEN constructions that differ in meaning between conventional programming and expert systems. This leads them into trying to crowbar their familiar method into the slightly different meaning that the construct has in expert systems. This doesn't work.

To show what we mean, look at Figure 12.3, written in a C-like code.

The code contains a lot of information and provides precise control to the programmer in a concise form. Here's what it means: If the variable *paperwork* equals a constant represented by the symbol *PASSES*, the program evaluates the next expression indented to the right. A similar evaluation takes place for *personality.* If it equals *VERY_GOOD,* then the innermost "if" tests to see whether *experience* equals the constant *VERY_GOOD.* If all three tests are true, the program prints the statement: "**Make a top offer.**"

If the first two tests pass but *experience* does not equal *VERY_GOOD,* the action following the inner ELSE takes place: print "**Make a good offer.**" If the second test fails, the action following the ELSE directly below its corre-

```
if (paperwork = = PASSES)
    if (personality = = VERY_GOOD)
        if (experience = = VERY_GOOD)
            printf("Make a top offer");
        else
            printf("Make a good offer");
    else
        printf("Make adequate offer");
else
    printf("Candidate fails: make no offer");
```

Figure 12.3. A "Nested-if" Structure Written in C Language.

sponding "if" statement is executed: "**Make an adequate offer.**" Finally, if the first test fails, the action following the bottom and last ELSE takes place: "**Candidate fails: make no offer.**"

Note several important things about this example. First, this single expression actually contains four separate actions—all of them a "printf()" function which displays a message. Second, the "if/else" code is a *control structure*; that is, the IF/THEN structures pass control to particular statements. Some action is guaranteed to take place once this code is encountered. This is because each IF/THEN has a corresponding ELSE. Without explicitly stating it, the ELSE condition holds the place of the test's negation. The first IF tests whether *paperwork equals PASSES*. Its corresponding ELSE has the implicit meaning: *paperwork does not equal PASSES*.

Third, each time one of the IF/THEN expressions is true, an implied control transfer takes place within the expression. That is, if *paperwork equals PASSES*, then it is mandatory that control be passed to the next test *(personality equals VERY_GOOD)*. One consequence of this control transfer is that the conclusion "**Candidate fails**" can no longer be obtained. Another is that the conclusion "**Make adequate offer**" becomes possible. Another way to look at this is to unbundle the expression into a series of separate tests connected by GOTOs (Figure 12.4).

Thus, what at first glance seems to be a single concise unit is actually a complex expression combining four different conclusions with a sophisticated control transfer mechanism enabled by the syntax of the language in which it is written. It combines knowledge and procedural control. Once considered, the expression is guaranteed to take *some* action. Most conventional programming languages offer this IF/THEN/ELSE type of expression.

In most expert systems shells, it is neither possible nor desirable to encode knowledge in this manner. Why? There are several reasons. One is that we want to avoid the procedural control that is implied in the expression. As a

```
        if (paperwork = = PASSES)
                GOTO ptest;
        else
                printf("Candidate fails: make no offer");
        break;
ptest:
        if (personality = = VERY_GOOD)
                GOTO etest;
        else
                printf("Make adequate offer");
        break;
etest:
        if (experience = = VERY_GOOD)
                printf("Make a top offer");
        else
                printf("Make a good offer");
        break;
```

Figure 12.4. A "Nested-if" Structure Rewritten with Explicit Control Transfers.

piece of knowledge, we want to declare it. It is the inference engine's responsibility to determine if the knowledge applies to the problem at hand.

Second, it is cryptic. The expression is not Englishlike. The knowledge base will be easier to read, debug, and maintain if we improve its readability. Third, there are actually four separate chunks of knowledge trying to get out of the one expression we examined. These should be separated into distinct rules (Figure 12.5).

Notice how these rules differ from the programming example. In the programming example, when the first test is true, certain new conclusions become possible as control is transferred to the next statement. This transfer excludes the possibility of other conclusions *("Make no offer")*. Using rules, no new conclusion is implied. For example, *Rule 1* continues to be considered if its first premise clause is true. The rule may yet fire or it may fail. We infer nothing about what happens elsewhere in other rules that make the same conclusion. We don't even know whether the user will be prompted, whether other rules are needed to establish a value for the premise, whether the inference engine already knows the value of the premise attributes, or whether there is any knowledge source that can conclude the rule.

At first glance, your reaction may be anxiety because of the loss of control you feel. "If I don't know what will happen when, how do I know that the result

RULE 1
IF   paperwork = passes
AND personality = very_good
AND experience = very_good
THEN recom = Make_a_top_offer

RULE 2
IF   paperwork NOT = passes
THEN recom = Make_no_offer

RULE 3
IF   paperwork = passes
AND personality = very_good
AND experience NOT = very_good
THEN recom = Make_a_good_offer

RULE 4
IF   paperwork = passes
AND personality NOT = very_good
THEN recom = Make_an_adequate_offer

Figure 12.5. A "Nested-if" Structure Written Using Rules.

is correct?" The answer is that if the rules truly reflect the knowledge at hand, then correct results will be rendered by the inference engine based on its ability to mimic problem-solving search techniques. What the inference engine needs is just that correct knowledge formulation.

Many conventional programmers also intuitively react against the redundancies rules may seem to contain. In Figure 12.5, *paperwork = passes* appears three times. *Personality = good* appears twice. There are four rules with up to three premises each. These rules don't seem to express the knowledge in its most compact and concise (and thus "best" in the conventional thinking) form. Thus, you may feel tempted to write knowledge bases that look like Figure 12.6.

Comparing Figures 12.5 and 12.6 shows how a programmer might try to create an implied nested-if structure by pruning possibilities with early rules that screen the consideration of later rules.

The misguided benefit that is sought is a "more concise" knowledge base—the rules have fewer premise clauses. Here's why it works. The inference engine chooses the first rule it finds that concludes *recom*. In Figure 12.6, *Rule 1* is considered first. If the rule fires, the sought attribute *recom* is instantiated and the search for a value for *recom* ends. If *Rule 1* fails, however, the developer counts on the unstated fact that *paperwork* does equal *passes* for

RULE 1
IF   paperwork NOT = passes
THEN   recom = Make_no_offer

RULE 2
IF   personality NOT = very_good
THEN   recom = Make_an_adequate_offer

RULE 3
IF   experience = very_good
THEN   recom = Make_a_top_offer

RULE 4
IF   experience NOT = very_good
THEN   recom = Make_a_good_offer

Figure 12.6. A Common Mistake: Trying to Write "Nested-if" Rules.

the remainder of the rules that conclude *recom*. If effect, each remaining rule begins with the unstated premise:

IF paperwork = passes

If *paperwork* didn't equal *passes*, *Rule 2* would never be considered—*recom* would have been instantiated by *Rule 1*'s firing and the search would be over. "Therefore," the developer might say, "it seems safe to omit the explicit declaration of the clause since the possible values for *paperwork* have been pruned."

The same phenomenon occurs in *Rule 2*. If it fires, the search for *recom* is done. *Rules 3* and *4* will not be considered. If it fails, there are now two implied premises in those remaining rules. *Rules 3* and *4* are considered in the same manner.

The knowledge base shown in Figure 12.6 works under the following circumstances:

- you can control and maintain the order in which the inference engine considers rules,
- the inference engine backward chains and chooses the first rule it finds that concludes the sought attribute,
- the inference engine stops seeking an attribute as soon as it finds a value for that attribute.

Since many inference engines offer this combination of choices, many new knowledge base developers fall into writing rules in this manner. While this knowledge base may operate correctly, it is a poor practice for the following reasons:

- Each rule does not reflect the actual knowledge as formulated by the expert. It is much more difficult to understand, debug, and maintain because of the implied dependencies on other rules.
- It is wholly dependent on a certain backward chaining search strategy. If some alternative consideration strategy is used, improper results may ensue.
- Its proper performance is dependent on rule order and the shell's idiosyncratic processing of the rules. You may get improper results if you add, delete, or change rules. You almost certainly will get improper results if you change rule order.
- Its proper performance is dependent on the inference engine's ending its search as soon as it gets its first value. If the attribute is *multivalued,* the approach may produce wrong results because every rule concluding *recom* is considered (we discuss this topic in Chapter 7).
- If you represent uncertainty in your rules, certainty factor results may differ from those of the example in Figure 12.5 (we discuss certainty factors in Chapter 8).

In short, by trying to reduce the number of premise clauses, you embed implied procedural content into the knowledge base by making a certain rule order mandatory to the successful processing of the knowledge base. This can only make the job of producing a successful expert system more difficult. It removes many of the benefits of expert systems. Therefore, do not write rules in such a way that a particular order is necessary in order to obtain correct results.

Realize that it is not redundant to restate premise clauses in different rules. Each rule is an independent chunk of knowledge. Each different piece of knowledge can, and does, often legitimately contain premise clauses that other knowledge items may also share. Because the job of the knowledge engineer here is to encode this know-how independent of how it is processed, *do not make it a priority to condense rules.* Your job is exactly the opposite: *to make the knowledge as clear and explicit as possible.* Because each rule ideally states a complete expression of some knowledge item, each factor affecting the conclusion should be present. The premise expresses knowledge, not conditional control. Thus there is nothing wrong with rules that contain many premise clauses if they properly represent that knowledge.

It may take time to get used to this approach. Knowledge engineers must put themselves at the service of the knowledge they encode. Their job is not to find clever, cryptic algorithmic solutions to programming. Their job is to flush out, declare, and preserve domain knowledge—to make intangible assets tangible. Restrain the temptation to find the terse solution. Declare assumptions. Do not add procedural content to rules.

Minimize Use of ELSE

Some expert systems shells offer the ability to add ELSE clauses to rules. For example:

```
RULE 7
IF      color = red
AND   size = like_a_rubber_ball
THEN fruit = apple
ELSE fruit = strawberry
```

Rules containing ELSE have a dangerous characteristic: they always fire. This again adds an often undesirable procedural content to those rules. If the premise is true, *fruit* is instantiated to *apple*. If the premise is not true, the assignment following ELSE *(fruit = strawberry)* is made.

Because of this procedural content, the relative position of a rule containing an ELSE clause can dramatically affect a consultation's results. Knowledge bases with many rules containing ELSE may behave more like conventional programs.

For example, what if we wanted to add a rule about *cherries?*

```
RULE 7
IF      color = red
AND   size = small
AND   stem = long
THEN fruit = cherry
```

```
RULE 8
IF      color = red
AND   size = like_a_rubber_ball
THEN fruit = apple
ELSE fruit = strawberry
```

Because *Rule 8* fires regardless of the value of *size, fruit* is sure to have a value instantiated. The proper processing of the fragment is dependent on *Rule 7* being considered before *Rule 8*. But if *Rule 8* happens to be considered first and *fruit* is singlevalued, *Rule 7* will never be considered and might as well be omitted from the knowledge base in spite of representing meaningful knowledge about *fruit*. The ELSE clause preempts all rules concluding *fruit* that follow the rule containing the ELSE clause.

RULE 8
IF   color = red
AND size = like_a_rubber_ball
AND stem = long
THEN fruit = apple
ELSE fruit = strawberry

RULE 7
IF   color = red
AND size = small
AND stem = long
THEN fruit = cherry

Within any one ELSE rule are two rules trying to get out. Because you want to strive for as clear and transparent a representation as possible, you clarify and improve the accuracy of your knowledge base by unbundling rules containing ELSE into two or more rules. For example, *Rule 8* could be rewritten as:

RULE 7
IF   color = red
AND size = small
AND stem = long
THEN fruit = cherry

RULE 8a
IF   color = red
AND size = like_a_rubber_ball
AND stem = long
THEN fruit = apple

RULE 8b
IF   color = red
AND size = small
AND stem = short
THEN fruit = strawberry

This more naturally represents the knowledge and allows the inference engine to determine which rule best applies. No conclusion is forced by the procedural nature of the rule. Moreover, it makes it easier to add rules without worrying about where in the knowledge base to place the rule. For example, add *Rule 8c*:

RULE 8c
IF   color = yellow
AND   size = long
AND   stem = short
THEN fruit = banana

Rule 8c can be placed anywhere in the knowledge base without concern for proper consideration. The inference engine will fire the rule if it applies. Finally, by using this method, you let the inference engine infer UNKNOWN when none of the rules apply. This helps you better identify knowledge gaps, and allows the possibility of adding rules that reason about the UNKNOWN.

All rules using ELSE can be rewritten to eliminate ELSE clauses. For example, the more complex *Rule 9* can be rewritten:

Original

RULE 9
IF   car_type = van
OR   car_type = truck
AND   amount = low
OR   amount = medium
AND   prestige = low
THEN advice = "Buy a truck or van"
ELSE advice = "Buy a sedan"

Two replacement rules

RULE 9a
IF   car_type = van
OR   car_type = truck
AND   amount = low
OR   amount = medium
AND   prestige = low
THEN advice = "Buy a truck or van"

RULE 9b
IF   car_type NOT = van
AND   car_type NOT = truck
AND   amount NOT = low
AND   amount NOT = medium
AND   prestige NOT = low
THEN advice = "Buy a sedan"

You can strengthen *Rule 9b* if you know that attributes *car_type, amount,* and *prestige* have preenumerated values as named in the EXPECT properties. For example, if they were defined as:

NAME: car_type
TYPE: symbol
EXPECT: (Truck, van, sedan, sports_coupe)
MULTI: yes

NAME: amount
TYPE: symbol
EXPECT: (low, medium, high)
MULTI   no

NAME: prestige
TYPE: symbol
EXPECT: (low, high)
MULTI: no

then you could rewrite *Rule 9b* more positively:

RULE 9b
IF   car_type = sedan
OR   car_type = sports_coupe
AND   amount = high
AND   prestige = high
THEN advice = "Buy a sedan or sports coupe"

Is it ever acceptable to use ELSE? There is one case in which it may be acceptable. It is when you positively know—for certain—that an attribute can have only one of two values and that the failure of one condition implies the other. For example:

IF   light_outside = yes
THEN time_of_day = day
ELSE time_of_day = night

However, even in these circumstances, we recommend avoiding ELSE. You may not yet completely understand the domain. There may be more than two possible values. Perhaps you have not anticipated every possible exception condition? For example, what if there is an eclipse? Is the question written clearly enough that no one could possibly misinterpret it? For example, could someone plausibly answer "no" if the day was overcast? These cases raise the possibility that the failure of one case does not necessarily imply the success of the other.

There are also technical factors to consider. Do you allow the user to respond with UNKNOWN? An "unknown" response will cause the premise to fail. This forces the rule to conclude that *time_of_day* = *night*. Are you using uncertainty? What if there is some evidence for light_outside, but not enough to put you over the truth threshold? Do you really want to conclude that *time_ of_day* = *night?* Consider all of these factors before using ELSE in rules. Better yet, don't use it at all.

Write Rules That Are Englishlike and Easy to Read

Make your knowledge base as Englishlike as possible. Here are some guidelines to help you do this.

Use Englishlike Names

Try to name attributes using the terminology of the domain you are encoding. Write out these names as fully as possible. This makes the knowledge base appear more Englishlike and helps the expert read your work.

If you enter rules with a word processor, there may be several shortcuts available. When entering a batch of rules, use a short one- or two-character symbol for each attribute. Then, after you've finished entering those rules, use the word processor's search-and-replace mechanism to change those abbreviations into the longer Englishlike equivalent. Some word processors have a key glossary, or shorthand capability. Define short key sequences that the word processor expands to a longer form you specify. This saves you keystrokes while making the knowledge base Englishlike.

Name rules in a manner which describes their function. Most expert systems shells allow you to name your rules. Many new developers simply give those rules numbers, only to quickly discover that numbered names don't offer much help in identifying their function. Instead, develop a system for naming rules. One useful method is to begin each rule's name with the attribute it concludes. Then provide a brief description of the rule's knowledge or conclusion. For example:

Rule recom_if_fails_test   Rule cherry_if_long_stem
Rule recom_top_offer   Rule apple_if_large

Some shells don't allow Englishlike rule names. Those that do sometimes have rule name length restrictions. Thus if the limitations of the shell cause your rules not to be self-explanatory, document them! Think of your knowledge base as a large formalized documentation file of the knowledge you've learned.

Convert Numbers to Symbols

When the domain expert makes decisions based on numeric data, it is usually best to convert these data into symbols, when rules will test these data in their premises. This improves the readability and meaningfulness of those rules. For example, examine the following rule:

RULE emergency_too_hot
IF sensor1 > (80)
THEN emergency_response = lower_heat

While the reader may infer that the problem is one of overheating, one can't be positive. In this way, the use of numeric values in premises often disguises the underlying knowledge for those who are not experts in the domain (this may include the person who maintains the knowledge base). There is nothing about the number 80 that necessarily means hot. The rule can easily be improved like this:

RULE emergency_too_hot
IF sensor_one_temp = too_high
THEN emergency_response = lower_heat

RULE define_too_high
IF sensor1 > (80)
THEN sensor_one_temp = too_high

When the rule *emergency_too_hot* is considered, the value for attribute *sensor_one_temp* is sought. *Sensor_one_temp* becomes the current goal and since the following rule concludes it, that rule is considered. In this manner, the number is turned into a symbol while documenting the fact that *IF the sensor's value is greater than 80,* THEN *its temperature is too high.* This technique of adding one chaining level enables you to use a single rule to turn the number into a symbol, improving the readability of the knowledge base, and explicitly defines what the value of "80" means in the context of the rule. You might then also add other rules that test other numeric values of *sensor1* to establish symbolic values for *too_low, just_right,* and so on.

SUMMARY

Use the rule-organizing strategy described at the beginning of this chapter. It will make it easier for you to debug and maintain the expert system. Refrain from trying to control and predict exactly when each rule will be processed. Instead, make every rule explicitly state the dependent conditions it requires to be true. Don't rely on implied premises or nested-if statements. Strive to remove as much procedural content from rules as possible.

13 | Fine-Tuning Consideration Order

Once the knowledge base correctly represents the domain's knowledge, you may want to fine-tune the order of how the expert system asks questions. During the prototyping and development phase, you focus more on getting correct results than tailoring when certain questions are to be asked. When it comes time to deploy the system, however, these fine-tuning points become important.

Refinement is an important "human factors" aspect. Because of the goal-directed nature of backward chaining, the consultation may appear to ask questions at random. The inference engine queries when *it* needs information. As it jumps from one line of inquiry to the next, there may seem to be no logical line of reasoning. This can be disconcerting to its human users. Users may have experience interacting with a human expert who asks questions in a seemingly more sensible manner. In order to increase the acceptance of your work, it is important to be able to refine the query process.

Refinement can also eliminate unnecessary inferences and optimize performance. Some rules may trigger a line of pursuit that is more involved than others. Some are more likely to be more relevant to the situation than others. By influencing the order in which certain lines are considered, you may be able to improve the performance of the knowledge base by reducing the number of fruitless paths it pursues for the most common cases.

You influence how the inference engine considers and fires rules by making minor adjustments to rules and rule order. The techniques are subtle and understated. In conventional programming, you make every decision. But you must coexist with the inference engine. Because it has a "mind of its own," you must first understand how it works and use that knowledge to "persuade" it to work in the way you desire.

FACILITIES FOR INFLUENCING RULE SELECTION

While most inference engines operate in a broadly similar manner, many have their own idiosyncrasies. We cover here how *most* inference engines work while noting possible areas of difference. In the Appendix, we show the order in which some popular rule-based shells consider rules.

Rule Order

When backward chaining, virtually every inference engine considers the first rule it finds that concludes the current goal. To take advantage of this capability, order those rules you want considered first among a group that make the same conclusion. Put those rules first that are most likely to apply.

Some expert systems shells don't allow you to control the order in which the rules occur. This is especially true of shells based on the LISP programming language. Many of these have an integrated rule entry and editing environment in which you don't have direct access to how rules are ordered. This may make it more difficult to control the rule consideration order.

Priority

Some shells give you an alternative way to influence rule consideration order, using a rule property you attach to each rule called PRIORITY. This property tells the inference engine which rules it should try first. For example:

```
RULE       more_likely
IF         employed = no
AND        win_lottery = no
THEN       college_savings_plan = interrupt
PRIORITY 35

RULE       least_likely
IF         win_lottery = yes
THEN       college_savings_plan = done
PRIORITY 20

RULE       most_likely
IF         employed = yes
AND        win_lottery = no
THEN       college_savings_plan = continue
PRIORITY 50
```

Without the PRIORITY property associated with each rule, *Rule more_likely* is considered first because it appears first. If it fails, *Rule least_likely* is considered second followed by *Rule most_likely*. This is because most inference engines select the first rule that concludes the current goal as it occurs in the knowledge base.

However, because *Rule most_likely* has a PRIORITY property whose value is greater than the other two, the inference considers it first even though it appears sequentially last. *Rule more_likely*, by virtue of its next highest PRI-ORITY, is considered second if *Rule most_likely* fails. *Rule least_likely*, because of its low PRIORITY representing the fact that its knowledge is unlikely to apply, is considered last.

PRIORITY is a weighting system for letting the inference engine know which rules to consider first. At each selection point, the next highest PRI-ORITY rule concluding the current goal is considered. When more than one rule concluding the same attribute has the same PRIORITY, the inference engine considers the rule occurring first in the knowledge base. The PRIORITY property allows rule consideration order to be controlled without changing the rule's relative position within the knowledge base.

Not all expert systems shells support PRIORITY, and many give it another name (see the Glossary for others). If yours does offer it, you may want to assign a PRIORITY to every rule in order to document its relative importance or likelihood. This adds to the knowledge content of the knowledge base and lets future maintenance engineers know exactly how (although not why) rules concluding like attributes stand in relationship to one another.

Cost

Some shells provide two weighting systems. For example, the expert systems shell Guru offers a COST priority system in addition to a PRIORITY system. This enables developers to weight the relative expense of using a rule as well as its importance or likelihood. Cost can refer to a number of different kinds of cost, including the amount of computing resources necessary to process the rule, the financial cost of using the knowledge contained in a rule, or the length or complexity of a reasoning line the rule will initiate. By independently weighting rules with COST and PRIORITY, developers can represent a rule's importance along with a measure of its cost. For example:

```
RULE       somewhat_sure_moderate_expense
IF         letter_there_by_end_of_week = important
THEN       delivery_method = overnight_mail
PRIORITY 80
COST       50
```

```
RULE       certain_but_expensive
IF         letter_there_by_end_of_week = important
THEN       delivery_method = courier
PRIORITY 99
COST       99
```

```
RULE      inexpensive
IF        letter_there_by_end_of_week = not_important
THEN      delivery_method = us_mail
PRIORITY 20
COST      5
```

By changing the inference engine's selection strategy between PRIORITY and COST, the same knowledge base can be processed in different order. If the consultation is run using PRIORITY as its selection strategy, the inference engine considers *Rule certain_but_expensive* first, because it has the highest priority. Next, it selects *Rule somewhat_sure_moderate_expense* and, finally, *Rule inexpensive* if the others fail.

If the same consultation is run using COST, those rules having the lowest COST rating are chosen first. In this case, the order is *Rule inexpensive, somewhat_sure_moderate_expense*, and *certain_but_expensive*.

Another use of PRIORITY and COST is for encoding both "best guess" and "most accurate or optimal" knowledge. This can be especially important for applications in which there may be many possible solutions, but you first need *any* solution. Later, you can run lengthier (more costly) consultations that seek the *best* solution. Substantial computing resources may be necessary to find that "best" answer, but the expert system may be able to quickly determine first if a solution is possible at all, and provide a "best guess." This can be done by assigning low COST to a set of rules employing "best guess" rules of thumb, and supplementing these with high COST "deep knowledge" rules that fire only when the longer, more tedious, but more accurate consultation is desired.

Note that the PRIORITY and COST factors do not affect *if* a rule fires, once considered. They simply let the developer control which rules get considered first. Also, many shells don't offer PRIORITY and COST. In those cases, you use rule order to influence which rules the inference engine considers first.

Certainty

A less frequently encountered rule selection strategy that some inference engines use is choosing rules by the certainty factor of the conclusion. This technique only comes into play when rules contain uncertainty in their conclusions. Consider the following example:

```
RULE moderately_certain
IF    pressure_dropping = yes
THEN chance_of_rain = yes CF 70
```

RULE more_certain
IF   conditions = cloudy_and_overcast
THEN chance_of_rain = yes CF 90

Using certainty as a selection criterion, the inference engine would first examine the relative certainty of the conclusions of these two rules when *chance_of_rain* is the current goal. In this case, even though it appears sequentially after *Rule moderately_certain, Rule more_certain* is processed first, because its conclusion contributes more certainty than the former.

This technique seems logical enough on the surface. Why not consider the most certain rule first? In practice, it offers significant disadvantages. Certainty and desired consideration order are not necessarily linked. It may be desirable to consider less certain rules first because they lead to fewer questions or to short reasoning lines. Thus, representing uncertainty in rules may give you less control over which rules are considered first. Fortunately, few shells use this approach.

Most "Known" Rule

Some shells let you instruct the shell to choose those rules with the fewest NOTSOUGHT premise clauses. Such shells preview each rule that concludes the current goal before choosing one for consideration. They first consider which rules can be evaluated without causing backward chaining on premise attributes. If such rules exist, they are considered first. If all candidate rules have some NOTSOUGHT attribute, the inference engine chooses those with the fewest. This selection strategy ensures that those rules that require the least amount of new information are considered first.

HOW RULES ARE PROCESSED

Once a rule is selected for consideration, the sequence in which attributes appear in the premise has a profound effect on the character of the consultation. By giving due attention to attribute order, you ensure efficient questioning and the shortest possible line of reasoning.

Conjunctions

When writing the premise of a conjunction rule, always order attributes from most independent to most dependent. This usually means asking for the most important information first. Consider this example:

RULE   wine_spicy_sauce
IF   has_sauce = yes
AND   sauce_type = spicy
THEN   wine = chianti

Property Lists

NAME: has_sauce
TYPE: boolean
EXPECT: (yes, no)
PROMPT: "Does the meal have a sauce?"

NAME: sauce_type
TYPE: symbol
EXPECT: (sweet, bitter, spicy)
PROMPT: "Is the sauce sweet, bitter, or spicy?"

When *wine* is the current goal and *Rule wine_spicy_sauce* is selected for consideration, the inference engine first seeks a value for *has_sauce*. If its status is NOTSOUGHT, *has_sauce* becomes the current goal. Because no other rule concludes *has_sauce*, its PROMPT property is used to generate the question, "Does the meal have a sauce?" If the user responds "*no*," consideration of the rule ends and no additional questions occur. If the user responds with "*yes*," the inference engine continues processing the rule by considering *sauce_type*. In order to conclude its value, the user is prompted, "Is the sauce sweet, bitter, or spicy?" The questioning order makes sense because the second clause is dependent on the first answer's being true. The second prompt does not get asked if the first clause is false.

Imagine if the rule looked like this:

RULE wine_spicy_sauce
IF   sauce_type = spicy
AND   has_sauce = yes
THEN wine = chianti

Although the two clauses are identical, here the order of the two premise clauses is inverted. This can produce a nonsensical line of questioning. When the rule is considered, the user must respond to the prompt, "Is the sauce sweet, bitter, or spicy?" If the client is having soup for dinner, this question does not make much sense. Moreover, if the client happens to have a sauce and responds that the sauce is *spicy*, the next question asks, "Does the meal have a sauce?" as the attribute *has_sauce* is sought. The value for *sauce_type* is relevant only if *has_sauce* is true. For this dependency relationship to be properly expressed in the consultation, *has_sauce* can only appear in conjunctions in which the attribute *has_sauce = yes* appears before it.

While the example is purposely simple to illustrate the point, more subtle variations can have a profound effect on consultations. For example:

GOAL: recom

RULE Is_domain_ok
IF   domain_well_formulated = yes
AND economic_need = yes
THEN recom = the_domain_is_ok

Imagine that *Rule Is_domain_ok* is the first rule considered in a consultation. It concludes the knowledge base goal *recom*. Its first premise clause causes an extensive series of rule considerations which evaluate whether a proposed expert systems domain is well formulated (see Chapter 2 for the knowledge that underlies this discussion). The second premise clause asks three questions which evaluate whether there is an economic justification for building the expert system. When the domain expert interacts with this expert system, she says, "I always check for *economic need* first because if the domain is not economically justified, I don't ask any more questions. I don't care if it's well formulated or not, since I won't recommend it." Thus, because the two premise clauses are inverted, the client is forced to engage in a lengthy dialogue consisting of many questions which may ultimately be meaningless when three simple questions might determine that the domain will not be recommended—regardless of how well formulated it is.

The rule for avoiding this kind of problem is simple: when creating a premise, always place dependent attributes after those attributes on which they depend. Because the *sauce_type* is meaningless when there is no sauce, *sauce_type* should not appear in a premise without *has_sauce* appearing first and being joined by AND. Similarly, questions of *domain_well_formed* are irrelevant unless *economic_need* is first established. Therefore, either *economic_need* must precede *domain_well_formed* in any premise in which the latter appears; or other attributes that precede *domain_well_formed* must themselves depend on *economic_need*.

Disjunctions: To Bundle or Unbundle?

While most expert systems shells process conjunctions in a similar manner, they use one of *two* ways to process disjunctions. Disjunctions are premises whose clauses are connected by OR. They are useful for representing knowledge in which any one of several conditions implies some conclusion.

RULE evaluate_rain
IF   barometer = falling
OR   temperature = dropping

OR   cloud_conditions = overcast
THEN chance_of_rain = high

The first method "short-circuits" rule evaluation as soon as one premise clause is true. In other words, as soon as one clause is proven, the entire rule is true and so consideration ends. This is desirable when you want to process a rule in the quickest manner. For example, if *barometer = falling* is true, the rule immediately fires and the remaining clauses are not considered. Because a disjunction requires that only one of the clauses in an "OR group" be true, it terminates consideration as soon as it determines that the rule will fire.

Other shells consider *every* premise in the rule, even if the rule has already been found true. Even if *barometer = falling*, the inference engine goes on to consider the next premise clause *temperature = dropping* and then *cloud_ conditions = overcast*. While backward chaining, it processes rules and prompts users just as if the rule's truth was as yet unresolved. The rule still fires even if the last two premise clauses are not true. But the inference engine goes through the extra work of considering each disjunctive premise clause.

The reason some shells are programmed to do this extra work is related to how they calculate certainty. As we saw in Chapter 8, these shells calculate each disjunction clause's certainty by figuring an intermediate certainty factor each time one of the premise clauses is true. The thinking behind this is that if more than one premise clause is true, the added evidence should be factored into the rule's overall certainty. For example, you could argue that the conclusion is more certain if *both* the barometer is falling and the cloud condition is overcast, compared to just one of those two conditions being true. So the inference engine checks each premise clause—even when it already knows that the rule is true. If more than one premise is true, the resulting certainty is higher.

The problem is that the inference engine uses this approach even if you are not representing uncertainty. Since the default certainty is 100 (or 1.0), and you can't have a higher certainty, the extra processing doesn't contribute anything. Yet the inference engine may force additional inferences, which can cause unwanted prompts, after the rule is already guaranteed to fire.

If your shell works this way, there is an easy technique to avoid these extra inferences. Simply split disjunctive premises into separate rules. For example, *Rule evaluate_rain* above can be expressed as three rules:

RULE rain_barometer
IF   barometer = falling
THEN chance_of_rain = high

RULE rain_temp
IF   temperature = dropping
THEN chance_of_rain = high

RULE rain_cloud_condition
IF   cloud_conditions = overcast
THEN chance_of_rain = high

These three rules express precisely the same knowledge as the earlier *Rule evaluate_rain*. However, because each is a separate rule with only one premise clause, consideration will end as soon as one of the rules fires (assuming that *chance_of_rain* is singlevalued). Thus, you can force processing to stop, as soon as *chance_of_rain* is instantiated.

SUMMARY

While the order in which you place like-concluding rules should not usually determine if your results are correct, it may influence how efficient or satisfying the consultation may seem to the user. Most shells provide some facility for letting you fine-tune the consultation order. Most shells allow you to do so by using rule order. Other shells use other means. By using such means and understanding how conjunctions and disjunctions are processed, the use of screening clauses, and other facilities your shell offers, you should find it easy to make whatever adjustments are necessary.

14 | *Testing the Knowledge Base*

In this chapter, we look at techniques that make knowledge bases easier to debug. We show how the testing challenges in expert systems are substantially different from those found in conventional programming. To minimize the difficulties in overcoming those challenges, we present a method of creating "structured rules" which loosely borrows from the well-accepted principles of structured programming. We also look at the importance of testing early and often. We examine the development of a requirements statement for the expert system and the importance of formulating a maintenance plan. We touch on the tools that various shells offer to ease the debugging task.

UNIQUE TESTING CHALLENGES

Expert systems pose a variety of testing challenges. Many of the testing problems found in conventional programming also show up in expert systems. You fight syntax problems, look for incorrect usages, and improve poor organization and structure. In addition, there are unique aspects to knowledge base testing. Because expert systems offer minimal direct control over the inference process, you may find it more difficult to follow consultation control flow and, therefore, more difficult to detect where wrong inferencing takes place. The human element also adds unique debugging challenges. Advice may be based on one expert's opinion. This can make the concept of "right" and "wrong" conclusions ambiguous, in a poorly defined expert system.

Many expert systems shells offer poor debugging tools. Does the shell flag rules with the same premises that conclude different values? Can the product detect contradictions? Does it assist developers in finding errors caused by the special problems of rules with more than one conclusion clause? Unfortunately, the answer is often "no." Thus you, the developer, must take responsibility for seeking out these potential problems. The special character of expert systems dictates a need for good diagnostic tools and techniques. If your shell lacks the tools, you must apply the techniques that test for these common problems.

MODULARITY AND TESTING

One of the key traits associated with the self-standing, modular nature of rule-based systems is that many rules may be eligible to fire at any time. A major implication of this behavior is that very little information about *when* rules fire (the control flow) is built into the knowledge base. Thus it can be said that rule-based systems have high *transparency*, but display low behavior *visibility*.[1] Rules are "transparent" because their meaning is relatively separate from their location in the knowledge base, and thus the meaning they have is contained within the rule. "Poor visibility" refers to the problem that the order in which rules will be processed is usually not apparent through casual examination.

Conventional program statements are not modular. Each statement contains little information about the program's overall function because much of its meaning is implicit—meaning depends on the statement's position within the script. On the other hand, determining *when* a given statement will be executed is much easier. The program, by definition, is a script detailing the order of execution. Conventional programs typically exhibit low transparency, but high behavior visibility.

This sets the stage for knowledge base debugging. Conventional debugging focuses around finding incorrectly defined script items. Bugs usually take the form of incorrectly stated or misordered program statements. The program's meaning is dependent on the aggregate impact of many statements. Each statement makes up only a small part of that meaning. Therefore, it can be difficult to detect which such statement causes a bug. Yet it is relatively easier to follow the order of execution because the program is, by definition, a script the computer follows. The debugging challenge is to isolate which statement is misstated or wrongly ordered. In other words, the task is to determine the unhappy meaning or implication of some wrongly written or ordered statement. The fight is against poor transparency.

Because rules are easier to understand, detecting ones that are wrongly stated is relatively easier. Since the meaning of well-written rules is more or less independent of position, incorrect ordering is less of a problem. However, most developers find the task of following the aggregate processing of the

---

[1] The terms *visibility* and *transparency* and the point of the trade-offs between them are established in Randall Davis and Jonathan J. King, "The Origin of Rule-Based Systems in AI," in *Machine Intelligence 8: Machine Representations of Knowledge*, ed. E. W. Elcock and D. Michie (Chichester, England: Eillis Horwood, 1977).

knowledge base much more difficult. Because it is true that any rule might be eligible for processing, following the flow can involve hopping throughout the knowledge base. The debugging challenge here is to follow, fine-tune, and influence the behavior of the inference engine as it processes rules. In other words, the task is to grasp *when* rules are processed. The fight is against poor visibility.

The above has an element of oversimplification. An Assembler program or one with many jumps or use of indirection may be difficult to follow. Structured programming techniques are designed exactly to reduce this problem. Too, good documentation, use of Englishlike variables, and well-designed code can minimize a conventional program's transparency limitations.

It is also easy to write knowledge bases that are as cryptic and meaningless to the casual eye as a C or Assembler program. This is poor development technique that the guidelines appearing in Chapter 12 and later in this chapter are designed to help you avoid. You use expert systems shells to increase the Englishlike content (the transparency) of your work. To ignore this benefit is like using a screwdriver to drive a nail. You may be able to do it, but you're not using the tool for what it was designed. Since you make tradeoffs (poor visibility) to get the transparency and humanlike advantages of shells, you shouldn't use the tool if you don't need, or aren't going to use, its advantages.

Conventional program debugging revolves around finding the wrong or misstated statement because each statement's ultimate meaning is not readily clear. Expert systems debugging tends to center around understanding the seemingly arbitrary processing of rules. The guidelines we offer here minimize the difficulties of fighting expert systems' visibility problem, while increasing the value of their good transparency.

Completeness

A unit of software must be complete to be tested. The notion of completeness does not mean that a user would regard the unit as a finished program or expert system. Instead, completeness here means that the unit in question is capable of producing some end result which can be evaluated.

In conventional software, the smallest testable software unit is usually the function, or subroutine. The function is a logically related group of instructions that produces some useful, coherent outcome. You can't test a conventional program below this level, just as you can't test the chain reaction of felling a row of dominoes until all the dominoes have been set up (Figure 14.1). The function's steps simply haven't yet been "set up" in order to be tested.

A function typically has one or more inputs and outputs. A function with only one output is easier to test than one with many outputs. You feed the function its inputs and evaluate its one output. If the desired output emerges,

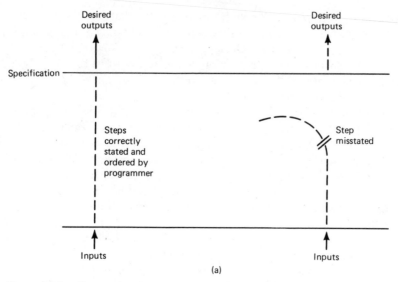

Figure 14.1a. Conventional programming relies on chains of instructions.

the function works. As soon as multiple outputs need to be produced, issues of side effects, technical implementation, and debugging increase exponentially. While the principle of one output is widely acknowledged, in practice it is used more as a guideline than a rule. Performance and other considerations make it sometimes necessary to produce two or more outputs from a given function.

The smallest unit in a rule-based expert system is the rule. Each rule is ideally a self-standing entity whose meaning is explicitly stated. A rule's inputs are its premise conditions. When input values are tested against a rule's premise conditions, the rule either produces conclusions or nothing (it fails or is "put aside"). In this sense, rules are analogous to functions or subroutines, except that you don't need to worry about setting up procedural steps. Since

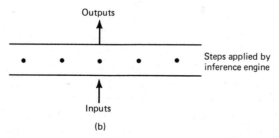

Figure 14.1b. Rules have no steps.

the inference engine performs the setup steps for you, you can test as little as a single rule. As with a function, it is highly desirable that—whenever possible—you limit a rule's outputs to one inference.

Test Now!

Since a function and a rule are both complete in the sense that we've defined, both can be tested. One of the most important parts of knowledge base debugging is taking advantage of the fact that you can test early. At any given time, an expert system can be seen as a complete system containing some amount of knowledge. That knowledge can be tested. Again, users may not perceive the expert system as being whole, because it does not perform all the functions (solve all the problems) specified for it. However, for whatever inferences it is capable of making, the expert system—in this technical sense—is complete and testable.

Unfortunately, many inexperienced expert systems developers, especially converted conventional programmers, resist the idea of testing early and often. This resistance is based on three facts of life to which they've grown accustomed in conventional software:

There Must Be at Least One Function to Test. Relatively large chunks of conventional code must be written (at *least* one function) before you have something that can be tested. A function may be made up of dozens of lines of code. Thus the conventional programmer gets used to writing much code before testing.

Conventional Programming Overhead. Just because a conventional function *can* be tested doesn't mean it is easy or practical to test. Since procedural languages only do what they're told, the programmer is still responsible for finding ways to get data into the function. This may include writing input and output routines as well as simulating or "dummying up" other functions on which the target function may depend. These functions, too, must be tested. Therefore, the up-front cost of early testing may be prohibitively high in the early stages of development.

The Resources Aren't There. Developers may be unaccustomed to frequent early testing because they previously didn't have the tools and computing resources. Traditionally, programmers have had to wait minutes, perhaps hours, to get their code compiled. This may be an unacceptable tradeoff for the benefits of early testing.

Test Early!

It shouldn't be necessary to justify the concept of early frequent testing. Frequent testing is inherently good and does not need much explaining. Nevertheless, the author's experience has been that adoption of this practice still lags among experienced conventional programmers. Here are four important reasons why you should test early.

Sooner Is Better Than Later. It is obvious that catching errors early is better than catching them late. It seems intuitive that verifying a rule now will often help avoid developing work under false assumptions. Imagine that you learned to multiply numbers incorrectly in fourth grade, but were not tested until college. Correcting the mistakes made along the way would be difficult, wouldn't it? Immediate feedback is better than delayed feedback. If immediate feedback is available (and it is in most rule-based shells), get it!

The Unit of Completeness Is Smaller. Rules are smaller and easier to write than functions. They are testable. However, because they are so easy to create, the tendency is to feel they are more analogous to program *statements* than functions. Fight this feeling. See a rule as an important subroutine you can test right away. This testing gives you immediate feedback as to the correctness of the rule as well as feedback on how the inference engine processes that rule.

There Is Little Overhead. Programming overhead is not an excuse for avoiding early testing. Remember that the inference engine takes care of the user interface for you. Thus, you don't have to write and test the supporting routines that a conventional program requires. The inference engine already "knows" how to deal with users. There is little cost associated with immediate testing.

The Nature of the Problem Dictates It. The challenge of knowledge acquisition is such that it is usually not practical or possible to grasp the entire domain before you start coding. This is why we use the rapid prototyping method to drive the engineering process. Frequent testing is another endorsement of the rapid prototyping method, a kind of prototyping within the prototyping process.

You may nod your head in agreement with these points, agreeing that early testing is good. We use these pages to argue for it for two reasons. First, most people seem to agree; but in practice, they don't do it, or don't do it often enough. Second, frequent and early testing is the number one single factor we've found to ensure the production of consistently good knowledge bases. Yes, there are important technical considerations which we discuss next. But no single technical consideration can compete against incorporating frequent testing *during development.* Whether this means testing after every rule, or every several or few rules, is a matter of style. But unless you integrate testing into the essential core of your development work now, you are compromising your ability to deliver a working, reliable expert system later. Test early, test often!

WRITING STRUCTURED RULES

In their purest form, rules are independent chunks of knowledge with no necessarily implied serial chain among them. We've established that as little as one rule is testable. We've also argued that early testing is a vital point of view you should bring to your development methodology.

Knowledge bases made up of rules that conclude a single inference are easier to test and maintain, just as conventional functions and subroutines that return or update one variable are considered well written for the same reason. Therefore, we call the following guidelines "structured programming for rules." Our experience has shown that this approach improves clarity, shortens development and debugging time, and makes the knowledge base much easier to maintain over time. There are two specific guidelines: *keep conclusions simple* and *push procedural content out of rules.*

Keep Conclusions Simple

Write rules whose impact on the consultation is as clear and simple as possible. Any one rule's firing should ideally make one change to the consultation state. To the degree that you follow this rule of thumb, you increase the ease of maintaining, debugging, and testing the knowledge base. Therefore, try to write rule conclusions so that they instantiate only one attribute. Here are some examples:

RIGHT

RULE Good_rule
IF   lights = dim
THEN problem = battery

RULE Good_rule2
IF   engine_sound = moans
AND lights = dim
THEN problem = battery CF 80
          problem = alternator CF 60

WRONG

RULE bad_rule
IF   engine_sound = moans
AND   lights = dim
THEN battery = poor CF 80
        alternator = poor CF 60

The first two examples both update a single attribute: *problem.* The meaning of each is clear and easy to understand. They produce no side effects. You do not have to worry about the possibly complex or idiosyncratic manner in which shells process rules with multiple conclusions.

Even though the second rule contains two conclusion clauses, both instantiate the same attribute. This meets the criteria of our test. The third sample rule's impact, however, is more difficult to measure. Tracking down which rules conclude which attributes becomes an order of magnitude more difficult when one rule updates more than one attribute. The role of these rules is no longer well focused. Tracing the cumulative effects of these updates becomes more complex. The clean inferencing line is lost, replaced by overlapping lines of responsibility for various consultation states. Inside a rule like *Rule bad_rule* are two or more rules trying to get out.

Figure 14.2 shows a well-structured relationship among attributes and rules. One or more rules are responsible for concluding any one attribute. Determining when and under what conditions the rule fires is a well-defined task. Figure 14.3 depicts a poorly structured relationship in which rules conclude more than one attribute. You can easily see the resulting added complexity in identifying which rules are responsible for a consultation state.

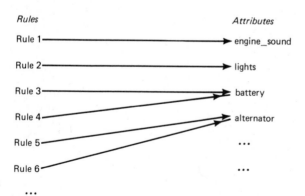

Figure 14.2. Well-Structured Relationships among Rules and Attributes.

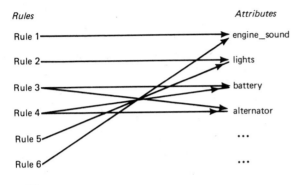

Figure 14.3. Poorly Structured Relationships among Rules and Attributes.

The appearance is reminiscent of conventional "spaghetti" code resulting from extensive use of GOTOs.

At a surface level, this issue may not seem serious. This is because you can conceptualize how each rule is processed on a rule-by-rule basis. You can follow the treatment for any one rule in isolation. This may be true, but it is the *cumulative* effects of many of these rules, combined with the complex and poorly visible behavior of an inference engine, that eventually make good testing of any sizable knowledge base virtually impossible. Even if the knowledge base is successfully tested, maintenance becomes difficult. The situation is directly analogous to the heavy use of GOTOs in conventional code. Any one GOTO can be understood. Reliance on it as a basic control technique causes poorly structured code that is difficult to follow and maintain. Rules with multiple conclusions are the expert systems equivalent of the "spaghetti code" caused by frequent use of GOTOs.

Other Problems

Besides the difficult-to-follow behavior they cause, multiconclusion rules raise questions about how they get processed and what they *mean*. In the sample *Rule bad_rule* above, these questions include:

Meaning. Does *alternator's* secondary position signal that it is a side effect associated with *battery*? Or does the presence of *battery* imply *alternator's* conclusion? Or do the two assignments flow equally and directly from the premise? The answer to these questions is not apparent by reading the rule.

Inference Engine Behavior. How does the backward chaining inference process this rule? Different inference engines process it differently. Here are three different approaches that are possible:

- The inference engine will process this rule when either *battery* or *alternator* is the current goal. If the rule is true, it instantiates both attributes.
- The inference engine will consider this rule when either is the current goal. If the rule is true, it instantiates only the attribute that caused the rule to be considered.
- The inference engine will consider this rule only when the first attribute appearing in the conclusion (in this case *battery*) is the current goal. If the rule is true, it instantiates both attributes.

In other words, the first case means: "bind both values regardless of what the current goal is." The second case interprets the rule to mean: "When backward chaining on *battery*, if the premise is true, there is only evidence that *battery = poor*. When backward chaining on *alternator*, if the premise is true, there is only evidence that *alternator = poor*." Finally, the last might be interpreted to mean, "When *battery* is needed, *battery = poor*, and as a side effect, *alternator = poor* too."

These differences make knowledge bases containing such rules less portable and point out the semantic ambiguities in what the rule means. It also raises additional highly technical questions, for example, "What if *alternator* already has a value *(alternator = good)* in the last case?" Is this a contradiction? If so, is it a "bug"?

Difficulties arise on two fronts. First, various shell vendors answer these questions in different ways. Thus if you choose to write multiconclusion rules, you need to determine exactly how the inference engine you use answers them and make no assumptions as to the applicability of this approach to other systems. Second, to the extent that you use multiconclusion rules, you add new testing requirements to the testing agenda, including contradiction testing and rule loops (more on these shortly).

Clear meaning is key to building clear, maintainable knowledge bases. The knowledge base's meaning must be as semantically clear as possible. Since rules containing multiple conclusions can have such profound differences in meaning, they must be extensively documented as to this point—or avoided. We urge adoption of the latter option.

Rule Loops. Rule loops may occur in rules containing more than one conclusion. Consider the following knowledge base fragment:

```
RULE 1
IF     total_evidence>(0)
THEN goal = found
```

RULE 2
IF   test1 = yes
THEN x = (econ_evidence + 1)
         total_evidence = . . .

RULE 3
IF   test2 = yes
THEN econ_evidence = (total_evidence + 1)

Assume that the premises in *Rule 2* and *Rule 3* are true. When the inference engine backward chains on attribute *goal* in *Rule 1*, it seeks attribute *total_ evidence*. *Rule 2* is considered because it assigns a value for *total_evidence*. In order to first assign *x* in *Rule 2*, attribute *econ_evidence* is required, so *Rule 3* is considered. However, *Rule 3* requires the value of *total_evidence* on the right hand side of the equals sign. At this point, the results become unpredictable because the knowledge base has now required the value of *total_evidence* twice. If the inference engine somehow establishes a value for *total_evidence* (perhaps by trying other rules or asking the user), one problem the inference engine encounters (among others) is that *total_evidence* will be assigned a value in *Rule 2* after it has already been used to calculate *econ_evidence* in the clause before it.

The style is deliberately appalling, for dramatic effect, but subtle versions of this problem are common. It shows how multiple conclusions can bury representation errors. Note that the three rules include four different conclusions. Only painstaking examination yields the fact that a circular loop is present. It may be virtually impossible to detect, if these rules reside in different locations in the knowledge base and the developer is not aware of this type of bug.

Push Out Procedural Content

The other major factor that increases the complexity of testing is rules that contain procedural content. By procedural content, we mean rules that do one or more of the following:

- change the current goal through means other than normal backward chaining.
- "call" outside programs or procedural subroutines that may produce hidden side effects.
- make other changes to the consultation state.

The guideline of removing procedural content from rules hits on the general style principle of emphasizing *what to know* as opposed to *what to do*.

This principle stresses separating the statement of knowledge from the processing of that knowledge, and letting the inference engine provide the explicit procedural processing. Abiding by this principle makes knowledge bases easier to read, test, and maintain. If you find that you absolutely cannot avoid adding significant procedural content to rules, you may be addressing a problem which could be better solved using a conventional language.

The problem of procedural content in rules is an exaggerated case of the same problem of rules with multiple conclusions. It is exaggerated because rules with procedural content can make dramatic changes to the consultation state without ever expressly stating those changes in the rule, as multiconclusion rules do, at least.

The procedural content problem is common in shells that offer procedural control sections (often called ACTIONS sections) or other procedural facilities. While these sections provide important functionality, they commonly are abused by inexperienced developers. These procedural commands are commonly allowed to reside in rules. Among such commands are "calls" to procedural code, like a subroutine call in conventional languages. These calls may modify the consultation state before returning control to the rule. Such actions may not show up when tracing the inference engine's path, and the developer may be left without a trail to follow, trying to determine how certain changes occurred.

Some shells with procedural modules identify the goal and start backward chaining using the verb FIND. Thus the phrase "FIND rec" means to make the current goal *rec* and find rules that conclude it. By burying goal-specifying verbs in rule conclusions, you can suddenly cause inferencing to go off on a tangent. The perceived need for this capability almost always arises from an improper conception of the expert's problem-solving strategy. The developer tries to force a line of questioning by using a FIND clause in the conclusion, instead of formulating the line of reasoning in the form of a control rule. The resultant rules steal control away from the inference engine and contain implicit procedural knowledge that can dramatically change the consultation character, depending on the position of the rule. In shells offering substantial procedural control components, such high-level commands should be used only in procedural code modules, *not* in rules.[2]

---

[2]The one exception to this is using FIND in a premise to force the binding of *any* value to an attribute when the keyword KNOWN or UNKNOWN does not cause backward chaining on the attribute. This is useful for causing the argument of the FIND clause to become the current goal as normal backward chaining would. You use it when you want to get *any* value for the attribute, e.g., when encoding rules that represent a problem-solving strategy. See the appendix section, "Unknown Handling" for more on this.

Contradictions. One example of the problems that procedural calls in rules and multiconclusion rules can cause is contradictions. Contradictions can occur in both single- and multiconclusion rules. For example:

RULE rain_yes
IF   barometer = up
THEN rain = yes

RULE rain_no
IF   barometer = up
THEN rain = no

A contradiction occurs when the same premise is inadvertently used to infer mutually several exclusive conclusions. This is a semantic problem; the shell may accept the two rules as properly written and have no way of knowing whether or not conclusions are mutually exclusive. Ultimately, a human must catch this problem through testing. With single-conclusion rules, this is not too difficult. You group like rules together as we have earlier recommended, and you can easily see that the two rules contradict each other.

On the other hand, multiconclusion rules can produce contradictions that are difficult to detect.

RULE color_blue
IF   texture = soft
THEN color = blue
        call colrproc

One can readily see some of the problems. *Rule color_blue* has poor transparency—we don't know what procedure *colrproc* does by looking at the rule. Thus the clarity of the rule is lost. Similarly, the multiconclusion problem also exists. Testing becomes more complex because individual responsibility for updates to the consultation state is difficult to assign and follow as the consultation progresses.

Worse, the procedure could cause instantiations that contradict inferences made so far. Perhaps the procedure could even deny the conclusions made in this rule. For example, if the procedure includes the assignment "*red*" to the singlevalued attribute *color,* the results could be erroneous or unpredictable.

The way to address the problem is to push procedural content out of rules. Rules are the expressive core of the rule-based expert system; they should reflect knowledge, not procedures. Such knowledge may include representations of the problem-solving strategy, but these representations should be expressly declared in the form of control rules.

There are three basic ways to push this knowledge out. If the shell has an ACTIONS section, design the expert system so that procedural actions occur there. This can be done by defining the knowledge base as a series of subgoals followed by procedural sections:

ACTIONS
find subgoal1
(procedural actions here)
. . .

. . .
find subgoal2
(procedural actions here)
. . .

. . .
find subgoal3
(etc.)

RULES
. . .

Second, use *procedural attribute properties* if your shell offers them. Procedural attribute properties are properties associated with an attribute just like EXPECTS, PROMPT, TYPE, and MULTI. They define some method for instantiating the attribute through means other than inferencing. For example, some shells define a dBASE data base query or Lotus 1-2-3 worksheet access as a property called METHOD, which the inference engine may use to get a value for the attribute owning it. When no rules or user prompt can provide the value, the inference engine invokes the METHOD as a last resort to provide a value. These procedural operations are associated with the attribute and serve as an additional knowledge source that the inference engine may pursue.

Finally, use demons and forward rules when possible. This is the topic we examine next.

Rewriting Multiconclusion Rules

The simplest way to avoid the problems discussed above is to avoid the use of rules concluding multiple attributes. This is what we mean by writing "structured" rules. Writing structured rules means writing rules that make one change to the current state of the consultation and do not produce procedural side effects. This simplifies testing and makes the consequences of additions and changes to the knowledge base much easier to gauge.

For Independent, Separate Conclusions. Rules like the example *Rule bad_ rule* used earlier can be remedied in a number of ways. First, you must determine what the rule is really trying to express. If the two conclusion clauses are independently true of each other, then only the current goal should be fired. The rule really is a shorthand version of the following two rules:

RULE better_1
IF   engine_sound = moans
AND   lights = dim
THEN battery = poor CF 80

RULE better_2
IF   engine_sound = moans
AND   lights = dim
THEN alternator = poor CF 60

When One Conclusion Clause Is a Side Effect. If the intent is rather that the rule applies only for *battery* problems and that the *alternator* conclusion is a side effect of the *battery* conclusion, then some form of forward chaining can be used to represent this. Forward chaining flushes out implications of previous conclusions. By representing side effects and subsidiary conclusions in a forward manner, you explicitly imply the cause and (side) effect nature of the problem. Representing the knowledge in this manner also allows for easy expansion. As other side effects are discovered, you simply add more forward representation structures.

What should those structures be? That depends on the forward representation your shell offers. It usually takes the form of "forward" rules, or demons. Here is a rewrite of *Rule bad_rule* using a forward rule:

RULE better_1
IF   engine_sound = moans
AND   lights = dim
THEN battery = poor CF 80

RULE better_2
IF   battery = poor
THEN alternator = poor CF 60
FORWARD YES

As you can see, the implied relationship is specifically stated: alternator's value is actually dependent on the *battery* instantiation, not the premise of *Rule better_1*. A rule with the FORWARD property is considered whenever its premise attributes are instantiated. In the example, whenever *Rule better_1* is fired, *battery* gets a value. This causes the inference engine to check whether there are any forward rules with *battery* in the premise. *Rule better_2* satisfies this condition and thus is immediately fired. Unbundling these implicit relationships into discrete rules improves the clarity of the knowledge representation, and eases testing by forcing each rule to make only one conclusion.

Conclusions Are Equal, but Jointly Implied. If the intent of the original multiconclusion rule is that both conclusion clauses are both implied without one being more important than the other, there are several possibilities. First, it is likely that the knowledge can best be represented by using a single attribute that may have several possible values. For example:

RULE single_concl
IF   engine_sound = moans
AND   lights = dim
THEN problem = battery CF 80
      problem = alternator CF 60

The knowledge is now formulated to reflect that the expert seeks possible solutions to a single *problem* as opposed to identifying multiple possible causes, each represented by its own attribute. Since the new rule concludes a single (multivalued) attribute, it is well structured.

If this is not acceptable, you might use a forward representation structure. Using forward rules, the knowledge becomes:

RULE forward_1
IF   engine_sound = moans
AND   lights = dim
THEN battery = poor CF 80
FORWARD YES

RULE forward_2
IF   engine_sound = moans
AND   lights = dim
THEN alternator = poor CF 60
FORWARD YES

In this case, the two instantiations are equal side effects, equally associated with the two premise traits. Each rule is independently considered and fired when the premise becomes known. The construction does assume that the values of *engine_sound* and *lights* are inferred from other sources, since forward chaining usually does not force backward chaining on NOTSOUGHT attributes. Thus, it is your responsibility to ensure that the knowledge base is capable of concluding a value for those two attributes during the consultation.

Screening Clauses. If the original multiconclusion rule was written with backward chaining in mind, the above solution may not work. This is because it depends on *engine_sound* and *lights* obtaining values from other knowledge sources. Without the value-seeking behavior of backward chaining, the consultation will fail to produce values for *engine_sound* and *lights* if they cannot be inferred elsewhere. In the original poorly written example, the inference engine would backward chain on *alternator* and *battery* to seek values for *engine_sound* and *lights*. By using two forward rules, *alternator* and *battery* no longer can become the current goal since they reside in the conclusion of a forward rule. Some other means are needed to cause *engine_sound* and *lights* to obtain values. This can be accomplished by adding a screening clause to those rules that require values for *alternator* and *battery* to be processed.

For example, if *Rule 9* required the value for *battery*, it may have looked like this:

RULE 9
IF   battery = poor
THEN rec = jump_start

To make sure that the attributes on which *battery* depends are known before *battery* is needed, you revise it to read:

RULE 9
IF   engine_sound = moans
AND   lights = dim
AND   battery = poor
THEN rec = jump_start

This now ensures that backward chaining occurs on the first two premise clauses, which assures that the forward rules depending on them will have a chance to fire. The rule could be streamlined further by adding an abstraction level:

RULE 1
IF   engine_sound = moans
AND   lights = dim
THEN electric_problem = found

RULE 2
IF   electric_problem = found
THEN alternator = poor CF 60
FORWARD YES

RULE 3
IF   electric_problem = found
THEN battery = poor CF 80
FORWARD YES

RULE 9
IF   electric_problem = found
AND   battery = poor
THEN rec = jump_start

The values of *engine_sound* and *light* are sought when *electric_problem* becomes the current goal. *Electric_problem* is an attribute representing the expert's problem-solving strategy which pursues a line of reasoning evaluating the evidence for electrical problems. When *Rule 9* is considered, *electric_problem* is sought. If it is instantiated, the inference engine immediately tries *Rule 2* and *Rule 3*, since forward rules are considered as soon as attributes in their premise clauses become known. *Rule 9's* first clause is a screening clause containing *electric_problem*. Its role is to cause goal-seeking on vital attributes to determine if the rest of its premise clauses are relevant. This lets all your rules remain well structured. Screening clauses may also create meaningful higher-level groupings (electrical problems) that summarize their components (battery, alternator) and explicitly state the problem-solving strategy. This enhances the clarity of the knowledge base.

When It's OK to Break the Rules

The above discussion is meant to emphasize that good design eases the testing and maintenance challenge. Writing concise rules that infer only one conclusion contributes to rule modularity and independence. This improves clarity, eases maintenance, and facilitates testing. Yet, there may be times when you will consciously decide that the guidelines should be disobeyed. We discuss these briefly here.

The Side Effects Don't Affect the Consultation State. This is not so much an exception as a clarification. Virtually all shells offer facilities for displaying messages and performing other nonknowledge-related housekeeping. Well-structured rules are permitted to have multiple *statements* as long as the rule makes only one change to the consultation state. Display statements actually help identify when a rule fires, aiding the debugging process and raising the visibility of the rule's behavior.

When There's No Other Way to Accomplish the Task. Some shells don't offer any forward processing features other than multiconclusion rules. In this case, you may have no way of encoding the knowledge other than coding rules with multiple conclusions. Check carefully to make sure that the inference engine does not have any forward processing capabilities, and ensure that it processes multiconclusion rules as you desire.

When the Procedural Content Is Closed within One Rule. Some shells are built specifically to support "procedural rules" which control integrated processes and execute outside programs as well as infer values. These shells are useful for building monitoring, process and control, and other cyclically running expert systems. For example, examine this LEVEL5 example:

RULE   Read sensor 12 and test
ACTIVATE   SENSORS.COM
DISK   c:\level5\sense.txt
SEND   sensenum
RETURN   sensor12
IF   sensor12 > (3000)
THEN   temperature is too high

This rule is essentially a small self-contained program. It executes a series of commands before the premise is considered, in order to obtain a value for the attribute *sensor12*. The *ACTIVATE* command causes execution of a program called *sensors.com*. The argument *sensenum* is placed in the DISK file *sense.txt*. After the program returns control to the rule, the returned value *sensor12* is read from the disk file. The premise *sensor12 > (3000)* is then evaluated. If true, the rule fires and *temperature is too high* is proven.

The rule plays the role of a procedural attribute property. The "program" does not affect other attributes in the consultation state. Its impact is local to this one rule. Thus its procedural impact is "closed," making its effect easier to evaluate. Because each procedural step is explicitly stated, there is little loss of clarity in the rule's meaning.

OTHER TESTING ISSUES

The course of normal testing and debugging includes a number of mundane, but common, problems. We describe some of the more frequently encountered problems, as well as some easy tests you can perform to get the most return from your testing time.

Typographical Errors

By far the most common debugging problem is the lowly typo. Typos are especially difficult to detect in expert systems for two reasons. In some shells, you don't need to declare attributes or their values before using them. Thus, virtually any string written in a premise or conclusion is accepted. Second, the values you assign are usually Englishlike symbols. If you happen to abbreviate an Englishlike symbol or use different words that symbolize the same thing, the rule may *appear* sensible. On the other hand, the inference engine simply matches patterns. If you write two different patterns, the inference engine treats them as two different attributes or values. For example:

RULE 3
IF   electricproblem = found
THEN battery = dead CF 80

RULE 1
IF   battery = bad
THEN rec = "replace battery" CF 80

You can readily see how both *Rule 3* and *Rule 1* make sense to the reader. However, *Rule 1* won't fire based on *Rule 3* succeeding because the value for *battery* is different in the two. In common usage, we may indeed refer to a "bad" battery as a "dead" battery. But the inference engine just matches patterns. To it, these are two discrete values.

If *Rule 1* and *Rule 3* reside in different parts of the knowledge base, your mind may impede the debugging of these kinds of errors. As you page between rules, you somehow ignore the fact that there is a different value in each rule because the *meaning* you assign them is roughly equivalent. To overcome this, you must learn to ignore the meaning and compare syntax when trying to find errors of this sort. Some shells make it easy to compare rules together on the computer. For others, you must print a listing and search through the rules.

Whenever you create a new attribute, immediately enumerate the possible values you know. Keep them ready at hand while you work. This helps you use the right syntax for those values from the start. Also, set up guidelines for hyphenating and connecting multiple word attribute names early on and be consistent. For example, earlier examples of *Rule 3's electricproblem* used an underscore, as in *electric_problem*. Unhappily, these are treated as two different attributes. We use underscores because some shells treat hyphens as subtraction symbols. Whatever you decide to use, make the rule and stick to it.

Falling Through

When no rule captures and matches the conditions of a consultation, it "falls through." By "falling through," we mean that the inference engine doesn't successfully match the actual conditions of its knowledge sources to any rules. In this case, when all knowledge sources have been considered and exhausted, the inference engine internally declares the goal UNKNOWN and ends the consultation. Some shells may display a brief message communicating the fact; many simply stop running.

"Falling through" is the expert systems version of a conventional programming "abend." It means that your knowledge base is incomplete for the case the inference engine just considered. Determine exactly what the state of that consultation was and either make changes that ensure that the case cannot happen (by trapping the inputs before they become consultation values), or expand the knowledge to handle that case.

Using UNKNOWN as a Non-Keyword

Another common and bothersome problem not related to knowledge representation is the way shells treat the strings "UNKNOWN" and "KNOWN" as reserved or keywords. Because your knowledge base may at some point include rules that reason about the unknown, you must determine whether these are keywords in the shell you use and, if so, how they are processed. This problem is explored more fully in Chapter 6. We iterate the point here because it is common to write rules that follow all the guidelines discussed here and to get results that simply don't work, based on an idiosyncratic handling of these keywords. See Chapter 6 and the Appendix for examples you can try, to determine how your shell treats the keywords UNKNOWN and KNOWN.

Answer UNKNOWN to Everything

Many shells let the user respond to prompts by answering UNKNOWN. This feature may be impossible to disable. Once you determine the role that UNKNOWN will play in your knowledge base, you must decide how to handle it. Test your knowledge base by answering UNKNOWN to every user prompt the expert system asks. If your reasoning fails to trap unknown responses, the knowledge base will fall through and conclude with no recommendation. Add rules that capture the response, disable the UNKNOWN input, or specifically document that the finished system simply will not handle this response.

TESTING FEATURES

Adopting the technique of writing "structured" rules is an important first step to writing knowledge bases that are easy to test. Regardless of how well a knowledge base is structured, the debugging features a shell offers can make a big difference in how easy an expert system is to test. We look at these features here.[3]

---

[3]Not all shells use the same terms to describe these facilities. Use the Glossary to cross-reference the terms used here with those in other products.

Trace

Trace lets developers follow the inferencing and consideration path of the inference engine as it processes a knowledge base. Each shell that offers trace capabilities displays differing levels of detail. "Events" that may show up include rule firings, rule consideration, rule "failings," attribute assignment, certainty assignments, and user input.

Contexts

Another feature many products offer is *context* saving and loading (also called "answer files"). This feature allows developers to "snapshot" the consultation's current state and save it to disk. Later, this state can be recalled, allowing the consultation to continue. This allows you to save and restore situations that cause errors or controversial recommendations. After updating the knowledge base, you can restore the case to test the effects of the changes you make.

Session Logging

Session logging allows an entire consultation to be printed or saved to disk. This feature lets you archive consultations for later examination. It is useful to have paper or disk archives when you are working with knowledge base listings away from the computer.

Review

Review allows developers to selectively change one or more attribute value(s) after a consultation. It then lets you test the effect of the single changes while keeping the rest of the consultation state constant. This quick method for rerunning consultations permits you to retest a knowledge base by changing only those responses you want which are different from the last consultation.

Validity and Contradiction Testing

This is a controversial but promising area that is vastly underdeveloped in most shells. These features warn you when you try to remove or change attributes already in use in the knowledge base. Others provide a "contradiction" testing feature. This finds rules which make different conclusions but contain identical premises. After entering a new rule, the shell checks it against other rules in the knowledge base. If it finds a rule with an identical premise, the shell alerts you. You can then accept, revise, or delete the new rule.

Automatic Query

One feature that is especially valuable for testing during the early stages of prototyping is automatic query or "auto query." This refers to the shell's ability to automatically ask users for attribute values when no knowledge source concludes them, even if the attribute doesn't have a PROMPT property. When you create knowledge bases, auto query lets you test high-level knowledge quickly, without writing the lower-level rules that conclude those higher concepts. This saves time and supports rapid prototyping, when the goal is to represent high-level concepts quickly in order to get feedback from the expert. Also, when these queries occur, the inference engine is letting you know that there is no other knowledge source for the attribute. This may flag missing or improperly written rules. If you receive a prompt from the auto query facility when you expected the attribute to be instantiated from a rule, you know there is a gap in the knowledge base. This is often more desirable than what would otherwise happen: the attribute receives an UNKNOWN status and the consultation continues. This status may cause other rules to fail. The implications of this failure may not show up until much later in the consultation. In such cases, you must trace back and discover what caused the incorrect result. Auto query gets to the problem at the source.

Graphics

Some shells graphically depict the relationships among attributes and rules. Such pictures display the inferential structure of the knowledge base. This can summarize significant amounts of knowledge in one picture. Using a picture makes relationships easier to see, thereby aiding debugging.

COMPLETION

Because expert systems development stresses the *what to know* over the *what to do,* it may be difficult to define when the expert system is completed. When the job is "to do" something, the job is done when the software "does it." When the job is "to know" something, how do you know when the software "knows it" well enough? Without a particular definition of when the project is finished, the project may grow to unmanageable proportions. Without a firm sense of focus and a definition of acceptable advice, the end result may not ever be accepted by the user community or management.

One of the most important steps in determining the perceived success of the expert system is establishing expectations about the milestones in the expert system's development and the problems it eventually will solve. It is critical you define as firmly as possible when the project is finished. However, this is a definition you must develop and refine over the development of the project.

Establish the Value of a Partial Solution

One of the most important steps you can take in addressing the completion issue is setting expectations for and establishing the value of a partial solution. We say partial solution here because, in an important sense, all but the most simple expert systems *are* partial solutions. An expert system virtually always is a subset of what the expert knows. By organizing your goals around solving some portion of the problems the expert solves, you acknowledge this fact up front and gain agreement for an achievable goal.

Initial Requirements: The Easiest and Most Common Problems

During the initial knowledge acquisition sessions, you strive to get a view of the expert's most frequently encountered symptoms, as well as most common and valuable conclusions. You also acquire the cases that are the easiest to solve. You brainstorm, encouraging the expert to think up as many scenarios and situations as possible. Once this is done, you prioritize and weight these. This process gives you a better sense of what the scope of the expert's activity is. If the expert's work is the solution of many individual and diverse sub-problems, you can create an initial statement in terms of percentages, for example, "solving 60 percent of the cases encountered in the domain." It builds in flexibility about which specific problems the expert system actually solves, and focuses on groups of problems that are most valuable and common.

Requirements Evolution

In an earlier chapter, we drew the analogy of knowledge as an iceberg. It is difficult for you to judge the project size early, because you don't have the knowledge. It is difficult for the expert to judge, because she or he does have the knowledge, and therefore often takes for granted the large chunks of foundation upon which the verbal top of the iceberg is built.

This trait makes it especially important not to commit to a final requirements statement until substantial knowledge acquisition has taken place. In fact, the requirements statement should be seen as a working document that is open for revision—or better, evolution. This evolution is documented after each knowledge acquisition phase.

Do not rely on the expert's preliminary or off-the-cuff judgments for defining the project. The only reliable measure of a particular expert domain's scope is thorough analysis supplemented by the prototyping experience and expert feedback. When the expert sees early prototypes, it often causes brainstorming behavior that pushes against the preliminary goals you may have set for the project. This is useful and productive behavior, since it can improve the conception of what a useful and reasonable final result is. Early on, this may cause you to rethink the requirements of the project. You may need to allocate more time or to narrow your expectations. Later, you may want to put aside this input to reach the previously established goals. The new input from the expert can then be evaluated for inclusion in a next stage in the project.

Regardless of how thorough your research, it is common to encounter new veins of reasoning or knowledge that widen the project beyond earlier projections once the work has begun in earnest. In these cases, it is wise to yet again revisit the original project definition. Thus, it is essential to have a management that understands the incremental nature of the acquisition process and sees value in the project, regardless of this fuzzy aspect of the development process.

Evaluating the Expert System

Much has been written on testing expert systems. From a commercial point of view, there has yet to be proposed an infallible method for evaluating the veracity of what the expert system concludes. How do you know when you've acquired all the knowledge an expert has to give? You don't. The system ultimately solves just those cases you and the expert have either encountered or been able to identify verbally. How do you know when the expert system is debugged? Again, you don't. You get to the point where it works for those cases you can test.

Nevertheless, there are two categories against which the expert system should stand up before it is accepted and deployed. The first requires the involvement of the developer, the expert or experts, and the user. The latter is of concern to the developer and those who will maintain the system.

Content Testing. Are the results the knowledge base gives correct? Can it solve for the cases it claims to solve? These are the two points content testing seeks to verify. This area needs two types of testing. First, the expert should verify that the results the system gives are correct. This can include one expert, or a panel of experts if there is more than one. Whatever diligent analysis is done on the decisions made by humans should also be applied to the expert system. Documenting the particular cases, or classes of cases, that the expert system can solve lends specificity to the testing phase, and increases the reliability of that testing. The goal here is to ensure that the advice given is correct.

As development proceeds, you should create and maintain a data base of common cases that you test against before prototyping review. Some shells make this easy by providing context-saving (case-saving) facilities that help you automate the testing process. In other cases, you will need to use manual methods. As you see the expert system grow, this testing responsibility becomes an essential part of the prototyping process, outside of the prototype reviews you hold with the expert.

It is essential to start user testing as early as possible. Users have certain expectations about what advice an expert should give. This may differ from how the expert sees the issue. Since expert systems are usually built for users other than an expert, this perspective is essential for ensuring acceptance and capturing the real-world cases the final user sees as important.

Thus the goal in user testing is twofold. First, ensure that the advice that is given is accepted. This includes evaluation of explanation facilities (if any), fine-tuning the expert system's role, and evaluating the need for integrated facilities. Users are the ultimate judges of success of the expert system as a software system. It must meet their needs on usability and human factors fronts, as well as on knowledge-based aspects.

The second front is as practical tester of the system. Because a rule-based system can be viewed as complete for some subset of the domain's final knowledge, it can be deployed early in the development cycle and used for those cases in which it is complete. Early deployment detects errors while they are still relatively inexpensive to correct. Users will quickly find missing cases and erroneous recommendations. During this stage, it is important to have the system running as a trainee. Usually, this means maintaining existing knowledge systems for solving the problem, while providing the opportunity for users to try out the expert system's problem-solving ability without the ultimate responsibility of solving the problem.

Technical Standards. The knowledge base should be examined for organizational and technical construction. This means rules should be well structured, as presented in this chapter, or their exceptions should be well documented. Care should be given to trying to rid rules of procedural content. Rules with multiple solutions should be avoided. The knowledge base should be organized in accord with the guidelines given in Chapter 12. It should be as

Englishlike as possible, and to the extent that it is not, should be extensively documented. In summary, the knowledge base should be viewed from the perspective of "Can this knowledge base be maintained by someone other than myself?" If the answer is "no," then its value as a reservoir of knowledge and a corporate asset is diminished.

ESTABLISHING A MAINTENANCE PLAN

Last, but not least, there must be an answer to the question of who will maintain the expert system. With so much concern for the choosing and implementation of the expert system, this is an easy area to overlook. However, it is important in guaranteeing the long-term payoff of the initial development effort. Failure to address this issue may have dire consequences. Users may continue using the expert system after it has become obsolete. Staff may act on wrong information. Hard-won confidence in the software may be lost, and be difficult to regain.

The maintenance stage can be seen as a normal iteration in the rapid prototyping process. In expert systems development, "maintenance" can be viewed as a name for continuing development, with the starting point of an existing base of code. Its key difference is that a basic version of the expert system has been installed. In formulating the maintenance plan, keep the following factors in mind.

How Quickly Does the Knowledge Change?

Domains that are relatively stable are better than those that evolve quickly. Unstable domains put pressure on organizations to formulate sophisticated maintenance strategies just when they should be winning payoffs from the original development. Moreover, those involved in the development, flush with a sense of accomplishment, are often eager to attack new problems and lose interest in the old project.

What New Knowledge Is Desirable?

As the original development progresses, new discoveries often add "wish list" items to the goals of the project. You will defer some of these until deployment of a system that meets more basic requirements. Therefore, even if the domain seems entirely static, count on the fact that some additions to the original formulation of the project will become desirable.

Can the Expert Remain Involved?

In almost all cases, plan to keep the expert involved. In some projects, the expert is trained in the use of the shell and takes over much of the maintenance task. In others, the developer works closely with the expert, but with the expert taking the lead for guaranteeing the veracity and currency of the knowledge. The expert provides the guidance for how new or updated knowledge should be adopted. Thus, the expert's job becomes maintaining the company's formal knowledge base in his or her area of expertise. This ensures a consistent availability of up-to-date expertise as that expertise evolves.

Expert systems maintenance has many analogies to conventional software. As the base of installed knowledge increases, so does maintenance overhead. As more and more systems are deployed, more emphasis must be placed on the maintenance of existing systems. In data processing, as much as 80 cents on the budget dollar gets spent on maintenance. Cross training should occur so that more than one individual is familiar with the system's contents. A log of sample cases should be updated to test changes to the knowledge base. It must be handled seriously and in a professional manner.

SUMMARY

Testing is one phase in the rapid prototyping loop. Like prototyping itself, you test early and often to secure frequent feedback as to conformance with your current conception of the domain. By using the guidelines for rule construction provided here, you will create knowledge bases that are easier to test and maintain. Testing is not strictly an activity for the developer. Recruit and involve the user and the expert in testing from the beginning. Take advantage of the fact that expert systems are testable from the earliest stages of development. Later, you supplement this with your own testing of a data base of common cases that is well understood.

Appendix

The Appendix details the basic knowledge structures this book uses to develop rule-based expert systems. It also provides discussions on some of the idiosyncratic methods that various products use to process their knowledge base, as well as how they represent uncertainty and unknown information within those knowledge bases.[1]

RULE PROPERTIES

Every rule has a **name** and a **conclusion.** It may also optionally have a **premise, priority, certainty factor, cost,** and **forward** property. A premise is made up of premise clauses, which may be linked by **AND** and **OR.** For example:

RULE 2
IF   color = red
AND   size = like_a_rubber_ball
THEN fruit = apple CF 80
PRIORITY 80

The name of the rule is *Rule 2.* The conclusion starts with the keyword **THEN.** The premise begins with the keyword **IF,** contains two clauses, the second beginning with the conjunction keyword AND. The certainty factor is signaled by the keyword CF; in this case its value is *80.* The rule has a PRIORITY of 80, meaning that the **inference engine** will select this rule from

---

[1]In the Appendix, the phrase "the TI products" means both of the Texas Instruments products, Personal Consultant Easy and Personal Consultant Plus. Words in boldface are the first use of terms defined in the Glossary. Words in capitalized italics are keywords in the software being discussed.

rules in the **conflict set** before those with lower priorities, and after those with higher priorities.

RULE 3
IF   conclusion_found = yes
OR   processing_done = yes
THEN DISPLAY "The consultation is complete"
FORWARD YES

The above rule contains a disjunction premise, signaled by the keyword OR. The rule is a **forward rule,** tested whenever a value for *conclusion_found* or *processing_done* is **instantiated** from some knowledge source. This is indicated by the presence of the keyword **FORWARD** in the rule.

ATTRIBUTE PROPERTIES

Attributes all have names and **types.** They may also optionally have **prompt, expects, if-needed, if-changed, if-added, multi,** certainty factor, and **default** properties. When omitted from an **attribute property list,** the attribute either does not own such a property or its value is set to "no." For example:

NAME: desired_car
TYPE: symbol
EXPECT: (truck, van, sedan, sports_coupe)
PROMPT: "What kind of vehicle do you prefer?"
MULTI: yes

The attribute name is *desired_car.* It may contain the symbolic values "truck," "van," "sedan," and "sports_coupe." If necessary, the user may be asked for this value with the prompt, "What kind of vehicle do you prefer?" The attribute is allowed to have more than one fully certain value. By omission, it does not have certainty factor, if-needed, if-changed, if-added, and default properties. Thus it may only have fully certain values, does not have a default value if all knowledge sources fail, and has no procedural actions associated with it when its values are needed, found, or changed.

For more specific information about any of these properties and how they translate to particular products, see the Glossary.

HANDLING UNKNOWNS

While most expert systems shells offer some way of representing unknown information, the particulars of that representation are usually idiosyncratic. We show here some examples of how particular shells handle the entry, representation, and testing of UNKNOWN. We also provide several examples so you can determine how other shells treat UNKNOWN. See Chapter 6 for details.

Products

EXSYS: EXSYS offers no built-in way to test unknowns. If you wish to allow users to enter UNKNOWN, add this item as an ordinary attribute value when building rules.

Guru: *UNKNOWN* is a keyword in Guru. Guru lets you test the status of an attribute using the *KNOWN()* function. If x in the expression *"KNOWN(x)"* has a value, the function returns true. If x is NOTSOUGHT, the function returns UNKNOWN. If x is UNKNOWN, the function returns false. The function does not cause backward chaining on x. Guru does not provide built-in user interface support for entering UNKNOWN from the keyboard. The developer, instead, manually builds a user interface that procedurally evaluates the user response and takes appropriate measures. Thus, the developer could build a menu containing the item "UNKNOWN," have software evaluate whether that option was chosen, and then assert *"x = UNKNOWN"* when the item is selected.

VP-Expert: *UNKNOWN* is a keyword in VP-Expert. It tests whether the status of an attribute is UNKNOWN. Given the following rule:

```
RULE 1
IF    x = UNKNOWN
THEN y = yes;
```

VP-Expert's inference engine does the following when evaluating *Rule 1:*

- If x is KNOWN, it fails the rule.
- If x is UNKNOWN, it fires the rule.
- If x is NOTSOUGHT, it makes x the current goal, and evaluates x's status when the search of x's value concludes.

VP-Expert supports entry of UNKNOWN using the "?" key. When users are prompted for a value, they assign it to UNKNOWN by pressing "?".

TI Products: Personal Consultant Easy and Personal Consultant Plus both allow developers to add "UNKNOWN" to menus by setting the attribute property CERTAINTY-FACTOR-RANGE to "UNKNOWN." When users select "UNKNOWN" from such a menu, the attribute's status is set to UNKNOWN.

The status of an attribute can be tested in rules using the "predicate functions" *IS KNOWN* and *IS NOTKNOWN*. *IS KNOWN* tests whether the attribute's certainty factor is greater than the certainty factor truth threshold (20).

RULE 1
IF   diagnosis IS KNOWN
THEN . . .

Conversely:

RULE 2
IF   interest_rate IS NOTKNOWN
THEN . . .

Rule 1 tests whether the certainty factor of *diagnosis* is greater than the truth threshold. *Rule 2* tests whether *interest_rate*'s certainty factor is less than 20. The *IS NOTKNOWN* verb returns "true" whenever an attribute is KNOWN with a certainty less than the truth threshold or is UNKNOWN.

M.1: Users can enter UNKNOWN by typing "unknown" from the command line or selecting the option from a menu of options. The product also offers a number of facilities for testing the status of attributes. The expression:

RULE 3
IF   cached(x is sought)
THEN . . .

fails the premise clause if *x* is NOTSOUGHT and fires the rule if it is KNOWN or UNKNOWN.

RULE 4
IF   cached(x is unknown)
THEN . . .

Rule 4 fires the rule if *x* is unknown, fails the rule if it is NOTSOUGHT or KNOWN.
The expression:

RULE 5
IF   x is known
THEN . . .

tests the certainty of *x.* If its cf is greater than 20 (the truth threshold), the rule is true. The clause:

RULE 6
IF   x is unknown
THEN . . .

is true if *x* is unknown or its cf is less than 20.

LEVEL5: Users enter UNKNOWN by pressing the UNKNWN function key. Developers can test for UNKNOWN by testing for a special case of an attribute's certainty:

RULE is it unknown
IF   conf(x) = − 2
THEN . . .

tests whether the current status of *x* is UNKNOWN. Similarly:

RULE is it notsought
IF   conf(x) = − 1
THEN . . .

evaluates whether the current status of *x* is NOTSOUGHT. Neither of these tests causes backward chaining on *x*. The verbs *UNKNOWN FAIL* and *UN-KNOWN CONTINUE* let the developer decide whether or not a line of reasoning should continue in the face of UNKNOWN information.

KES: Users may enter UNKNOWN from the keyboard. KES provides two functions for evaluating the status of attributes. The expressions *IF status(x)* = *KNOWN* and *IF status(x)* = *UNKNOWN* return true or false depending on the resulting status of *x*. The expression causes backward chaining on *x* if *x* is NOTSOUGHT. By substituting the keyword *determined* for *status*, you may make the same test without causing backward chaining.

Test for Other Products

Enter the following rules in your shell's syntax:

GOAL z

RULE 1
IF   y = yes
THEN z = yes

RULE 2
IF   x = UNKNOWN
THEN z = maybe

RULE 3
IF   y = UNKNOWN
THEN z = no

RULE 4
IF   x = yes
THEN y = yes

RULE 5
IF   x = no
THEN y = yes

NAME: x
PROMPT: "What is x?"
EXPECTS: yes, no, maybe;
MULTI: no

When you enter "yes" or "no" to x's prompt, the conclusion "yes" should result. If you select "maybe," one of two things will occur. If UNKNOWN is a keyword, the answer "no" will occur. If UNKNOWN is a value similar to "yes," "no," or "maybe," the consultation will end without concluding z.

If the shell supports some way to enter UNKNOWN from the keyboard, run the consultation and enter UNKNOWN. You should see the final answer "maybe" if UNKNOWN is a keyword. If "maybe" does not result, add the word UNKNOWN to x's EXPECTS list. Now enter "UNKNOWN" when you run the consultation and the answer "maybe" should appear. This means you can manually add the option "UNKNOWN" to menus and write rules that reason explicitly about unknown information.

RULE ORDER

When backward chaining, inference engines have various methods of deciding which rule to consider among a group that concludes the current goal. Here is how some popular tools' inference engines make these decisions. The lists appear in the order that each product's inference engine considers each option.
LEVEL5:

- Consider the rule with the highest certainty factor.
- If more than one have the same cf, choose the rule that occurs first.

TI Products:

- Choose the rule with the highest UTILITY (TI's PRIORITY feature)
- Choose the rule that occurs first.

VP-Expert, Guru, M.1, EXSYS, KES: Choose the rule that occurs first.
Guru: Guru provides additional methods for directing the inference engine on how to choose a rule from a conflict set. This is done using the *e.sord* environment variable. These include:

- Choose the rule with the lowest COST.
- Choose the rule with the highest conclusion certainty.
- Select the rule with the highest PRIORITY.
- Pick rules in random order.
- Choose the rule with the fewest NOTSOUGHT attributes in its premise.

ORDER OF KNOWLEDGE SOURCE CONSIDERATION

Inference engines have different sources from which they seek values for NOTSOUGHT attributes when backward chaining. Here is the order in which some popular tools perform this search.

Default Method

Many shells use what we call the "default method." Here is the default method:

1. Is the attribute in an arithmetic expression in the premise? If so, compute it.
2. Is the value already known? If so, use it.
3. If not known, are there rules which conclude the attribute? If so, process them.
4. If there are no rules, or the existing rules fail, is there a PROMPT property for the attribute? If so, prompt the user.
5. If there is no PROMPT property, or the user enters UNKNOWN to the prompt, make the attribute's status UNKNOWN.

Note that many shells have an automatic prompting mechanism, generating a default prompt if no text is provided by the developer. This may cause automatic user prompting even if no PROMPT property is specified. Most shells usually provide a way to suppress this behavior.

M.1: M.1 uses the default mode except that it considers "facts" and "meta-facts," as well as rules, in step three.

LEVEL5, EXSYS, VP-Expert: These use the default method.

KES: KES uses the following method.

1. Is the value already known? If so, use it.
2. Can the EXTERNAL section assign a value? If so, invoke the external program.
3. If there is no external program, are there rules that conclude the attribute? If so, process them.
4. Is there still no value assigned? Check to see if there are DEFAULT or "calculation" properties defined for the attribute. If so, use them.
5. If none of the above returns a value, PROMPT the user.
6. If none of the above returns a value, or if the user responds to a prompt with UNKNOWN, make the attribute's status UNKNOWN.

Personal Consultant Easy: PCEasy uses the following method:

1. Can the attribute be computed? If so, do it.
2. Is the value already known? If so, use it.

3. If not known, are there rules that conclude the attribute? If so, process them.
4. If there are no rules, or existing rules fail, is there a PROMPT property defined for the attribute? If so, prompt the user. If the user responds with UNKNOWN, make the attribute's status UNKNOWN.
5. If there is no PROMPT property, is there a METHOD property defined? If so, apply it.
6. If no METHOD, is there a DEFAULT property defined? If so, use it.
7. If none of the above, make the attribute's status UNKNOWN.

Guru: Guru provides several methods for controlling the order in which the inference engine seeks a value. This is controlled by the *e.whn* environment variable. The default method is:

1. Can the attribute be computed? If so, do it.
2. Is the value already known? If so, use it.
3. If not, are there rules which conclude it?
4. If not, or if existing rules fail, have actions been specified in the attribute's FIND clause? If so, take those actions.
5. If no FIND actions, prompt the user.
6. If still no value, make the attribute's status UNKNOWN.

DISJUNCTION "SHORT-CIRCUIT" TREATMENT

VP-Expert, M.1: Both these products evaluate all premise clauses in a disjunction, whether or not the premise is found.

RULE 3
IF   color = orange
OR   juice = orange_juice
THEN fruit = orange

Regardless of whether *color = orange* is true or false, VP-Expert and M.1 evaluate the second premise clause *juice = orange_juice.* If you want to cause the inference engine to avoid considering the second clause if the first is true, you must break the rule into two:

RULE 3a
IF   color = orange
THEN fruit = orange

RULE 3b
IF   juice = orange_juice
THEN fruit = orange

Now if *Rule 3a* fires, the inference engine will not consider *Rule 3b* (assuming *fruit* = *orange* is singlevalued).

LEVEL5, TI Products, EXSYS, KES: These products "short-circuit" consideration of disjunctions as soon as one of their premise clauses is found to be true. Therefore, in *Rule 3* above, if *color* = *orange* is found to be true, the inference engine does not consider the second premise clause. Instead, the rule is immediately fired after the first clause is found to be true.

Guru: Guru defaults to the "short-circuit" mode of consideration. This behavior can be overridden by setting the environment variable *e.tryp* to "p," in which case all clauses are sought before the premise is evaluated.

Other Products

To determine how other rule-based products treat disjunctions, create a knowledge base representing this knowledge:

```
GOAL:    fruit
TYPE:    symbolic
EXPECT: orange
MULTI:   no

NAME:    juice
TYPE:    symbolic
EXPECT: orange_juice
PROMPT: "What is the juice?"

NAME:    color
TYPE:    symbolic
EXPECT: (orange, white)
PROMPT: "What is the color?"

RULE 3
IF      color = orange
OR      juice = orange_juice
THEN fruit = orange
```

Run this knowledge base. Enter the value *orange* when prompted for *color.* If the consultation proceeds, the inference engine does not short-circuit premise consideration. If the consultation ends immediately with no further prompts, the inference engine does short-circuit disjunctive premise clauses. If this is not the behavior you want, you can cause the inference engine to act as though it does "short-circuit" disjunctions by breaking up rules whose premise clauses are connected by *OR*.

CERTAINTY FACTORS

While there are many similarities among shells in the way that they handle uncertainty, there are also important differences. In this section, we look at some of these differences. See Chapter 8 for details.

Level5

Facts. Truth Threshold (called *THRESHOLD*): Default: 50, may be changed. Certainty factor range: 0 to 100.

Premise certainty.
Simple premise: itself.
Conjunctions: "minimum" method.
Disjunctions: "maximum" method.
Rule uncertainty. "product" method.
Previous certainty. "maximum" method.

VP-Expert

Facts. Truth Threshold (called *TRUTHTHRESHOLD*): 50, may be changed. Certainty factor range: 0 to 100.

Premise certainty.
Simple premise: itself.
Conjunctions: "minimum" method.
Disjunctions: "probably sum" method.
Rule uncertainty.
Simple premise, conjunctions: "product" method.
Disjunctions: "probability sum" method.
Previous certainty. "probability sum" method.

M.1

Facts. Truth Threshold: 20. Certainty factor range: – 100 to 100.

Premise certainty.
Simple premise: itself.
Conjunctions: "minimum" method.
Disjunctions: "probability sum" method.[2]

---

[2]When both cfs are positive. When both are negative, apply the same formula and reverse the sign. Combinations in which one factor is positive and one negative are outside the scope of this book.

Rule uncertainty.
Simple premise, conjunctions: "product" method.
Disjunctions: "probability sum" method (see previous footnote)
Previous certainty. "probability sum" method. (see previous footnote)

EXSYS

Facts. Offers a wide variety of systems including ranges 0/1, 0/10; – 100/100, "increment/decrement"; and "custom formulas." These systems do not fall within the certainty factor systems discussed in this book.

KES

Facts. Truth Threshold: 0.0. Certainty factor range: – 1.0 to 1.0.

Premise certainty.
Simple premise: itself.
Conjunctions: "minimum" method.
Disjunctions: "maximum" method.
Rule uncertainty. "product" method.
Previous certainty. Outside the scope of this book.

TI Products

Facts. Truth Threshold: 20. Certainty factor range: – 100 to 100 (called *FULL*), or 0 to 100 (called *POSITIVE*).

Premise certainty.
Simple premise: itself.
Conjunctions: "minimum" method.
Disjunctions: "maximum" method.
Rule uncertainty. "product" method.
Previous certainty. If both positive or negative: "probability sum" method with same sign. Else outside the scope of this book.

Guru

Guru offers a wide variety of certainty factor blending algorithms from which the developer may choose. The first named in each category is the default.
Facts. Truth Threshold (called "unknown threshold"): 20, may be changed. Certainty factor range: 0 to 100.

Premise certainty.
Simple premise: itself.
Conjunctions: "minimum" method (also: "product" method, two others).
Disjunctions: "maximum" method (also: three others).
Rule uncertainty. "product" method (also: "minimum" method, two others).
Previous certainty. "probability sum" method (also: "maximum" method, two others).

Glossary

Items in italics are the associated product keywords that invoke a feature. Items in quotes are the terms as described in the product documentation. Words in boldface are defined elsewhere in the Glossary. The phrase "the TI products" means both of the Texas Instruments products, Personal Consultant Easy and Personal Consultant Plus.

AND: The keyword used in this book to declare the beginning of a **conjunction premise** clause within a rule.
  VP-Expert, M.1, LEVEL5, TI Products, EXSYS, Guru, KES: *and.*
  See also: **conjunction, premise.**

Answer file: A disk file containing **attribute** assignments for use by an expert system. Often used to bypass user prompting or ease the testing process. Some products allow **context** saving for future use as answer files.
  TI Products: "playback file."
  M.1: "cache file." *savecache, loadcache.*
  KES: "case data." *freeze, defrost.*
  VP-Expert: *loadfacts, savefacts.*
  EXSYS: "saving data." *recover.*
  Guru: "saving the context." *save to, load from.*
  LEVEL5: "context." *context save, context restore.*

Antecedent: In some products, a rule premise. In the TI products, a **forward rule property.** See also: **forward rule.**

Artificial intelligence: Artificial intelligence (AI) aims to make computers capable of displaying behavior that is considered intelligent when observed in humans. Besides expert systems, AI covers a wide variety of areas including natural language processing, vision systems, voice recognition, and robotics.

Assertion: An **instantiation** not caused by a **rule.** Also called a **fact.**
  Guru: "assignment statements."
  M.1: "facts," "proposition."

Atom: The smallest nondivisible knowledge structure of an **expert system**. In rule-based expert systems, an **attribute**.

Attribute: The basic representation unit in most rule-based **expert systems**. Similar to **variables** in traditional data processing, but different in that they may own **properties**, and do not necessarily represent memory storage locations.
   TI Products: "parameter."
   EXSYS: "condition" for symbolic attributes, "variable" for numeric attributes.
   LEVEL5: "fact," "object-attribute."
   Guru, VP-Expert: "variable."
   M.1: "fact," "expression."
   KES: *attribute.*
See also: **variable**.

Attribute properties: Characteristics associated with an **attribute** that influence its processing by the **inference engine**, e.g., **certainty factor, multi, prompt**, and **status**. See also: **procedural attribute property, name, type, expect, prompt, multi, method, if-needed, if-changed, if-added, status**.

Attribute property list: The notation used in this book to name the properties of an attribute and their values.

Attribute/value pair: An **attribute** bound to a value.

Backward chaining: The goal-directed search strategy used in many rule-based **expert systems shells**. Backward chaining begins by attempting to seek a value or values for a known **goal**. Processing continues by seeking values for those **attributes** on which the goal depends. Commonly used in diagnostic, classification, selection and repair/debugging **expert systems**. See also: **forward chaining, mixed chaining**.

Bind: The act of linking a value to a particular **attribute**. See also: **instantiation**.

Boolean: A **type property** value which permits an **attribute** to represent only two values: yes and no.

Boolean fact: An **attribute** whose only valid values are YES and NO.
   LEVEL5: *simplefact.*
   TI Products: a "yes/no" type.
   KES: *truth.*

Cache: The working memory of an **expert system** in which user entries, calculations, and other conclusions are stored.

Certainty blending: See **certainty factor algebra**.

Certainty cut-off: See **truth threshold.**

Certainty factors (cfs): Property associated with **attribute/value pairs** and **rules,** commonly used to represent uncertainty, likelihood, or ranking. Certainty factors are usually maintained automatically by the **expert systems shell.**
LEVEL5: "confidence," measured from 0 to 100. CF.
VP-Expert: "confidence," measured from 0 to 100. CNF.
EXSYS: "probability," measured from 0 to 10, 0 to 100, or − 100 to + 100.
M.1, TI Products: "certainty factors," measured from − 100 to 100. CF.
Guru: "certainty factors," measured from 0 to 100. CF.
KES: "certainty factors," measured from − 1.0 to + 1.0. CF.

Certainty factor algebras: The algorithms used by rule-based **expert systems shells** to calculate certainty factors. The algebras consolidate the uncertainties associated with **premises, rules,** and prior **attribute** uncertainties.

Cfs: See **certainty factors.**

Compile: In some **expert systems,** the act of processing a knowledge base into an intermediate or machine readable form.
LEVEL5, Guru: "compile."
KES: "parse."

Conclusion: The action or **instantiation** portion of a **rule,** executed or "**fired**" when its **premise** is determined to be true.
KES, M.1: consequent.
TI Products, EXSYS: "Then" statement.
See also: **then.**

Conflict resolution: The process used by an **inference engine** to select a **rule** from the current **conflict set.**

Conflict set: A group of **rules** logically related to the current **line of reasoning** at a particular time. In **backward chaining,** those rules concluding the current **goal.**
LEVEL5: "Or class."
Guru: The "candidate" or "competing" rules.

Conjunction: A **premise** made up of clauses connected by AND, as in:
RULE 1
IF   temp_direction = dropping_fast
AND   cloudy = yes
THEN rain_likely = yes
For a conjunction to be considered true, each clause connected by AND must be true.

Consultation: The interaction between user and **expert system** arising from the expert system's use.

Context (also, **consultation state**): The state of an **expert system's** working memory. The context includes **instantiated attribute/values**, environment settings, defaults, and modes. Contexts may be saved for later restoration. This is useful in debugging. See also: **answer file, cache.**

Control rule: A **rule** whose knowledge represents a **problem-solving strategy** designed to control the order in which reasoning lines are considered, rather than representing declarative knowledge about the **domain.**

Conventional software (also, **conventional programming**): A software paradigm which relies on the developer to specify the steps and the order of the steps the computer should execute.

Cost: A **rule property** found in Guru, representing relative cost versus other rules making the same **conclusion.** The **inference engine** can be made to use cost as a "tie-breaker" when determining which rule to choose from the **conflict set.** See also: **priority.**

Current goal: In **backward chaining**, the **attribute** whose value the **inference engine** is seeking at a particular time. Either the **knowledge base goal** or a **NOTSOUGHT** attribute appearing in a **rule premise.**

Data-driven chaining: See **forward chaining.**

Default: An **attribute property** whose value is assigned when no other knowledge sources can provide a value.
LEVEL5, M.1, EXSYS, VP-Expert: No facility.
Guru: No facility, can be procedurally represented in an attribute *FIND* clause.
KES, TI Products: *default.*

Demon (also, **deamon**): A **property** that associates a set of actions with an **attribute.** The actions are triggered when the attribute's value is added or changed. Demons may usually fire more than once.
KES: *demon.*
Personal Consultant Plus: *active-values.*
VP-Expert, M.1, Personal Consultant Easy: No facility, but can be simulated with forward rules, with the limitation that forward rules may fire only once.
EXSYS, LEVEL5, Guru: No facility.
See also: **frames, default, if-needed, if-added, if-changed, procedural attribute property, forward rule.**

Disjunction: A **premise** made up of clauses connected by OR, as in:
RULE 1
IF   temp_direction = dropping_fast
OR   cloudy = yes
THEN rain_likely = yes
For the rule to fire, only one clause connected by OR must be true.

DISPLAY: The keyword used in this book to instruct the **inference engine** to display a message.
VP-Expert, M.1, LEVEL5: *display.*
TI Products: *print, show.*
Guru: *output.*
KES: *message.*

Domain: The subject area explicitly included within the scope of an **expert system**. Aspects of the target knowledge included within the expert system are said to be "within the domain." Portions outside its scope are "outside the domain."

ELSE: A **rule** action taken when the **premise** is found to be false. Use of *else* can be dangerous because, once considered, the rule containing it always fires. This makes the rule's proper placement in the knowledge base crucial and builds unwanted procedural content into the knowledge base.
EXSYS, LEVEL5, VP-Expert: *else.*
Guru, M.1, TI Products, KES: No facility.

Expect: An **attribute property** whose contents are the specific allowed values for the attribute.
VP-Expert: *choices.*
M.1: *legalvals.*
TI Products: *expect.*
EXSYS: "value list." Specified during "qualifier" creation.
KES: specified as a symbol list after the attribute definition.
LEVEL5: Automatically determines the list from the contents of the knowl-
      edge base.
Guru: No facility

Expert system: Computer programs that give the appearance of humanlike reasoning for problems ordinarily requiring expertise.

Expert systems shell: A software development tool designed to enable the creation of **expert systems**. Usually consists of an **inference engine**, user interface facilities, and optional productivity tools like **knowledge base** editor, debugging aids, and testing facilities.

Fire: The act of taking the **conclusion** of a **rule**. An **inference engine** performing the action named in a rule conclusion is said to "fire" the rule.

Forward chaining: A **search strategy** used for processing **knowledge bases** in which solutions or recommendations are inferred from known facts. Commonly used in configuration, design, planning, prediction and interpretation expert systems. See also: **backward chaining, mixed chaining.**

Forward rule: A **rule** which is considered whenever the value of one of its **premise attributes** changes. **Inference engines** do not **backward chain** on forward rules. If any of the forward rule's premise attributes are not known, the rule is put aside for later consideration. Forward rules differ from demons in that they usually may fire just once, while demons may fire many times.

    KES: No feature. Can be simulated with a *demon.*

    TI Products: *antecedent.*

    VP-Expert: *whenever.*

    M.1: No forward rule, but can be equivalently represented using *whenfound* and *whencached.*

    Guru, EXSYS, LEVEL5: No facility.

See also: **if-changed, demon.**

Frame: A set of values, definitions, **properties**, and procedures grouped for the purpose of representing an object. In cognitive psychology, a set of related assumptions, expectations, and previous experience brought to bear at the onset of a situation or object in an attempt to understand and interpret it. See also: **default, if-added, if-needed, if-changed, method, instantiation.**

Goal: The **attribute** or attributes whose value is sought by the **expert system**. **Knowledge base** processing is usually concluded when the goal is **instantiated** or found to be **unknown.**

    VP-Expert: *find* x (x is declared the goal).

    KES: *obtain* x (x is declared the goal).

    LEVEL5: *goal.*

    Guru: *goal.* Developers also may force x to become the current goal, using the expression *consult to seek x.*

    M.1: *goal.* Developers also may force an attribute to become the current goal from within a premise, using the expression "x is SOUGHT."

    TI Products: "goal." Developers also may force a parameter to become the current goal from within a premise, using the verb *FINDOUT x.*

Goal-directed reasoning: See **backward chaining.**

Heuristics: The high-level, often imprecise rules of thumb and intuitive reasoning that experts use to solve problems.

IF: The keyword used in this book to declare the beginning of a **rule premise.**
Guru, M.1, EXSYS, TI Products, LEVEL5, KES, VP-Expert: *if.*
See also: **premise.**

If-added: A **property** that associates a set of actions with an **attribute**, triggered when a value is added or the attribute is **instantiated** for the first time. The if-added property can be represented with **forward rules** and **demons.**
KES: No facility, can be represented using a *demon.*
Personal Consultant Easy: No facility, can be represented using an *antecedent* rule with the premise: *IF x IS KNOWN.*
VP-Expert: No facility, can be represented using a *whenever* rule with the premise: *IF x < > UNKNOWN.*
EXSYS, LEVEL5, Guru: No facility.
M.1: *whencached, whenfound.*
See also: **frames, default, if-needed, if-changed, demon, procedural attribute properties, method, forward rule.**

If-changed: A **property** that associates a set of actions with its **attribute**, triggered when the attribute's value changes. The if-changed property can be represented using "**demons.**"
KES: No facility, can be represented using a *demon.*
Personal Consultant Plus: *active-values.*
EXSYS, VP-Expert, Personal Consultant Easy, LEVEL5, Guru: No facility.
M.1: *whencached, whenfound.*
See also: **frames, default, if-added, if-needed, demon, procedural attribute properties, method.**

If-needed: A **property** that associates a set of actions with an **attribute**, triggered when an attribute value is needed and cannot be obtained using other knowledge sources (e.g., **rules** or **prompts**). This property is sometimes called a **method.**
TI Products: *method*
Guru: Developer may specify actions in the attribute's *find* clause.
KES: *external.* Requires that the actions be specified in an external program. Considered *before* rules.
See also: **frames, default, if-added, if-changed, demon, procedural attribute properties, method.**

Inference engine: A computer program which processes the contents of a **knowledge base** (in rule-based systems: rules) by applying one or more **search strategies** against its contents and deriving whatever **conclusions** can be made.

Instantiation: The creation of an instance of a knowledge structure, and optionally assigning a value to all or portions of that structure. In most rule-based products, it is functionally equivalent to a **conventional** data processing "assignment" statement. However, in systems supporting **o/a/v triplets** (M.1, KES, and Personal Consultant Plus), the term additionally refers to the software's ability to dynamically create indefinite numbers of object instances without specific developer control (referred to as multiple instantiation).

Knowledge acquisition: The activity of gleaning and organizing knowledge in a form suitable for codification in an **expert system**.

Knowledge base: The **rules, assertions**, procedures, descriptions, and other knowledge structures that represent domain knowledge. When processed by an **inference engine**, the two together are called an **expert system**.

Knowledge engineer: Developer of **expert systems**. Term used to connote the special activities related to acquiring, organizing, and coding knowledge.

Knowledge engineering: The activity of representing and coding knowledge into an **expert system**.

Known: In some products, the state of an **attribute** when it has been **instantiated** to a value with a **certainty factor** greater than the **truth threshold**. In some products, the state of an attribute that has been instantiated to a value regardless of certainty. See the Appendix for more. See also: **notsought, unknown, status.**

Line of reasoning: The path taken through an **expert system** to arrive at a **conclusion** or recommendation.

Metaknowledge: Literally: "knowledge about knowledge." Describes **expert systems** facilities in which the software can in some way reason about its own knowledge. Features under this category include the ability to reason and delete rules based on some condition, to reason about the **status** and uncertainty of **attributes**.

Metarule: A rule containing **metaknowledge**.

Method: A **property** that associates a set of actions with an **attribute**. Methods are triggered when a value for the attribute is needed by the **inference engine** and the value cannot be obtained using **rules** or **prompts**.
   TI Products: *method*
   Guru: Developer may specify actions in the attribute's *find* clause.
   KES: *external*. Requires that actions be specified in an external program.
      Considered *before* rules.
See also: **if-needed, frames.**

Mixed chaining: A **search strategy** which uses both **backward** and **forward chaining** during a single processing of a **knowledge base**.

Guru: A mixed chaining mode can be selected using the *e.mix* environment variable, in which the inference engine temporarily treats all rules containing a newly instantiated attribute in their premise as forward rules. After processing these rules, the inference engine reverts to backward chaining until the next instantiation, at which time the process is repeated.

Multi or **Multivalued**: An **attribute property** denoting whether or not an attribute may have more than one fully certain value.
> VP-Expert: *plural.*
> TI Products: *ask-all* or *multi-valued.*
> M.1: *multivalued.*
> LEVEL5: *multi, exhaustive.*
> KES: *mlt.*
> EXSYS, Guru: No facility, all attributes treated as potentially multivalued.

Name: A **property** associated with a **rule** or **attribute** denoting the name by which the rule or attribute is referenced.

Notsought: The **status** of an **attribute** whose value has not been assigned, considered, or sought during an expert systems consultation.
> M.1: "not noted in the cache."
> KES: "undetermined."
> VP-Expert: "undefined."
> Guru: "unknown."
> LEVEL5: "not known yet."
See also: **known, unknown, status.**

O/A/V triplet: See **object/attribute/value triplets.**

Object/Attribute: In LEVEL5, the term for referring to symbolic **attributes.**

Object/attribute/value triplets: Knowledge structures containing three information levels, usually associated with **frames** and objects.

OR: The keyword used in this book to declare the beginning of a **disjunction premise** clause within a **rule.**
> VP-Expert, M.1, LEVEL5, TI Products, Guru, KES: *or.*
> EXSYS: No facility, except for testing alternate values for a single attribute.
See also: **disjunction, premise.**

Parameter: An **attribute** in the TI products. See also: **attribute.**

Preenumerated: An **attribute** trait, meaning that the possible allowable values of an attribute can be named in advance of their use. These values will appear in the attribute's EXPECTS property if one exists.

Premise: The portion of a **rule** that is tested by the **inference engine**. If the premise is found to be true, the corresponding action specified in the rule conclusion is taken. See also: **IF**.

Priority: A **rule property** representing a rule's relative importance or likelihood versus other rules making the same conclusion. The **inference engine** can be made to use priority as a "tie-breaker" when determining which rule to choose from the **conflict set**.
 TI Products: *utility*.
 Guru: *priority*.
 VP-Expert, M.1, KES, EXSYS, LEVEL5: No facility.
 See also: **cost**

Problem-solving strategy: The step-by-step approach used by an expert to attack a problem.

Procedural attribute properties: Properties that associate a set of actions with an **attribute**. The actions in the property are triggered under particular circumstances—for example, when the attribute owning the property is changed, or its value is needed but cannot be inferred from **rules** or **prompts**. See also: **demon, method, if-added, if-needed, if-changed.**

Prompt: An **attribute property** determining whether the user may be prompted for a value. The prompt is used when other knowledge sources, most commonly **rules**, fail to provide a value for the current **goal**.
 LEVEL5: *text*.
 TI Products: *prompt*.
 VP-Expert: *ask*.
 M.1: *question*.
 KES: Prompt text is specified with *question*. KES always prompts if prior knowledge sources fail to generate a value for a sought attribute. This behavior can be defeated by assigning the attribute's *default* property to *unknown*.
 Guru: *input*. Used in *find* clauses in the variable description.
 EXSYS: "qualifier text."

Property: A characteristic belonging to some **expert systems** knowledge structure (usually a **rule** or **attribute**) that dictates or influences how an **inference engine** processes that structure.

Prototyping (also, **rapid prototyping**): An approach to **knowledge base** construction in which developers quickly build a preliminary representation of **domain** knowledge. This is done while realizing that this early conception of the knowledge may be incomplete or wrong. It is pursued with the goal of getting quick feedback from the expert. After feedback is received, the developer abandons, revises, or expands the prototype. Prototyping acknowledges that it may be difficult or impossible to completely understand knowledge without first building preliminary models of that knowledge.

Review: An **expert systems shell** feature, enabling users to selectively change **attribute** values while maintaining the remainder of the consultation **context**. This is convenient for rerunning **consultations** while testing the effects of one or two changes.

Rule: A self-contained knowledge structure consisting of a **premise** and **conclusion**. When the premise is true, the conclusion's action is taken. See also: **premise, conclusion.**

Screening clause: A **premise** clause whose role is to ensure that certain **attributes** have been sought and **instantiated** (perhaps to particular values) before the premise clauses that follow it are considered. Screening clauses are used to represent **problem-solving strategies**, to help formulate **well-structured rules**, and to ensure that necessary preconditions for pursuing a **line of reasoning** are fulfilled.

Search strategies: The approaches available to a developer or **inference engine** for interrogating and processing a **knowledge base**. See also: **backward chaining, forward chaining, mixed chaining.**

Shell: See **expert systems shell.**

Short-circuit reasoning: The processing technique applied by some **inference engines** of processing a **rule** without considering every **premise** clause in that rule. Most shells process **conjunctions** in this way, ending consideration as soon as one clause fails. Some products apply this approach for processing **disjunctions**, ending consideration as soon as one clause is found to be true. See also: **conjunction, disjunction.**

Simple fact: See **boolean fact.**

Singlevalued: An **attribute** whose **multi-property** value equals "no" is said to be singlevalued. Such an attribute may contain exactly one fully certain value. Most shells let singlevalued attributes have multiple uncertain values. This allows the **inference engine** to continue seeking values until the most certain is found. If a fully certain value is concluded, all uncertain values are purged.

Status: An **attribute property** containing the attribute's epistemological condition. Status plays a major role in influencing inference engine behavior during backward chaining. The status will be either **known, unknown,** or **notsought.** See the Appendix for more. See also: **notsought, known, unknown.**

Structured rule: A **rule** which changes exactly one **attribute** and minimizes or eliminates procedural actions which might change the current **goal**, or cause hidden changes or side effects to the **consultation state.**

THEN: The keyword used in this book to declare the beginning of a rule conclusion.

Guru, M.1, EXSYS, TI Products, LEVEL5, KES, VP-Expert: *then.*
See also: **conclusion.**

Threshold: See **truth threshold.**

Trace: A diagnostic feature enabling developers to view the **inference engine's** consideration pattern as it processes a **knowledge base.** Monitored activities may include showing **rule** firings, consideration, "failings," attribute assignments, certainty assignments, and user input.

Truth threshold: The **certainty factor** value above which a less than fully certain **attribute** is regarded as true by an **inference engine.** This judgment affects **rule** evaluations, certainty factor blending, and the result of functions that test the **status** of attributes.

VP-Expert: *truththreshold.*
LEVEL5: *threshold.*
Guru: "unknown threshold." Controlled by the environment variable *e.unkn.*

Type: An **attribute property** whose contents are the allowable types of values for that attribute. Some common types are "boolean," "numeric," "symbolic," and "text."

Guru: Not explicitly typed. Text strings, symbols, and boolean attributes are treated as a single type, identified by quotes (e.g., "yes," "no," "blue," "I don't know"). Attribute values not in quotes are treated as numeric values.

M.1: Using the legalvals() *meta-fact:* "integer," "real," "number," symbol (allowable responses named in an EXPECTS list).

KES: *sgl, mlt* (symbol: both with associated EXPECTS list), *truth* (boolean), numeric, string, class.

EXSYS: "string," "numeric," "choices" (symbols).

TI Products: *YES\NO* (boolean), *ASK-ALL, SINGLEVALUED, MULTI-VALUED* (last three are all symbolic), "text."

LEVEL5: *STRING* (text), *ATTRIBUTE* (symbolic), *NUMERIC, SIMPLEFACT* (boolean).

VP-Expert: All attributes are treated as symbolic, constrained by their EXPECTS property if one exists. Attributes may have a numeric value taken by using parenthetic notation, as in:

RULE 1
IF   heat>(80)
THEN . . .

Unknown: The **status** of an **attribute** which has been sought, but for which the **inference engine** failed to find a value. Unknown often may also be entered from the keyboard by users. For more, see the Appendix.
Guru, VP-Expert, M.1, KES: *unknown.*
TI Products: *is unknown.*
See also: **known, notsought, status.**

Variable: In **conventional** programming, a symbol representing a storage location in memory. The name some **expert systems shells** use to describe **attributes** (Guru, EXSYS, and VP-Expert), or PROLOGlike place-holding symbols (M.1). See also: **attribute.**

Well-structured rule: See **structured rule.**

Index